THE PIONEER HISTORIES

EDITED BY V. T. HARLOW, D.LITT., AND J. A. WILLIAMSON, D.LIT.

THE INVASION OF CHINA
BY THE WESTERN WORLD

The
INVASION OF CHINA
by
THE WESTERN WORLD

by

E. R. HUGHES, M.A.
READER IN CHINESE RELIGION AND PHILOSOPHY
IN THE UNIVERSITY OF OXFORD

THE MACMILLAN COMPANY

NEW YORK

1938

PRINTED IN THE UNITED STATES OF AMERICA
BY THE POLYGRAPHIC COMPANY OF AMERICA, N.Y.

EDITORS' PREFACE
TO THE SERIES

THE Pioneer Histories are intended to provide broad surveys of the great migrations of European peoples—for purposes of trade, conquest and settlement—into the non-European continents. They aim at describing a racial expansion which has created the complex world of to-day, so nationalistic in its instincts, so internationalised in its relationships.

International affairs now claim the attention of every intelligent citizen, and problems of world-wide extent affect the security and livelihood of us all. He who would grasp their meaning and form sound judgements must look into the past for the foundations of the present, and, abandoning a local for a universal perspective, must take for his study the history of a world invaded by European ideas. It was less so in the days before the Great War. Then the emphasis was upon Europe itself: upon such questions as that of France's eastern frontier inherited from Richelieu and Louis XIV, the militarism of Germany derived from Frederick the Great, and the Balkan entanglement which originated with the medieval migrations of Slavonic peoples and with the Turkish conquests of the fourteenth century. Now the prospect is wider, for these ancient domestic difficulties in modern form cannot properly be estimated except by correlation with the problems of a Europeanised outer world.

The Orient is in ferment and Asiatic difficulties compel the attention of Geneva because long ago the Portuguese, followed by the Dutch and the English, rounded the Cape and came to India. For the same reason, Africa is no longer an unknown continent but a vast area in which civilised enterprise demands direction and control. Knowledge of the process by which North America was discovered and gradually filled with Europeans is the necessary basis for an understanding of the modern reactions upon each other of the new continent and the old. In South America the same process is to be seen at work, though incomplete while Nature is yet unsubdued. Similarly, it may be appreciated how the search for an unknown but credited continent lying about the South Pole has helped to shift the centre of gravity to the Pacific, and has created a white Australasia. The present series will show how the permanent factors in these great regions first presented themselves to European minds and how achievements were then effected which have governed all subsequent relationships.

But if the subject has this interest for students of affairs, it has also its appeal to those who dwell most on individual character, courage and ingenuity. Movements are made by men, and in these stories of European expansion are to be met men worth knowing, whose deeds carry inspiration for this generation as for all others.

Each volume takes for its subject the history of an important movement and, while related to others in the series, is thus complete in itself. The authors whose co-operation we have been fortunate to secure have all had experience of research in the original evidence pertaining to their subjects, and in their contributions to this series they give the results of that research in narratives which should appeal to the general reader. Each book is designed to embody the most recent information available, and some will be found to deal with subjects of which no full treatment has hitherto been accessible in English.

V. T. HARLOW

J. A. WILLIAMSON

AUTHOR'S PREFACE

WHEN the Editors invited me to write a book for the Pioneer Series on the cultural penetration of China by the West, I was attracted to the proposition because it seemed to me that such a book was needed at this particular time. Also I may perhaps claim some of the necessary qualifications, namely, long residence in a rural interior district, later residence in Shanghai and Peking with first-hand acquaintance with the new forces, new men, and new literature. I recalled too that Professor Tawney had urged on me the task of writing on the Chinese side to this subject. At the same time, the earlier part of the period was not one to which I had given special attention, nor the theme one to which I was warranted in devoting a large part of my time as University Reader in Chinese Religion and Philosophy. A solution of the difficulty then presented itself, namely, that my wife might join with me in the necessary work. In the authorship of this book, therefore, my wife has a joint share.

The Editors of the Pioneer Series state in their general preface that 'international affairs now claim the attention of every intelligent citizen' and that the said citizen 'abandoning a local for a universal perspective must take for his study the history of a world invaded by European ideas'. As regards this second statement, the question arises how is a man to achieve a really universal perspective. To do so, or to approach as nearly as is humanly possible to such an omniscient position, requires some high quality of imaginative sympathy, which enables a man to hold fast to that which he knows to be good and at the same time to lay hold of the good which is in his neighbour, whether that neighbour be yellow or black or brown. It means an appreciation of things alien to his own way of thought. Applying this to an understanding of the spread of European ideas, it involves an appreciation of the mind of the man who accepts many of those ideas and proceeds to adapt them to his own spiritual and intellectual needs. This as a stage, and not more than a stage in the history of cultural penetration, has to be recognised wherever it is going on. It can be studied from one point of view where European culture is meeting and affecting the minds of primitive and inarticulate peoples. A different point of view is necessary where, as in China, European culture has met a civilisation as old or older than itself in the past. That civilisation has expressed itself nobly in literature, poetry, and art, and in the present is competent to give reasoned reflection and have a critical reaction to the results of its contact with the West.

My aim has been to make such a study as will enable the general reader to arrive at this sympathetic point of view. If, further, it enables him to appreciate the greatness of the qualities which distinguish the nations of Europe and China, and the fact that between the representatives of two ancient and virile civilisations there exist no ultimate grounds for quarrel, then some small contribution will have been made to that exploration of ideas which is the logical and necessary continuation of the geographical explorations of earlier generations.

This book is not, therefore, a history of trade or war or diplomatic contests. No one is more conscious than I am that these also are in themselves cultural relations, but in order to bring the story within the prescribed limits I have had to exercise the severest restraint. Thus in the first chapter the record of major political events is given to provide an outline into which the developments referred to in the other chapters may be fitted. It could not include an adequate account of relevant political events in Europe and America. To supply this gap the reader may profitably turn to *The Far East in European Politics*,[1] which was published just as the writing of this book was being finished. With regard to the chapter on missionary influence, the reader with a special interest will feel that scant justice has been done to many important aspects and personalities. If so, he should read Professor Latourette's *History of Christian Missions in China*. He will find there all the detail systematically presented by a master hand: also a place given to Roman Catholic missions which is not given to them in any other work by a non-Catholic historian. This brings the whole missionary picture more into true perspective.

It will cause surprise and disappointment to some readers that there is little or no reference to the influence of the West on Chinese art, more particularly in its two master fields of ceramics and painting. As I see it, there is very little that can be said with any assurance of right conviction. The loss of confidence which the Chinese people experienced late in the nineteenth and early in the twentieth century, had its effect on art. There was a decline, one already heralded by the development of luxury art in the first half of the Manchu régime. Then the

[1] G. F. Hudson: Clarendon Press, 1937.

Renaissance Movement twenty years ago brought a renewal of confidence, and with this came a new enthusiasm for the traditional art of which such a wealth had come down from the past. But the inspiration which the Renaissance has been, the new power of experiment which it has brought in literature, has not become creative in the field of art. With regard to porcelain, the standard has steadily gone down. There has been an irresistible temptation in these hard times to make curios for the foreign market. Then a certain amount of attention has been paid to the principles and practice of painting in the West, with results which seem to me about as lifeless as they are meretricious. None the less, I cannot believe that the Chinese people are in real danger of losing their aesthetic genius, just as I cannot believe that they may lose their reverence for Nature. It can hardly be long now before developments will take place, and it is only reasonable to suppose that the West will be found to have exercised some sort of influence. Here a prophet might speak. My task, however, is not to prophesy but to record and appraise what has already happened.

The list of books given at the end is not intended to be in any way a complete bibliography of such an immense subject. They are merely suggestions, based on my own experience as to books specially reliable or specially illuminating, which will serve to lead the student into a more profitable consideration of the historical questions with which I have attempted to deal. I have included Mr. W. C. Costin's *Great Britain and China, 1833–1860*, which I was only able to read after this book was in the printer's hands. Mr. Costin and Mr. Hudson have each his own subject and his own angle of approach to far-eastern questions. These differ from mine. In some important respects, however, the three works seem to me to show a certain affinity of outlook. I trust I am not deceived in this, and so may hope for my book to prove soundly complementary to theirs.

E. R. HUGHES

OXFORD, *April* 1937.

CONTENTS

MAPS

MATTEO RICCI'S MAP OF THE WORLD

THE map reproduced as a frontispiece to this book is taken from the *Yue Lin Kuang I*, chuan 1, page 60, by Feng Mu-kang, published in 1602. It is, therefore, a contemporary reproduction of the original map, of which Ricci's contemporary, Father Nicholas Trigault, writes in his *de l'Expédition Chrétienne*: 'Father Ricci being well versed in mathematics, which he had learned from Christopher Clavius, the prince of the mathematicans of his century, applied himself to the construction of this map. . . . I will not either omit to mention a contrivance of his to gain the good graces of the Chinese. They believe that the sky is round but the earth square and that their empire is situated in the midst of it; and they are for this reason very angry when they find our geographers in their maps putting it in a corner of the extreme East. Now, they are not capable of understanding any mathematical demonstration, by which it might be proved to them that the earth and the sea together form a globe and that by the nature of the spherical figure there can be neither beginning nor end to it. He, therefore, altered a little our plan for maps of the world, and by placing the first meridian of the Fortunate Islands at the margin, right and left, he brought the Empire of China into the centre, to their great satisfaction.' (Quoted by Abbé Huc, *Christianity in China, Tartary, etc.*, vol. ii, p. 68. London, 1857.)

Wu Chung-ming's Commentary on the map is quoted in the *Yue Lin Kuang I (ad loc)*: 'The philosopher Tsou [third century B.C.] said that the nine countries outside China were also surrounded by sea. His statement is exaggerated and not exactly correct. It has been said that south-east of the Kun Lun Mountains a spur runs out into China, therefore all the rivers flow to the east; and that a similar spur runs out to the north-west, but it is difficult to know its extent. The earth is wide and great, but anything that has shape cannot but have limits. Thus the provinces of China do not extend beyond the sea on the south-east, the Kun Lun Mountains on the west, or the desert on the north. But to know all about the regions of heaven and earth, is not this difficult? One who only knows what he sees will think that the earth is small; one who can imagine what he does not see will perhaps think it very large. Both are wrong. The monk Li [Matteo Ricci] who came to China from Europe has made a map of the whole world, for the people of his country and the Franks like to wander in far places. With regard to the south polar region, no one has explored it, but it is important to note that he infers from the north, east, and west corners what the rest must be like. The monk has studied deeply with reverence for Heaven. The calculations which he has made of the size and the relative distances of the heavens, the sun, moon, and stars are probably trustworthy and are here appended.'

Then follows Matteo Ricci's own description of his map, in which he states that 'the earth is round, the shape of a ball and lies in the middle of the heavenly sphere like the yoke of an egg surrounded by the white'. He divides the land surface of the earth into six great continents, Europe, Libya, Asia, North America, South America, and Mo-wa-la-ni-chia. This last, as the map shows, is the continent south of the Cape of Good Hope and Cape Horn. Ricci gives detailed boundaries for the other continents, but of this he says, 'we do not entirely know the boundaries and so cannot fix them'. The Holy Land is described as an isthmus connecting Libya and Asia.

THE INVASION OF CHINA BY THE WESTERN WORLD

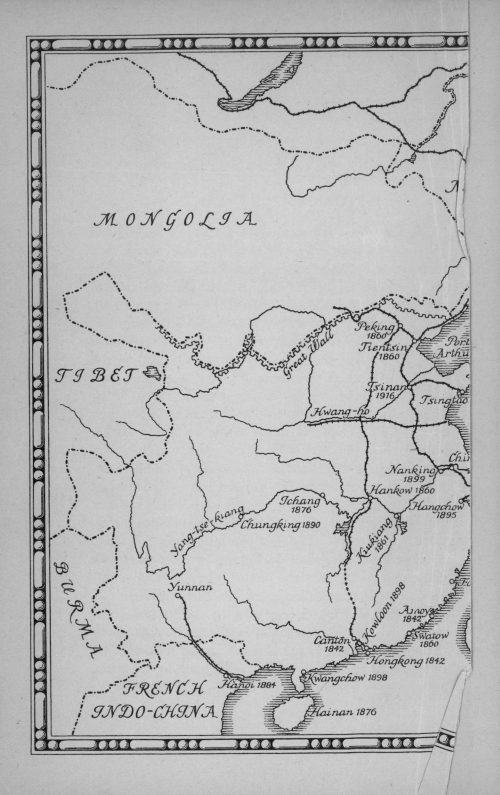

MONGOLIA

TIBET

Great Wall

Peking
1860

Tientsin
1860

Port
Arthu

Tsinan
1916

Tsingtao

Hwang-ho

Nanking
1899

Chi

Hankow 1860

Hangchow
1895

Ichang
1876

Yang-tse-kiang

Chungking 1890

Kiukiang
1861

BURMA

Yunnan

Kowloon 1898

Amoy
1842

Fo

Canton
1842

Swatow
1860

Hongkong 1842

Hanoi 1884

Kwangchow 1898

FRENCH
INDO-CHINA

Hainan 1876

CHAPTER I

HISTORICAL INTRODUCTION

'IN the year 1723 there was a Chinese in Holland who was both a learned man and a merchant, two things that ought by no means to be incompatible: but which thanks to the profound respect that is shown to money, and the little regard that the human species do, and ever will, pay to merit, are become so among us.' These, the opening words of Voltaire's *A Conversation with a Chinese*,[1] serve well as an introduction to the history of cultural relations between the West and China. Learning and trade 'ought by no means to be incompatible', indeed given reasonable conditions they can and do go hand in hand, as the history of Indian and Arabian contacts with China goes to prove. But during nearly two thousand years, from the fifth century B.C. to the sixteenth century A.D., Europe and China were reaching out to find each other and did actually meet for purposes of trade, yet under conditions which militated against the interchange of ideas. The arrival of the Jesuits in Peking in 1601 marks the beginning of the modern period when cultural influences as well as trade began to find their way.

The fifth and fourth centuries B.C. saw in the Greek world that amazing uprush of intellectual power which the West acclaims as the birth of its civilisation. The same centuries saw a similar phenomenon in north

[1] Voltaire, *Romances, Novels and Tales*, vol. i. London, 1806.

China, an equally amazing uprush which also gave birth to a civilisation. Then on the western side came Alexander and his establishment of Greek influence in Western and Central Asia, an influence traceable in art forms though not otherwise making a deep and lasting impression. After Alexander there was the consolidation and extension of the Mediterranean civilisation by means of Rome's imperial power. On the eastern side there was the same process under the Han Emperors (206 B.C.–A.D. 256). Sinitic civilisation became a superior cultural force and made itself felt as far south as the borders of modern Burmah, and as far west as the Caspian Sea, to which Chang Ch'ien and Pan Chao, the two heroes of Han imperialism, carried the prestige of their royal masters. Thus Rome and China came within meeting distance, in fact became fully aware of each other's existence, and a trade of considerable dimensions grew up. The chief commodity was silk, so that Ammianus Marcellinus (*circa* 380) could say 'the use of silk which was once confined to the nobility has now spread to all classes without distinction, even to the lowest'. The Romans paid partly in glass and woollen textiles but also in large quantities of specie.[1] But the power of Parthia lay across the routes of communication, and the Parthians were too good business men to allow their middleman profits to go into other hands. Rome never succeeded in binding Parthia to her will, whilst the Chinese for their part failed to establish any permanent hegemony over the medley of peoples north and west of Parthia. Communication therefore was largely indirect even into the days of the Byzantine Empire. Trade missions, possibly embassies, continued to be dispatched to China at rare intervals, and in the seventh

[1] G. F. Hudson, *Europe and China*, p. 98.

4

century Nestorian Christianity reached out and planted a church in China which for a time had considerable success. The China of the T'ang Dynasty (620–907), stronger culturally than any preceding era, had regular communication with India, and the records of the court at Ch'ang-an contain information about Fu Lin (Byzantium).

Thus at more than one point of time the two cultural streams were on the verge of mingling, did indeed seep across into each other's area of influence. But the cultures neither of Europe nor of China were strong enough to penetrate the barbarian territories of Central Asia. At one time it looked as if Indian Buddhism with its quietist principles would prove capable of bringing peace and harmony and a highway for all nations. Among the Central Asian peoples and tribes it set up 'a standard of the spirit to which the thing achieved is little and the quality of mind that achieves it much'.[1] Again there was failure to secure permanent dominance. Then a fourth culture intervened, the Moslem, and from the seventh to the eleventh century the Arabs with their capital at Bagdad were by far the most potent influence in Central Asia, where there were Buddhists, Moslems, Nestorians, Zoroastrians, and Manicheans living alongside each other, with a background of the old paganism.

What the Arabs meant to the weak and divided peoples of Europe we know. They not only threw them on their defence and so brought a measure of cohesion, but also passed on in due course the ancient Greek science of which they had made themselves masters. Most immediately significant, however, was the fact that the Arabs stirred Europe to a consciousness of itself as

[1] Gilbert Murray, The Legacy of Greece, p. 1.

Christendom. From that came the Crusades, and with them and the mobilisation of religious zeal in the new religious orders of St. Francis and St. Dominic, there sprang up the sense of a world to be won for Christianity. On the one hand, how superbly convincing was that faith as now interpreted by the dialectical genius of St. Thomas Aquinas and touched with the poetic fire of Dante! With the truth of Reason harnessed to the truth of the Holy Ghost, with salvation as the sole property of Holy Mother Church, Christendom could now engage with the intimidating East. On the other hand what a world it was that now began to open to their view! The further east their monks and traders might go, the more strange and yet more humanly real it became. As one of them naïvely confessed, 'I asked about the monsters or of these monstrous men of which Isidore and Solinus speak. They tell me that never the like was seen, and I was greatly astonished at it'.[1]

It was at this juncture that the situation was changed by the sudden emergence of the Mongol tribes as an imperial Power. It is characteristic of the new energy and hope in Europe that in spite of the devastating force with which these hordes swept over Russia, southwest Europe was not intimidated. For a time it was believed that the Mongols were already Christian, or at any rate prepared to become so. In the space of ten years four religious embassies were sent to the Grand Khan, that of Friar Lorenzo, of John de Plano Carpini, of Friar Andrew of Longumeau, and of William of Rubruck. They came back with facts built on observation, description of rites and customs, details of local products and trading facilities. Within the same generation there was a yet more striking and informative

[1] Manuel Komroff, *Contemporaries of Marco Polo*, p. 164.

exploit. Two Venetians, Nicolo and Maffeo Polo, bent on trade, suddenly found their way open to 'far Cathay'. From Bokhara to Cambaluc (Peking) was a journey of twelve wearisome months, but they were rewarded by their welcome at the court of Kublai Khan. The Emperor invited them to return and bring with them a hundred teachers of religion. This request was presented to the Pope, but the Church was too much occupied at that time with internal dissension to be able to undertake such a mission. Two friars only accompanied the Polos when they, with their nephew, Marco, set out on their second journey. The friars' courage failed half-way, but the merchants went on; and the upshot was Marco Polo's seventeen years in China, part of the time as a high official of the Khan, then his return to Europe and the writing of his famous book. The challenge to the Church was taken up later by the Franciscan Order, through whom John of Monte Corvino was sent with a letter from Pope Nicholas IV to Kublai Khan. In a letter dated 1305 and written from Cambaluc, John reported that though the Emperor himself had grown old in idolatry, yet some 6000 persons had been baptized and a church had been built. The Franciscan Mission flourished for three-quarters of a century and spread as far south as Zaitun (Chuan chow) in Fukien, before it collapsed after the fall of the Mongol Empire (1370).[1]

With the fifteenth century we enter on a new stage in the process which was bringing Europe and China nearer to each other. It was Europe which made the move. The Chinese, on their side, having rid themselves of their Mongol rulers and the tribe of Moslem and Nestorian officials from Central Asia, accepted with

[1] A. C. Moule, *Christians in China before the year 1550, passim.*

7

profound relief the purely Chinese authority which the first Ming Emperor gave them. The century which in Europe was to prove so stimulating, was for the Chinese a time of getting back to the old ways, of consolidating the State on the old T'ang foundations. With this came a feeling of caution towards foreigners. Political and intellectual leaders seem to have felt that the infusion of alien blood and alien customs had gone too far and that it was now time the sons of Han concentrated on being themselves. In educated circles the rationalist re-interpretation of Confucianism by the Sung philosophers was widely accepted, and knowledge of it became indispensable for success in the imperial examinations. The spirit of the men who made the Ming era was that same schoolman spirit, part rationalist, part dogmatically theological, which had served Europe so well a century earlier.

In the West, however, a new spirit was awake: the Renaissance spirit with its insatiable curiosity and taste for bizarre luxury. The kings of the new states and their courtiers, prelates and monks, and a new type of merchant-adventurer were beginning to study maps and charts. To all of them China was the wonder of the world, a country rich beyond the dreams of avarice. Prince Henry 'the Navigator' pored over Marco Polo's book and sent out Portuguese sailors to find their way round Africa to India (1416–98). From there they went on to the Moluccas and so to Canton, which they reached for the first time in 1514. Columbus also was inspired by Marco Polo and decided to try a western route. It was on his way to China that he discovered the Americas. In spite of the prodigious wealth which that discovery brought to Spain, she too pushed on until she found and conquered the Philippine Islands. There the

Spaniards met Chinese, both resident traders and sea-farers; but the contact was not a happy one. Finding that the Chinese by their numbers and trading ability were likely to hinder their own success, the Government cleared them out of the islands by a wholesale massacre in which 20,000 people were killed. Both the Spaniards and Portuguese showed a ruthless com-bination of religious zealotry and lust for money, and when their ships put into Chinese ports they came armed to the teeth and carrying priests fired with the conviction that the Cross must be made to triumph. Those were the days of the Inquisition in Southern Europe and America, and the secular and ecclesiastical arms were one force for the glory of God and the in-crease of wealth and power for his most Christian servants. If a Chinese port did not welcome the visitors, or trade was not to their liking, they had no scruples about the use of violence. Thus to the Chinese they appeared as nothing but marauding pirates.

While Spain and Portugal were developing the southern routes, English merchant-adventurers too were seeking a road to Cathay so that they might find a market for their woollen goods and bring back rich cargoes of spices. John Cabot (1497) and later Gilbert and Frobisher, Davis and Hudson, for more than a century sought in vain for the North-West Passage. Better fortune attended those who turned to the north-east, though their exploits are not so famous in history. Willoughby and Chancellor, in charge of an 'expedi-tion for the discoverie of Cathay and divers other regions . . . unknowen', left England in 1553 and reached Moscow by way of the White Sea. The same route was followed four years later by Anthony Jenkin-son, who, fired by his experience of the trade from the East which reached the Levant, now hoped to find a way through Russia and so tap the source without going through Turkish dominions. He reached Bokhara, where he learnt that Cathay was still beyond his reach, but where he opened trade with Persia and established relations with Indian merchants.[1]

The defeat of the Spanish Armada and the ending of the war with Spain opened to England the use of the sea route and obviated the necessity for seeking a lengthy and expensive overland route. There was need, however, to develop the sea trade speedily, for there was another competitor. Holland had been accustomed to get her spices and other Indian produce from the ports of Spain and Portugal. When they were closed through her war with Philip II, she began to send her own ships direct and thus challenged the supremacy of Portugal in the Moluccas.

In order to compete with the Dutch, English merchants formed the East India Company on the last day of December 1600. For a century England and Holland were building up their empires in India and the East Indies at the expense of Portugal. But though Portugal almost disappeared from the scene of trade, it was through the Portuguese settlement at Macao that the next contact was made with China. The Dutch and English, ardent Protestants and upholders of the Reformation as they were, seem to have had no interest in the propagation of their religion among the heathen. It was through Roman Catholicism that Christianity was again introduced into China. After several attempts had failed, most notably that of St. Francis Xavier, two Italian Jesuits succeeded in 1583 in obtaining residence

[1] See *England's Quest of Eastern Trade*, by Sir William Foster, in this same series, chaps. i, ii, and iii.

in a village near Canton. One of these was Matteo Ricci, who eighteen years later won his way to Peking and was able to establish himself and his fellow Jesuits there.

The Ming era was the least progressive of the settled periods in Chinese history, but in the seventeenth century there were signs of new life stirring in the nation. One of these signs was the popularisation of printing.[1] Another was the revival of interest in foreign travel, this time by sea. There are records of voyages going as far west as the Persian and Arabian ports and the coast of Africa.[2] More significant still was the stimulus afforded by the teaching of the great intuitionist philosopher, Wang Yang-ming (1473-1529). A new liberalism began to emerge, as we can see from the conversion to Christianity of two such outstanding scholar-officials as Li Chi-tao and Hsü Kuang-chi, and the new attitude to classical studies shown by the great geographer, Ku Yen-wu. Seventeenth-century Europe too was different from any earlier age. Under the influence of the Renaissance and of the great humanists, Erasmus and Sir Thomas More, Francis Bacon and Galileo and others, men began to see a new heaven and a new earth. Religion could not remain where it was, much less theology. Most important of all was the sense that knowledge was not what was to be found in time-honoured books but in what this vastly surprising world had in it to reveal.

The discoverers and missionaries of the sixteenth

[1] Block printing had existed in China since the ninth century. Movable type was invented in the fifteenth century, and by the sixteenth century there was in China a great development in publishing, both private and official. *Vide* T. F. Carter, *The Invention of Printing and its Spread Westward* (1925).

[2] By Cheng Ho, Yung Lo's famous eunuch, see *Ming History*. Also cp. MS. of a log-book, probably sixteenth century, in the Bodleian Library.

century had at last found the road to Cathay and brought that land out of the mists of romance into the world of practical politics. We have indeed reached the point in time when after attempts ranging over so many centuries the two great cultural streams of East and West might really intermingle. The point of contact was the Jesuit mission in Peking. The missionaries were not only teachers of their religion but some of them were trained scientists and as such were welcomed by Chinese scholars. They were also the means of introducing Chinese scholars to Europe through their colleges in Italy and France. One such scholar was even found in Oxford in 1687.[1] There was here the opportunity in both Europe and China for a fertilising of mind and spirit with fresh ideas born from the older philosophies of each culture. In the West this actually happened. The Catholic missionaries and their Chinese colleagues supplied a steady stream of works on China. These aroused such interest that by the eighteenth century there was quite a literature on the subject by men who had no first-hand knowledge of China at all. Dr. Fisher's description of the eighteenth century in England and France[2] shows how widely this influence penetrated and how much the thinkers of the Enlightenment owed to Chinese humanism and nature philosophy. Here we have one of history's striking ironies, that this philosophy, wedded in politics to a paternalist monarchy, should have been one of the forces which brought about the French Revolution.

In the East the scientific treatises published by the

[1] Andrew Clark, *The Life and Times of Anthony Wood*, vol. iii, p. 236. There were some 80 Chinese works by that time in Bodley's Library apart from western works on China.

[2] *A History of Europe*, chap. xxii.

Jesuits created much interest and were included in the collections of learned studies to be found in every well-stocked library. But, unfortunately, circumstances again intervened to prevent the mind of China co-operating with that of Europe in the development of scientific knowledge. The quarrels between the Jesuits and Dominicans, ending in the denunciation of the Jesuits in the Bull *Ex illa die*, broke the connection between western and eastern learning for nearly two hundred years. Moreover, the conquest of China by the Manchus threw the whole weight of imperial authority on the side of a hard, stereotyped form of Confucianism. By the lavish endowment of classical studies K'ang Hsi and his successors won the support of the *literati*, and liberalism in scholarship as in politics was only able to live underground. Thus in China the ultramontane temper came into the ascendancy, and orthodoxy reigned.

While China was thus closing the doors which had seemed to be opening to religion and science, it proved impossible for her to do the same in the face of the trade invasion in the south. From the time that the Portuguese seized Macao and made it a naval and trading base there was never again complete severance of relations with the European countries which were pressing in from the Dutch East Indies, from British India, and from the French settlements. The Emperor Ch'ien Lung (1736–96) attempted to control this trade by confining it to the port of Canton and making it all pass through the hands of one Chinese guild, known as the Co-hong. Towards the end of his reign efforts were made to open direct diplomatic relations with Peking. Russia had been the first European country to make a treaty with China, when in 1689 they came to an agreement as to the frontier between Siberia and

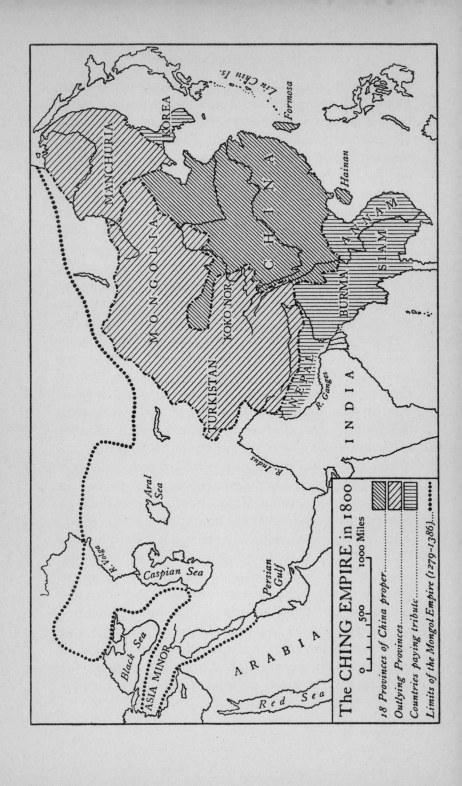

The CHING EMPIRE in 1800

1000 Miles

18 Provinces of China proper..........
Outlying Provinces...................
Countries paying tribute.............
Limits of the Mongol Empire (1279-1386)......

0   500

KOREA

MANCHURIA

MONGOLIA

Liu Chiu Is.

Formosa

Hainan

ANNAM

SIAM

BURMA

CHINA

KOKO NOR

TURKISTAN

NEPAL

R. Ganges

INDIA

R. Indus

Aral Sea

R. Volga

Caspian Sea

Persian Gulf

Black Sea

ASIA MINOR

ARABIA

Red Sea

Manchuria; and Russian envoys continued to visit Peking from time to time, three supplementary treaties being signed, the last in 1792. In the same year George III sent an ambassador, Lord Macartney, who was received by the Emperor but did not succeed in obtaining the concessions he sought. A Dutch mission in 1795, a Russian mission in 1806 and a second British mission under Lord Amherst in 1816, all failed to achieve their end. One difficulty was the Chinese insistence on the performance of the *kowtow* by anyone admitted to the imperial presence, a ceremony which the Europeans considered wholly beneath their dignity. On the Chinese side the position was that from time immemorial foreign envoys had been received in the Colonial Office: there was no Foreign Office. Whatever other countries there might be in the world, they must all acknowledge the supremacy of the Son of Heaven, and the status of their envoys could only be that of tribute-bearers. As to trade with foreigners, the Empire had all that it required within its own borders and felt no need of the goods they offered.

Europe, however, increasingly demanded Chinese silk, porcelain, lacquer and, above all, tea. As the foreigners had nothing China wanted with which to barter in exchange, payment had to be made in silver. This was a serious problem until it was found that the Chinese could be induced to buy opium. Then the principle of exchange began to work to the advantage of the foreigner. Big profits were made by the merchants and the export duty on opium from India brought a huge increase to the Indian revenue. But the conditions under which the trade was carried on were galling in the extreme. As everything had to be done through the Co-hong and there was no fixed tariff, constant oppor-

15

tunities arose for the Chinese to demand bribes or impose irritating restrictions as they felt inclined. Residence was confined to a narrow strip of land on the river bank, in the so-called 'factories'. Women and children found an asylum in Macao, where the conditions were somewhat better. Any attempt to communicate with the Viceroy or other officials had to be couched in the form of humble supplications. For, as the Viceroy wrote in reply to a protest from Captain Elliot, the Superintendent of Trade: 'Between him (the Emperor) and the small and petty how can there exist anything like "bonds of peace and good-will". . . . Not only is this offensive to the dignity to be maintained but also the ideas therein expressed are absurd and ridiculous.'[1]

The expiration of the East India Company's Charter in 1834 brought matters to a crisis. Trade now being open to private merchants who had no official representatives, the English Government made another effort to open diplomatic relations. Lord Napier was sent out with instructions to arrange for some kind of consular official. He died within a year, and the only result of his mission was his report advising the acquisition of the island of Hongkong as a naval and commercial base. The Chinese absolutely refused to make any concessions. They, on their side, were alarmed at the growth of the opium trade, which had increased from some four thousand chests imported in 1821 to thirty thousand in 1839. The trade was highly objectionable to them both on moral and economic grounds. Since edicts had no effect, a special Commissioner, Lin Tse-hsü, was sent to Canton in 1839 with instructions to put

[1] Quoted in a pamphlet on *The Management of our Affairs in China* in the library of the London Missionary Society, probably by Dr. William Lockhart.

an end to the whole business. The action which he took was to order the confiscation of all stocks of opium, and the signing of an agreement that no more should be imported. The opium was burnt, the bond signed, but opium continued to be smuggled in. The murder of a Chinese by drunken British sailors and the refusal of the British authorities to hand them over to Chinese justice raised the other burning question of whether or not foreigners were to be amenable to Chinese law. War broke out between England and China and continued for three years until it was ended by the Treaty of Nanking.

This treaty marks the opening of China to the western influences of the nineteenth and twentieth centuries. The story of these different influences and their effect on men's minds and souls, not to speak of their bodies, will occupy the pages of this book. Since the growth of these influences came in well-defined stages, it will be convenient to note certain dates which are landmarks, and then to refer briefly to the main historical events of the periods thus outlined.

(1) 1839. The outbreak of the Opium War, ending with the Treaty of Nanking, 1842.

(2) 1857. The outbreak of the Arrow War leading to the Treaty of Tientsin, 1858; and then the renewal of hostilities with the sack of the Imperial Summer Palace and the Conventions of Peking, 1860.

(3) 1894. The war between Japan and China with its revelation of China's inability to resist any aggression and the consequent excitement of strong national feeling in China; this followed by the Hundred Days of Reform, 1898, and this in turn by the Boxer Outbreak, 1900,

and the vengeance taken by the Western Powers.

(4) 1911. The Fall of the Manchu Dynasty and the establishment of the Republic in 1912.

(5) The Shanghai Incident of May 30, 1925, followed by the Nationalist Revolution, 1926–27, and the establishment of the Nationalist Government at Nanking and the theoretical unification of the country.

FIRST PERIOD, 1839–57

The war of 1839–42 is generally known as the Opium War. The point at issue was, however, a bigger one than the importation of opium: it was the whole question of what the terms were to be on which Europeans were to be allowed to trade with China. By the Treaty of Nanking, the five ports of Canton, Amoy, Foochow, Ningpo, and Shanghai were opened to the residence and trade of British subjects. The island of Hongkong was ceded to Britain for development as a naval and commercial base. Agreements were made for a footing of equality between British and Chinese officials, for the establishment of a regular tariff, and the payment of an indemnity for the opium destroyed by Commissioner Lin.

A year later an agreement was reached on two further issues. British subjects were to be placed under the law of their own country and offenders to be judged by their own consular officials in the consular court—the system which has come to be known as 'extra-territoriality'. China also agreed that whatever privileges she might grant any other nation, she would also grant to Britain. This is the 'most-favoured-nation principle' which came to play so great a part in later treaties. Within ten years, France, Belgium, America, Sweden and Norway, and Russia had also obtained treaties on the same basis.

The next eighteen years saw the building-up of the foreign communities in these Treaty Ports. Foreigners now had the right to build houses, wharves and warehouses, churches, schools, and hospitals, so that some of the more acute difficulties of residence and trade were solved. They were assigned special areas in which to live, and thus came the beginning of those self-governing foreign settlements on Chinese soil which have been such a peculiar feature in the history of the relations between China and the West. Through contact with these communities a growing number of Chinese became accustomed to the presence of the foreigners, and ideas of many sorts began to filter through into Chinese life. But the problem of the relation between these new communities and Chinese society was in no way solved. There were merchants prepared to do business, but neither officials nor common people were any more desirous than formerly to have these foreigners in their country. They brought guns, opium, and Bibles, and to sober peace-loving citizens there was no distinction between the three: they were all equally obnoxious and deleterious. The imperial policy with regard to opium remained the same; protests were repeatedly made against the extensive smuggling which went on. Since the smugglers were Chinese subjects, and it was known that officials connived at the business for the sake of the bribes which they received, foreign traders were able to argue that they could not help it if the authorities were not able to enforce their own laws. But, since the traders would allow no one to interfere with their bringing of the opium to the door of China and their governments

19

regarded themselves as having treaties of amity, this argument can only be regarded as dubiously moral.

Two further sources of difficulty must be mentioned. One was the action of the Roman Catholic missionaries who came into the Treaty Ports. Through the French consuls they presented claims for buildings and land in the interior which had belonged to the Church during its earlier period of expansion. This property had now been in Chinese hands for several generations, and the attempts to recover it caused much ill-feeling. The other trouble was the coolie traffic from south China to California and South America. Shiploads of coolies were taken over to develop the gold mines and other connected industries. On arrival they were sold into virtual. slavery under agreements which they did not understand and over which there was no legal supervision. The conditions during the voyages were comparable to those of the African slave trade, and mutinies and massacres were not unknown. Efforts made by the British Government to close the traffic from Hongkong were successful, but it continued from Macao and the other southern ports until the second half of the century. To the Chinese, with their mordant sense of humour, this came to be known as the 'pig-selling' trade.

Meanwhile the general condition of the country had begun to deteriorate. Prosperity under the earlier Manchu Emperors had induced a rise in population, but there had been no new economic developments to increase trade or provide new sources of food supply. In the nineteenth century, therefore, there came a slump. This was accentuated by the degeneration of the Manchu Court, which gave itself up to extravagant luxury, entailing heavier taxation. Then came the opium trade which, by creating opium addicts, increased the number of non-producing consumers, already large, owing to the peculiarities of the Chinese family system. As the consumption of opium grew the payment of imports by silver instead of by goods further impoverished the country.

In 1851 a new Emperor, Hsien Feng, came to the throne, a weakling quite incapable of dealing with the troubles that arose. Chief among these was the Taiping Rebellion, which lasted for seventeen years and caused a casualty list estimated at twenty million lives. Its story falls into three sections: its rise, 1849–53; its period of power, 1853–60; its decline and fall, 1860–1865. It has a peculiar interest for us because its chief leader, one Hung Hsiu-ch'üan, from the far interior of Canton province, was stirred by contact with Christianity and the study of some of the Protestant missionaries' tracts. The initial impulse came from a special revelation in a vision, that he was called by God to destroy the Manchu tyranny and set up a 'Great Peace Heavenly State' (Tai Ping T'ien Kuo). Armed with this commission from Heaven, he attracted followers from all over south China, particularly members of the secret revolutionary societies. The *literati* on the whole were unsympathetic: the teachings of the leaders were both too radical and too mystical for them. This eventually proved the downfall of the rebellion. The strain on the Heavenly State Emperor (Hung Hsiuch'üan) and his group of advisers became too much for them. They lost their nerve and found refuge in fantastic visions, though to the very end the distinctively Christian side to the movement was quite clearly marked.

Starting in the far south in 1849, the Taipings developed a fine military organisation with some very able army leaders at the head. They proclaimed their Emperor in 1851 and very soon after were in possession of a large quantity of arms taken from defeated Government troops. In March 1853 they captured Nanking and had most of southern China under their control. The Emperor appointed civil officers, collected taxes, destroyed idols and, at any rate in some areas, arranged for education on the basis of Christian teaching. Meanwhile his ablest commander, the Chung Wang, set out to attack Peking. In a few months he was within striking distance of Tientsin. The approach of winter and the lack of supporting troops then made retreat necessary, and the Taipings never again came so near to their final objective. The scene of conflict developed in the Yangtse valley. The Manchu Court had by this time discovered that they could not rely on their regular troops, but that there was a force of effective loyalty to be found among the Chinese people. Tseng Kuo-fan, the grand old man of Hunan province, was called on to save the country. Reluctantly deciding that he must leave his scholarly life to obey the call, he raised an army from among his fellow provincials. Time after time he suffered reverses, but he refused to be beaten, and his sober, patient gallantry inspired all those who mistrusted the Taiping régime. The final stage came when the Western Powers decided that it was to their profit to maintain the Manchus in power. At this time the Taipings were in the neighbourhood of Shanghai and were greatly interfering with trade. This was made the excuse for official support of a force raised by a filibustering American, Frederick Ward. Eventually Charles Gordon, 'Chinese Gordon', was brought out and lent to the Chinese Government, together with a number of other foreign officers, to help Tseng Kuo-fan's army. The attacks which finally captured the Taiping strongholds in 1864 were under Gordon's generalship.

The Taiping Rebellion gave an impetus to the study of foreign shipbuilding and the manufacture of guns. Tseng Kuo-fan needed ships to carry on the campaign against the rebels along the Yangtse and among the inland lakes, so ships had to be built. Foreign guns were purchased to equip these, and also for the use of the army. After the rebellion was over, Tseng as Viceroy interested himself in the manufacture of guns and ammunition and the building of ships. He established arsenals first at Anking, then at Nanking and later at Kiangnan, near Shanghai. At first he had no foreign experts or any Chinese who had studied abroad. In order to get foreign machinery he used the services of Yung Wing, the first Chinese graduate in America. With the equipment thus obtained, the first steamship was built and launched in 1868. Later six or seven foreign engineers were employed, and so began the training of Chinese engineers. Before Tseng's death in 1872, five steamers had been built, and his coffin was escorted by them up the Yangtse on its way to his native city of Changsha: a fitting escort for the greatest Chinese statesman of the nineteenth century, a scholar and official of the old school, who had vision and ability to begin to meet the challenge of the West where it was strongest. His dreams of a modernised navy, however, were not realised, either then or later. Li Hung-chang, his former subordinate, followed him in making plans and preparations but, as we shall see later, he did not succeed in creating an efficient navy. What he did do was to lay the foundation of a merchant service by the organisation of the China Merchants' Steam Navigation Company, which has ever since had its share of the coast and Yangtse traffic. Even in this direction the success was very partial, in no way to be compared to the development of the Japanese merchant service.

SECOND PERIOD, 1857–94

During our first period England was the western country chiefly concerned with China. When we come to the middle of the century, we find France, Russia, and America taking their part. The Crimean War brought about the Anglo-French Alliance which made for joint action in the East. It also caused Russia to push forward her frontier along the Amur River in order to reach her settlements on the coast, when naval communication from the Black Sea was cut off. Thus between 1856 and 1860 China had to deal with England and France in the south and Russia in the north.

As with the war of 1839, there was trouble brewing for years before the actual clash took place. Again opium smuggling was the bone of contention, with the additional complication of whether China had the right of search over vessels manned by Chinese crews but sailing under the British flag. There was also the irritation caused by the failure to provide better living arrangements for the foreign community at Canton. People's tempers began to give way. Harry Parkes, the British Consul at Canton, was never known for a patient man, whilst Viceroy Yeh was just the man to do the job which had been given him, namely, to obstruct in every possible way. Since the early treaties had expired, the time had come to apply the screw. The arrest of the crew of the Chinese lorcha *Arrow*, flying the British flag, furnished the *casus belli*, and the British

bombarded the Viceroy's *yamen*. France joined in on the
pretext of satisfaction for the murder of a French priest
in Kwangsi, protection of Catholic missions being at
the time part of Napoleon III's policy. In due course
Canton was captured by a combined force of British and
French sailors. The Viceroy was caught as he tried to
escape and sent to Calcutta, where he died a few months
later. But that was not the end of his influence. He was
a Hunan man, and the Hunanese are known through
all China as having both a specially strong sense of
provincial loyalty and a militant sense of nationality. It
was from Hunan that a flood of anti-foreign literature
came during the next twenty years.

The British having taken the lead at this critical
time, it is interesting to see what opinion in England
was. The *Arrow* incident caused a violent debate in the
House of Commons. Cobden brought in a vote of want
of confidence against Palmerston's administration, and
Gladstone supported the motion in one of his greatest
speeches. As early as 1840 he had expressed himself on
the subject of the Opium War: 'although the Chinese
are undoubtedly guilty of much absurd phraseology,
and of no little ostentatious pride and of some excess,
justice in my opinion is with them, and whilst they the
pagans and semi-civilised barbarians have it, we, the
enlightened and civilised Christians, are pursuing objects at variance both with justice and with religion'. In
1857 he again pleaded for justice: 'that justice which
binds man to man; which is older than Christianity
because it was in the world before Christianity, for
Christianity itself appeals to it'.

Cobden's motion was carried by a majority of sixteen
in a full House. Palmerston's reply was that 'there
would be and could be no change in the policy of the

Government in respect to China'. He went to the country and was returned to office. The 'vigorous policy' was therefore endorsed, and Lord Elgin went east as Her Majesty's Envoy Extraordinary with plenipotentiary powers. His diary makes interesting reading.[1] 'I thought bitterly of those who for the most selfish object are trampling underfoot this ancient civilisation.' 'There is a word called "loot" which gives unfortunately a venial character to what would in common English be styled robbery.' The so-called vigorous policy he described as consisting in 'resorting to the most violent measures of coercion and repression on the slenderest provocation'. His general impression of British trade was that 'it is carried on on principles which are dishonest as regards the Chinese and demoralising to our own people'. With regard to Chinese officialdom also he formed the worst impression, and in one passage he wrote: 'I now know what fools they are and what calamities they bring upon themselves, or rather the wretched people, by their pride and treachery'.

Whatever Lord Elgin might feel, he was committed to the policy of his Government. In pursuance of that policy he went north with the British forces, Baron Gros going with the French. The aim was twofold, to force an audience of the Emperor without the indignity of the *kowtow*, and to get new Treaty Ports and other trading privileges. That meant war. A preliminary skirmish occurred which hustled the Chinese into the Treaty of Tientsin, and then, a year later, further hostilities which brought about the capture of Tientsin, the treacherous imprisonment and ill-treatment by the Chinese of a party negotiating terms of truce, and in

[1] *Letters and Journals of James, Eighth Earl of Elgin*, ed. by T. Walrond (1st ed. 1872), pp. 213, 227, 232.

retaliation the capture of Peking and the sack and burning of the Summer Palace. This was the 'thrashing such as they have never had before' for which the Hongkong papers at the time made vociferous demands.

Sir John Bowring was then in charge at Hongkong. Like Lord Palmerston, the idol of John Bull of that generation, Sir John was always sure that he was right and could show where England's enemies were wrong. Unlike 'Pam' he had in him a strong religious strain, the strain which went with the outlook of the new middle class and its belief in the civilising mission of British commerce and manufacture. The Great Exhibition (1851) had been a resounding success, with the 'works of all nations' assembled in Hyde Park. That display of England's power and prestige had an intoxicating effect. If anyone knew the way to peace and prosperity and the triumph of right, surely it was England. Was she not blessed with wealth, the fruit of her own probity and industry, mistress of the seas, able and just administrator of vast colonies, benefactor of the Indian peoples, and denouncer of slavery? Must it not be for China's good to share this beneficent influence?

The Treaty of Tientsin (1858) and the Conventions of Peking (1860) to all intents and purposes laid China open from end to end. The powers concerned in those treaties were England, France, Russia, and the United States. Russia had taken no part in the hostilities and appeared in the negotiations as a friend and counsellor of China, but she also played her cards to further strengthen her position on the Amur. America, who had been occupied with the naval demonstrations which led to the opening of Japan to the West, now demanded her share in the privileges granted by China to the European Powers. Ten new Treaty Ports were arranged for, some of them far up the Yangtse River. Ministers with their staffs were to have the right of residence in Peking. An indemnity for the recent operations was exacted and its payment guaranteed from the Maritime Customs Service, which had come into existence as a temporary measure of convenience during the troubles and was now established under foreign supervision. Kowloon, a stretch of territory opposite Hongkong, was ceded to England, and the import of opium was legalised by the imposition of a tax. Finally, toleration was given to missionaries and converts to teach and practise Christianity throughout the country. The Russians and Americans were the first to get this clause accepted.

According to Wells Williams's account, he being secretary to the United States Envoy and himself a missionary, the Russians had no difficulty, as their priests were well known in Peking and not disliked; but the Chinese Commissioners objected firmly to the Protestants claiming the same privileges. A long tussle ensued, and the United States Envoy finally told Williams that he was prepared to give way and be content with toleration in the ports. Williams was greatly distressed by this. He and his fellow secretary, W. A. P. Martin, went the next day with a new amendment and informed the Chinese that 'this was the form *we* were decided on and they must approve it as it stood'.[1] The amendment was as follows: 'The principles of the Christian religion as professed by the Protestant and Roman Catholic Churches are recognised as teaching meant to do good and to do to

[1] Vide *Life and Letters of Samuel Wells Williams* (New York, 1889), p. 271. The italics are not in the original text.

others as they would have others do to them. Here-after those who quietly profess and teach these doctrines shall not be harassed or persecuted on account of their faith. Any person whether citizen of the United States or Chinese convert who according to these tenets shall peaceably teach and practise the principles of Christianity shall in no case be interfered with or molested.' The Commissioners agreed, thinking presumably that Reed, the Envoy, was behind the amendment. Wells Williams then returned and informed his chief that the Commissioners had consented to sign. The Chinese, having given way here, also gave way to the British and French. In addition the latter secured the return of all the church property lost by the Roman Catholics during the last hundred years of persecution and the right for missionaries to buy and rent land and houses anywhere in the country. At least that was what was stated in the Chinese version of the Treaty, as distinct from the French, where there was no such clause. The missionaries, with the French authorities backing them, insisted on taking the version which suited their interests as the authentic one. The exercise of this doubtful right had far-reaching consequences, for Protestant missionaries also came increasingly to claim the same privilege as the Catholics. The Chinese government continued to object that this was not included in the Treaty.[1]

From 1860 to the end of this period was a time of incessant expansion of foreign interests. The Powers were firm supporters of the Manchu Dynasty, a posi-

---

[1] The mystery has never been cleared up. Professor Latourette remarks: 'Since the chief interpreter for the French was a missionary, Delamarre, it is supposed that he introduced the changes, perhaps surreptitiously'. *Hist. of Christian Missions in China*, pp. 276-7. For the Catholic side see *Variétés Sinologiques*, No. 18.

tion profitable to both sides but having a disastrous effect on Chinese domestic politics. In previous ages the Chinese had had their own traditional way of getting rid of a régime which had outlived its value, and they had already been estimating that the time had come for a revolution. Now fear of what the foreigner might do came in as an incommensurable factor. The result was that the Manchus hung on for another fifty years, during which time very valuable concessions were given to foreign interests.

The missionary movement now made enormous strides. At the beginning of the century there had been only a handful of Roman Catholic missionaries with some 200,000 converts. By 1897 the number of Catholic missionaries totalled 750. Among the Protestants the number of missionaries in 1864 was 189, in 1893 nearly 1300, representing forty-one different societies organised from England, and America, Germany, Norway and Sweden, Switzerland, Denmark, and Finland. Among these societies was the China Inland Mission, founded in 1866, and numbering 600 missionaries by the end of the century. This society was committed to the policy of preaching specially in those provinces into which foreigners had not yet penetrated, and its missionaries carried out this aim with a high degree of courage and devotion.

This expansion of effort met with a certain amount of success. It is difficult to give accurate statistics as a basis of comparison, but by 1897 the Roman Catholic Church would seem to have more than doubled its numbers as compared with the beginning of the century, while the Protestants had built up a church of over 50,000 members. The much more rapid increase of the Catholic Church in spite of fewer foreign missionaries was due partly to the fact that it was already established long before the beginning of Protestant missions, and partly to its methods. While the story of Protestant missions during this period is largely that of single-handed pioneer evangelists, the Catholics were building up their congregations with the help of a Chinese priesthood.

The growth of the Christian Church, whether Roman Catholic or Protestant, was achieved, however, at the expense of a great deal of bad feeling. Hardly a year passed without a riot in one province or another, involving destruction of property and in a number of cases, loss of life. The immediate cause of these riots was nearly always connected with mission work. As to what really lay behind them opinions varied very much. Some people came to the belief that the Chinese as a nation had an ingrained hatred of foreigners, others holding that this was not true and that the mobs were maliciously stirred up by the Government and the *literati*. Foreign officials were more and more convinced that the Government was responsible, endeavouring in this way to take back by force privileges which had been won by force. Even missionaries were convinced that such an attitude must be met with the utmost firmness. The saintly David Hill said at a protest meeting in 1895: 'I class these outbreaks with the kidnapping of slaves, and as in this matter the Powers have determined to seize a slave dhow wherever it is seen, so let Christian nations combine to suppress this mad rioting. . . . In negotiating with the representative of the Viceroy it was forced upon me that he was seeking how little he could cede to the foreigner rather than what it was right to do.'

The French, and later the German Foreign Offices

were not embarrassed by such events. In fact they rather welcomed them as opportunity for further advance. The British Government, however, had no such clear-cut policy. *The Times* said on March 10, 1869: 'Parliament is not fond of missionaries, nor is the press, nor is general society.' On the other hand one consul in his official report said:[1] 'There is no doubt that Christian education tends to raise the Chinese to a higher intellectual level . . . that correlated with this will arise a greater desire of comfort and luxury and consequent extended commerce. The labours of the missionaries indirectly benefit our merchants, manufacturers, and artisans.'

The question of benefit to British trade was a matter of some concern at this time. The opening of the Treaty Ports had been hailed as the dawn of an immense expansion of trade among the millions of China. But this optimistic view did not allow for the solid weight of conservatism and prejudice among the Chinese of the interior, nor perhaps for their poverty. There was some growth in the import of kerosene oil, matches, and a few other kinds of goods; but until 1870 more than half the total imports were made up by opium and cotton goods, and there was little extension of trade beyond the Ports and their immediate neighbourhood.

The establishment of the legations in Peking proved on the whole disappointing to those who hoped that better relations would result. That remarkable and—one must add—sinister woman, Tzu Hsi, mother of the baby placed on the throne in 1862, held the reins from then until 1908. She was pure Manchu and never thought of anything but Manchu interests. In pursuing

[1] C. T. Gardner, *Official Report from Newchang*, 1884.

these she showed brilliant gifts of the Machiavellian order. She could back her friends and ruthlessly destroy her enemies, and it is safe to say that she never once thought of foreigners as anything but alien barbarians whom it was one's business to hoodwink by every possible means. She called the tune for the new Foreign Office, the Tsungli Yamen; and the eminently safe Manchu grandees who were put in charge of it solemnly followed her lead. The less they saw of the foreigners the better they were pleased, and there was only one of the Ministers who gained their confidence. This was Anson Burlinghame, the American, who came to see that China's diplomacy was inevitably doomed to failure unless she could use her own diplomats at the different courts in Europe and America. The first step taken in this direction was an invitation to Burlinghame himself in 1867 to go to Europe and America, taking with him some budding Chinese diplomats, and as envoy extraordinary of the Chinese Court to try to put relationships on a more equitable basis. In both America and England his mission was a success, but he died in Russia before it was concluded. The Manchu Government, however, was encouraged to proceed along this line, and in 1873 a Minister was appointed to the Court of St. James to be followed by the establishment of legations in the other main European countries. This change proved more productive of mutual understanding.

Outside diplomatic circles there was a distinct improvement of relations in a number of quarters. July 12, 1854, was a notable date in the history of international relations, for on that day three foreigners entered the service of the Chinese Government as inspectors of Maritime Customs. The need for this step arose from

33

the difficulties of trade in Shanghai during the troublous years of 1850–54. The purpose was originally to guard the interests of British trade, but by reducing smuggling a more regular revenue was ensured for the Chinese Government. By the Conventions of Peking the indemnities demanded by the Powers were secured on this revenue, and foreign inspectors were appointed at all the ports. Although he was not the first Inspector-General, the name of Robert Hart is always associated with the Customs Service. As an organiser he built up a remarkably efficient system on an international basis. As a servant of the Chinese Government he never forgot his loyalty to his masters; and he won their confidence to a high degree both by his sense of dignity and by the integrity of his word and deed. Not only he but also the Inspectors of Customs in the different Ports—British, French, American, Dutch or Japanese, whatever they might be—were brought into constant relations with local Chinese officials on quite a new footing. This gave opportunities for intercourse between men of education with the will to appreciate each other, and this led to much better understanding. While the higher appointments in the Service were reserved for foreigners, the lower grades provided a training-ground for Chinese who, in positions which were free from the disabilities attaching to most official appointments in China at the time, learned western methods of administrative efficiency. The steady revenue derived from the Customs proved of immense advantage to China, even though after 1900 it was made the security for a second and enormous indemnity. On the other hand, it was humiliating; and the fixed tariff which was part of the Treaties favoured foreign trade and has been regarded in recent years by Chinese Nationalists as one of the factors hindering the growth of Chinese industries.

To Hart also is due the credit, in the first instance, for the modernisation of the Chinese Postal Service. Imperial couriers had transmitted dispatches with amazing speed by means of an organisation dating from very early times. Also from Ming times there had existed private posting companies which operated very efficiently over a limited area: that is to say, they developed only the profitable routes where trade was brisk. As the Treaty Ports grew, foreign post-offices were instituted by the different nations for handling mail from abroad. When Hart began to study the situation he had, therefore, these three systems with their special interests to combine into one national service. It was a long and difficult business which was begun after the Chefoo Convention of 1876 and was not finally completed until China entered the Postal Union in 1914. The foreign post-offices were closed in 1922. Like the Customs Service, the Post Office has a record of devoted service from foreigners of many nationalities and has trained many Chinese. The way in which the mail service was carried on even in remote districts through all the disturbances of 1911–28 is the best testimony to the success which has crowned this joint enterprise of Chinese and foreigners to adapt and develop native practice to the more exigent requirements of modern life.

Another similar experiment in a different sphere was the college for the training of diplomatic agents, the Tung Wen Kuan, which for many years had as president the American W. A. P. Martin. He and his foreign staff got to know and respect their Chinese colleagues. They met on a basis of common love for learning, an appeal to which Chinese always respond. In the Ports, too, business men on both sides learned to distinguish between rascals and men of honour. Good men learnt to trust each other, though unfortunately with but few individual exceptions they everywhere tended to restrict their intercourse to business relations only. Among missionaries appeared such men as the Englishman Timothy Richard and the American Young J. Allen, who took pains to make themselves conversant with Chinese culture, and when they met an official showed that they expected to meet a scholar and a gentleman and to be treated as such themselves. The result was seldom a conversion, but they discovered each other's human qualities and came to a mutual respect and feeling of friendship. There had been from the beginning able students of the Chinese language, men like James Legge in Hongkong and Sir Thomas Wade in Peking, who became well versed in the classical literature, and did much to make it accessible to other foreigners. Mission schools also had their influence. They were increasing in numbers and efficiency, and in some of them teachers and students began to understand and respect each other's culture.

As early as the Opium War a few Chinese had raised a cry for 'self-strengthening', a demand which the Peking Court heartily endorsed. By the 'sixties there was a distinct movement which as the years went on became more and more conscious of the fact that behind the technical achievements which seemed to make the West so strong there lay a western culture which was worth consideration. This created a demand for translations of western books, first technical works, then works on international law and western history and even novels. These books became an important factor in the situation, as appeared with great force in the 'eighties, when one of the most brilliant and distinguished scholars of his day, the Cantonese K'ang Yiu-wei, gathered round him a group of disciples and stirred them with his exposition of western culture and its significance for China. During this period also Chinese began to go abroad to Europe and America, at first for technical education and later to study other subjects.

THIRD PERIOD, 1894–1911

While the Peking Court was still resisting the on-coming tide of western influences, the leaders of Japan had accepted them and in particular had remodelled her army and navy. China reckoned to have been doing the same, but in 1894 a clash over Korea revealed that she had only been playing at it. Special taxes had been levied, large sums had been spent—other sums had disappeared into private pockets—and men had come back from abroad prepared to train the new army and navy. The result was forces which could parade but could not fight. China was defeated by her small neighbour, and by the Treaty of Shimoneseki (1896) she had to acknowledge the independence of Korea and cede to Japan Formosa and the Liaotung Peninsula, besides paying a heavy indemnity.

The result was a conviction in foreign diplomatic circles that the Manchu Government was past praying for, and that the thing to be done was for each Power to decide on what area it could hope to exploit with the most profit and to go ahead with plans for doing so. France had already since 1885 annexed Annam, and Russia with the Trans-Siberian Railway to help had been pushing forward on the Manchurian border.

England wished to make sure of the Yangtse valley, France of Yunnan, Russia of Manchuria, Germany—a very late comer and all the more anxious to make up for lost time—of Shantung province. To balance the concessions given to Japan, England secured the 'lease' of Wei-hai-wei, France of Kwangchow, Germany of Tsingtao and Russia of Dairen.

These leased territories differed from the earlier 'settlements', and were more in the nature of colonies. Those were the days when the cry of 'the white man's burden' was at its height. High-minded men were persuaded that the benefits of their material civilisation must be an unmitigated blessing to 'the coloured races'. Southern Asia had come under foreign dominance and Africa was being colonised. Why not China? By railway and mining concessions spheres of economic influence could be built up, and the question of political control could be left to a convenient time when one's competitor was not watching so carefully. So the race for concessions went ahead. Agents of railway and mining corporations flocked to Peking; Ministers calling at the Tsungli Yamen eyed their colleagues, each wondering what schemes the other had in mind.

The first railway in China had been built from Shanghai to Woosung in 1876 and had been torn up again two years later by Government orders. But four years later Li Hung-chang, being in charge of foreign trade in the north, had secretly, without imperial permission, built a small line from Tongshan to Tientsin for the transport of coal. By the time it was completed he had won over the Court to agree to making it the first section of a line to connect Tientsin with Peking. So the first steps had been taken in overcoming the fear that the 'fire-carriages' would upset the *fengshui*—the

'wind and water influences'—which are so much con-
cerned with anything affecting the land. But now that
China was in no position to go forward herself, she had
to concede railway rights all round: in Manchuria to
Russia, in north China to England, in Yunnan to
France and in Shantung to Germany.

Foreign capital was invested not only in railways and
mines but also in a loan to pay off the Japanese indemnity of £30,000,000. The European Powers were
seriously perturbed at this indemnity, which threatened
to give Japan a hold on what they had come to regard as
their 'rights' in China. France, therefore, with England,
Russia, and Germany made a combined loan to China to
enable her to pay off Japan.

All this foreign activity made the Chinese feel that
their country was about to be 'carved like a melon', and
a movement for reform began to take definite shape.
Older officials, men in high positions like Li Hung-
chang and Chang Chih-tung, Viceroy at Wuchang,
were not prepared to risk the anger of the Empress-
Dowager, but there were others who saw that her
power must come to an end if the country was to be
saved. Among them was a young western-trained doctor, Sun Yat-sen, who in 1894 began collecting arms in
Hongkong for a revolt in the south. The plot was discovered, and Sun became an exile with a price on his
head. The scholar K'ang Yiu-wei, with his group of
ardent disciples, learned that the young Emperor,
Kuang Hsü, had progressive leanings and was anxious
to be free from the Empress-Dowager's leading-strings.
Through their influence there was in 1898 a complete
revolution in the Manchu policy. The Emperor turned
his back on his old advisers and issued edict after edict
organising a new régime. The period is known as the

'Hundred Days of Reform', for the reactionary forces rallied round the Empress-Dowager. With the help of Yuan Shih-kai who commanded the new foreign trained army, she achieved a *coup-d'état* by which she got power entirely into her own hands, thus flying in the face of Chinese tradition and Manchu dynastic law. The Emperor was imprisoned on an island in the Palace lake, and edicts issued in his name ordered the arrest of K'ang Yiu-wei and his associates. K'ang and the subsequently famous Liang Ch'i-ch'ao escaped to Japan, but six of the band were caught and executed. All the reform measures were annulled, and the Empress-Dowager was confirmed in her belief that it was possible to put the clock back. The foreign diplomats looked on and did nothing.

The country, however, was in a state of nervous excitement. A wave of hysteria, part religious, part political, swept over the north, and an insignificant secret society called the *I Ho Tuan* (known to the West as Boxers)[1] suddenly assumed alarming proportions. The Empress and her advisers saw the danger to themselves, saw also an opportunity for diverting public indignation away from their own acts and concentrating it on the foreigners. The Boxers were given imperial support; Prince Tuan became their leader and later was made head of the Tsungli Yamen. So came the tragic outbreak of 1900. Orders were issued from Peking to all provincial governors that foreigners were to be executed: the troops in Chihli with the aid of the Boxers would deal with the Legations and the Tientsin foreign community. In the weeks that followed, over two hundred foreign missionaries were murdered and a

[1] The three characters I Ho Tuan mean justice harmony band. The members were trained in a special art of boxing.

vastly larger number of Chinese Christians: one estimate puts it at about 30,000 Roman Catholics and
nearly 2000 Protestants.

The majority of the provincial governors did not act
according to instructions. A few took strong measures
to repress anti-foreign outbreaks. In Peking and
Tientsin, however, the situation became very critical.
The German Minister was killed and for two months
the refugees in the Legations were closely besieged.
The Powers took combined action and an international
force first relieved Tientsin and then fought its way to
Peking. The Court fled and the capital was at the mercy
of the foreigners.

For six months Peking and the province of Chihli
were in a state of chaos. Both the diplomats and the
Allied commanders suspected each other of secret
schemes for reaping the harvest to their own benefit.
Meanwhile public opinion in Europe and America was
urgent in its demands for retribution. That retribution
was taken in the first instance by widespread looting in
Peking in which civilians as well as soldiers joined. The
troops also marched all over the province taking toll of life
and property as they willed, without distinguishing friend
or foe. Finally peace was made by the signing of the
Protocol on September 9, 1901. The terms included the
punishment of the officials responsible for the murder
of foreigners and the suspension for five years of the
State examinations in the towns concerned; the pro-
hibition for two years of the importation of arms or
ammunition; the maintenance of free communication
between Peking and the sea with the right to keep
guards at the foreign legations; the reconstruction of
the Tsungli Yamen into a Ministry of Foreign Affairs
taking precedence of all the other ministries of State;

and the payment by China of an indemnity of 450,000,000 taels (£67,500,000) with interest at 4 per cent. in thirty-nine annual instalments. This sum was secured on the Maritime Customs, the Salt Tax, and the native customs. China's humiliation was complete. In 1898 the foreign diplomats had done nothing, and in the spring of 1900 they were careless of the warnings which they received. But after the crash had come, the violence of their action was as unstatesmanlike as their former inaction. Moreover, the fact that the Manchus were allowed to return and again enjoy imperial power while so enormous an indemnity was laid upon the country as a whole, was in Chinese eyes a confounding of the guilty and the innocent.

From 1902 the Manchus, to all intents and purposes, reigned by sufferance of the foreign Powers. Of this they were perfectly well aware, as their policy showed. The radical reform of the State examination system for which Chinese reformers had so long pleaded in vain was now granted. A Ministry of Education was set up to promote modern education and a commission was sent to Europe to study constitutional government. In 1908 an elected assembly of provincial representatives was promised, and this met two years later. The foreign concessionaires were allowed to complete and start operating their railways. Most of the main lines of railway in China as they are to-day were built at this time by foreign engineers with foreign capital. The contemplated mining development has not, however, taken place to any great extent, chiefly because by the time the railways were finished the Manchu régime came to an end and the country was thrown into confusion. The British coal mines at Kailan and Japanese coal and iron mines in Manchuria are the most noteworthy exceptions. The

Japanese treaty of 1896 conceded the right to build factories in the Treaty Ports, and this was followed by a British treaty in 1902. Cotton and flour mills were opened by the Japanese and British in Shanghai and Tientsin, and their example was soon followed by Chinese companies. Another new enterprise was telegraph cable construction, for which loans were made by Britain and Denmark.

Meanwhile missionaries had gone back to their stations and opened new ones, for the sufferings of the Church aroused great sympathy in religious circles, and it was felt that here was a challenge that must be met. More money was subscribed, especially in America where a great interest in Chinese education was aroused. The United States Government took the far-sighted step of devoting half of their share of the Boxer Indemnity to the providing of opportunities for Chinese to study in American universities. The feeling grew in liberal circles in China that America was not only China's best friend but also the outstanding example of a free and enlightened country.

In 1902 England allied herself with Japan. Both were afraid of Russia's advance in Manchuria, where she controlled the newly built Chinese Eastern Railway. In 1904 the inevitable war came between Japan and Russia, and Russia was defeated, leaving Japan, by the Treaty of Portsmouth, heir to her interests in south Manchuria. This was for the time being a gain for China, for the Powers insisted on Chinese territorial integrity being preserved. They also insisted that the agreement which America had sponsored in 1898 for an open-door policy in trade should be applied to south Manchuria. To this Japan submitted unwillingly.

Already since the Boxer trouble the 'self-strengthening' idea had taken a number of students to Japan for technical training. Now that she had demonstrated her superiority to a Western Power, the attraction was all the greater, and students went over in thousands. The result was one not anticipated by the authorities. The remaining leaders of the 1898 reform movement were in exile there. So also was Sun Yat-sen, with his newly founded League of Sworn Brothers (Tung Ming Hui). Liang Ch'i-ch'ao and Sun Yat-sen came to an agreement that the Manchus must go and a republic be founded. To such radical proposals the students turned an enthusiastic ear, and thus as they returned to China were primed with revolutionary ideas. Liang, the most brilliant writer of his day, wrote many articles which penetrated far into the interior of China.

In 1909 the Emperor Kuang Hsü died, followed very shortly after by the Empress-Dowager. Immense pains were taken to make these events impressive, and to arouse the veneration of the people. But the new Emperor was only a baby, and in any case the time was past for a revival of loyalty to the Dragon Throne. The provincial governors, specially in central and south China, had tended since Taiping days, and even more since the Boxer year, to think for themselves. In 1911 the proposal of a railway loan brought a clash between the interests of the Peking Government and those of the Yangtse provinces. In October a mutiny of the troops in Hankow was engineered in order to make Peking pause, and then, before anyone could realise it, the end had come. One after another the provinces declared their independence, and in February 1912 the child Emperor's advisers were led to see that the only thing to be done was for him to resign the throne. The revolutionary leaders who were assembled in Nanking had already declared Sun Yat-sen President of the Republic of China. The country agreed, province by province, the more enthusiastically since Dr. Sun and his following came to the decision that he should resign in favour of Yuan Shih-kai, the one man who could bring in the north, and the one man also who controlled a modern army. On this basis it was thought that a place could be found for the old officials as well as the new men. Thus China took her stand before the world as a modern democratic nation.

FOURTH PERIOD, 1912–27

The change was effected with the minimum of disturbance; and this produced a general feeling of optimism throughout the country. People both in China and abroad expected that the Parliament in Peking would support President Yuan while the necessary work of reconstruction was carried out. These expectations were doomed to disappointment. A clash came at once over the question of the President's authority. Sun endeavoured to raise public opinion against him,[1] but Yuan was backed by the army and by a £25,000,000 loan which the foreign diplomats engineered for him from a bankers' consortium. Under the circumstances, being discredited by a futile appeal to arms, Dr. Sun had no option but to retire from politics for the time being, whilst Yuan Shih-kai carried on the business of administration and showed no hurry about the constitution. In 1915 came his attempt to make himself Emperor, a failure, since the provinces were prepared to fight. He was already a sick man and died soon after. The popular Vice-president, Li Yuan-hung, was

[1] Cf. Chapter III.

recognised all over the country as the right man for President. He called all parties together and reinstated the Parliament in Peking. But agreement proved impossible, the cleavage being roughly one of north versus south, and military leaders versus supporters of parliamentary authority. While the quarrel was in full swing an attempt was suddenly made by a small group to reinstate the Manchu ex-Emperor. This also was a complete failure, but to Li Yuan-hung it meant a loss of face, and he resigned from the presidency. Civil war broke out, and for the next ten years the 'war-lords' were competing among themselves with incessant fighting in one area or another. Sun Yat-sen and his party in Canton were feebly trying to work for a national constitutional government, while the Powers continued to recognise whatever party held Peking. The warlords, with the exception of Chang Tso-lin, who started an arsenal in Mukden, drew on Japan and the West for war material—the Chinese market was a godsend after 1918 to Governments and firms with munitions to dispose of. Though the Maritime Customs Service did their best to stop the trade, any general with access to the sea was able to smuggle in all he wanted. The more influential of them kept foreign experts to conduct the arrangements abroad.

One of the most striking results of the revolution in 1911 was the wave of good-will towards foreigners which swept over China. In spite of the disturbed state of the country, foreigners everywhere were received with friendly courtesy and also with eager admiration, until the Great War began to throw a lurid light on western civilisation. The effect of this attitude on missionary influence was very great. Another period of expansion took place. Large and influential congregations came into existence in the big towns, ecclesiastical organisation developed, Chinese priests and clergy, as well as laymen, began to reach positions of equality with foreigners. Most striking to the public eye were the number of colleges becoming universities, and small dispensaries becoming great hospitals and medical schools, all with fine foreign buildings. The peak of Protestant endeavour came in 1922, when the World Student Christian Federation met in Peking and a National Christian Conference (Protestant) in Shanghai. In both conferences Chinese distinguished themselves by their powers of leadership; and it was said 'the Chinese Church comes of age'. As an outcome of the Shanghai Conference a National Christian Council was formed in which Chinese were in the majority. The same influences were at work in the Roman Catholic Church, where there was a marked increase in the number of Chinese priests and preparations were made for the national organisation of the Church.

The Great War at first seemed hardly to concern China, though as time went on it gave an impetus to manufacturing developments in Shanghai and elsewhere. However, in 1915 China declared war on Germany and sent her battalions of labourers to France. Japan had acted earlier. In 1915 she seized control of German interests in Shantung, and then took the opportunity to press her Twenty-one Demands on China. Submission to these demands would have put not only Shantung but all China under Japanese control. A storm of anti-Japanese feeling was aroused, but none the less the military leaders in Peking agreed to the greater part of the demands and further in 1918 pledged national property such as railways and mines as security for the Nishihara loans. The China of 1918, however, was not the China of 1894. She had now a complete telegraphic system, an efficient postal service, and a number of daily papers which circulated to the remotest towns, whilst in Peking there were the universities. The students there had already been stirred in 1917 by Hu Shih and Ch'en Tu-hsiu and their appeal for a revolution in literary expression, an appeal which started the movement known as the Renaissance. The appeal had been enthusiastically endorsed by youth, and a perfect spate of popular writing ensued. To youth thus invigorated, not to say slightly intoxicated with its new powers of self-expression, came the challenge of the country's danger from Japan's aggression. In 1918 over the Japanese loans, and again in 1919 over the betrayal of China's interests at the Versailles Conference, Peking students engineered a nation-wide agitation. Also a new weapon of defence was discovered in the trade boycott. The consequences of this were important, because between 1911 and 1922 there was a large development of modern industry. This was partly due to the progressive attitude induced by the revolution, and partly to the war. The Japanese especially had taken advantage of the decline of European trade to increase their factories and their imports. But the Chinese also were coming more and more to the use of industrial machinery, though still only in a few places, for the most part in Shanghai and Tientsin.

The Versailles Peace Conference was the first occasion on which China met with the nations on a footing of equality. Although she had no option but to refuse to sign the treaty which gave Shantung to Japan, she yet joined the League of Nations, and was in a position to send notable jurists and able diplomats to represent her on the Council and at the assemblies. This did much to make the West realise that there was a new China to be taken into account. The Government of the United States, recognising this and perturbed at the trend of Far Eastern affairs, invited the Powers in 1922 to confer in Washington. There, much against her will, Japan became party to the Nine-Power Agreement to preserve Chinese territorial integrity and the open-door policy in trade. China was promised sympathetic attention to her grievances and, in relation to her import tariff, the removal of the restrictions which had been in force since 1842 and now militated heavily against her infant industries.

As an expression of good-will the Washington Conference and the Nine-Power Treaty were admirable in every way, and the effect in China was correspondingly to the good. Unfortunately, apart from the return by Japan of German property in Shantung, no immediate steps were taken to implement the various schemes of readjustment. The battalions of the war-lords were still operating in north China, and it was perhaps difficult to know where to begin. But Chinese opinion became cynical of western help and began to speak of vested interests and of 'a tiger having once tasted blood'.

In the south also a new spirit was at work. The Kuomintang[1] under Sun Yat-sen was in desperate need of help. They appealed to England, but the diplomats still considered themselves bound to the shadow Government in Peking. Sun Yat-sen then turned to Russia, Soviet Russia as it was now, and there found a friend. In 1923 a posse of Communist agitators under Michael Borodin's leadership arrived in Canton, and in January 1924 Sun Yat-sen issued his famous Three Principles of Democracy. The technique of the Bolshevik Revolution

[1] *I.e.* Nationalist Party.

began to lay hold of the Kuomintang, and violent emphasis was laid on the injustices and oppressions to which China had been subjected by the imperialist and capitalist West. The Chinese people, not only the Government, were bidden 'to arise and break their chains'.

In January 1925 Sun Yat-sen went north in response to an invitation to try and bring all parties together. But he was a sick man, and in March he died in a Peking hospital. His private will revealed that he had nothing to leave to his family except a house in Shanghai and a library of western books. His public will called for united efforts to prosecute the real revolution to a final conclusion. Devotion to the dead leader proved far more powerful in arousing the country than his living influence had been. Then came the incident of May 30 in Shanghai when the police of the International Settlement fired upon a demonstration of students and killed some twenty of them. In a week a nation-wide campaign of anti-imperialism was in full swing, and consuls were calling their nationals in to the Treaty Ports. An anti-British boycott was declared, and violent demonstrations took place in Canton and Hankow. Since 1922 an anti-religious movement had been in existence, sponsored by the young intellectuals. This became a predominantly anti-Christian movement, Christianity being identified with western imperialism. Thus the years of foreign popularity and missionary success came to an end, and for the time being most Chinese believed that the source of all their troubles was foreign aggression, political, economic, and cultural.

On the crest of the nationalistic wave, Sun Yat-sen's intimate disciple, Chiang Kai-shek, marched out from Canton with his 'save-the-country' army and his corps of propagandists. Its slogans were 'Down with Imperialism' and 'Down with the War-lords'. This army with the allied forces it gathered on its way reached Peking in 1928. The war-lord of Manchuria joined the Party, and the reunification of the country was declared on the basis of the dead leader's programme. The country thrilled with new hope and confidence. But the Kuomintang leaders had two dangers to face. One was foreign intervention. Foreigners had been killed in the occupation of Nanking, a large amount of foreign property had been destroyed in the interior, refugee missionaries had suffered indignities, and propagandists were vociferously demanding the abolition of extra-territoriality and the rendition of the foreign concessions. Two of these were forcibly seized by mob violence. The Nationalist headquarters had officially notified the various Governments that the 'Unequal Treaties' would not be renewed when they expired. On the foreign side a large expeditionary force was on guard at Shanghai and Tientsin with British troops in reserve at Hong-kong. Fortunately the situation was simplified by German and Russian interests having already come under Chinese protection. The nations chiefly concerned were England, France, America, Italy and, last but not least, Japan. The Americans were naturally less under suspicion of imperialism: the British for the time being were regarded as the worst enemy. To many business people in Shanghai and elsewhere the situation seemed to call for forcible measures, such as had been used in the past, but fortunately there were statesmanlike minds in the English Cabinet. Mr. Austen Chamberlain's Note in 1925 had revealed an intention to deal fairly and equally with the new China and her new needs. The other western nations followed Britain's lead, and the crisis passed over, though public excitement and foreign nervousness lasted on into 1928 and 1929.

The other danger was the Communist wing of the Kuomintang. In the full tide of the Nationalist success the Communists decided that the time had come to swing the revolution without compromise into line with the full Soviet programme. To this end they gave every provocation they could to arouse foreign suspicion and resentment, and at the same time organised labour unions with highly radical programmes directed against all capitalists whether foreign or Chinese. Hankow was their headquarters: Borodin was there with Madame Sun and Eugene Chen, Foreign Minister of the Nationalist Government. But the military ascendancy was with Chiang Kai-shek and the Right Wing. In the autumn of 1927 the Hankow group was eliminated and Borodin turned out of the country. One section of the army, however, broke away and succeeded in establishing a Communist régime in Kiangsi with a number of pockets in Hupeh and elsewhere. These were a serious embarrassment, not to say danger, to the Government. The Kiangsi régime was broken up in 1933, but the Red Army has now emerged in the northwest. It is not the danger which it was in the central provinces, but it is still a challenge to the Central Government's authority.[1]

In 1929 the Nationalist Government made Nanking the capital and settled down to put the Three Principles of Democracy into practice. How it has succeeded and what is the present situation in China we shall be better able to estimate in our last chapter, after considering in detail the different aspects of western cultural influence.

[1] Since the above was written the situation has changed for the better.

CHAPTER II

THE MISSIONARY INFLUENCE

AMONG western cultural influences in China the missionary influence claims right of way for consideration. In point of time it was the earliest, whilst in scope of operations it has been the largest. Whether it has been the profoundest or the most successful is another question, one on which there is the widest divergence of opinion. It is certain that the mass of the Chinese people still regard Christianity as essentially a foreign religion, as being, indeed, the religion of the West; and there are grounds for doubting whether any considerable section of the three million who make up the Christian community have really come to feel at home in their new faith. In a book such as this which is concerned with western influences as such, theological considerations have to retire into the background. The subject is not whether Christianity is the world religion it claims to be, but what has been the effect of that kind of Christianity which missionaries from the West have inculcated. It is necessary also to remember that it has not been only one kind of Christianity. Both Roman Catholics and Protestants have inculcated those forms with which they were familiar in their own countries, or which have appealed to them personally.

When Christian missionaries began to arrive in China in the late Middle Ages, there were already a number of religions in the country. Some, such as

53

Mohammedanism, had only a restricted geographical range. The main religions were three in number (the *San Chiao*), Confucianism, Taoism, and Buddhism; two of them indigenous, one from India. Christianity was therefore not the first religion coming from outside and claiming to be the truth for all mankind. Buddhism was introduced by Indian missionaries somewhere about the first century A.D., and the Chinese proved so susceptible to its influence that about the seventh to tenth centuries it came near to superseding Confucianism. It had a lasting effect on the old pagan beliefs and practices preserved in Taoism.

With these three religions living side by side the situation from the point of view of religious psychology embodied features which were remarkably alien to the western religious mind. In Europe, Christianity, a religion from the East, was thought to have overcome all the old pagan faiths and made itself supreme as the one and only source of truth about the order of the universe and man's place in it. In China, the great orthodoxy of Confucianism stood its ground as the pillar of the truth—the dogmatism of Christian theologians had its exact counterpart here—but there was so much of the more personal and colourful side of religion which the austerity of Confucianism ignored and which Buddhism and Taoism could supply, that room had to be made for them as well. Of the two, Buddhism was generally recognised as making a loftier appeal than Taoism. A scholar, therefore, never questioned the divine logic of his Confucian faith, but in all except the most puritan circles he could indulge as he felt inclined in these other attractive cults. It was even felt to be a matter of temperament. In some respects the situation reminds a westerner of the different orders in the Catholic Church, each meeting some particular need and being recognised by the Papacy as legitimate for that purpose, but only on the strict understanding that in the last resort the Church and the Pope were supreme and their enunciations the ultimate truth. In other respects, since Confucianism was predominantly of this world, the Confucianist may be compared to a type of modern business man who will not allow religion to obtrude into the realm where he feels economic factors must govern the serious business of life, but who at the same time proclaims his belief in religion, takes his family to church on Christmas Day, and looks to the Church to marry and bury him. To most Chinese, Confucianism was the practical truth of life. To this day they are loth to call it religion, and that name is reserved for the frillings of personal, private cults.

In the city of Hsianfu in Shensi province, there is still to be seen an engraved stone monument which is evidence of the first attempt to introduce Christianity into China. It records the 'diffusion through the Middle Kingdom of the Brilliant (or Luminous) Teaching of Ta-chin'. The characters are those of the T'ang Dynasty when the name Ta-chin was used for what we now call the 'Near East' or perhaps for Syria. From other evidence it is possible to re-create the story. The Christian Church in Mesopotamia which is associated with Nestorius (died *circa* 451) became independent of Rome and spread eastwards to Bagdad and Central Asia. In 635 a monk named A-lo-pen arrived at Ch'ang-an, the capital of the T'ang Empire, where he was welcomed in the cosmopolitan society which included Buddhists, Zoroastrians, and Mohammedans. He founded a Nestorian Church which existed in China

for two and a half centuries, but it is probable that the
larger part of its adherents were non-Chinese from
Central Asia of whom there were a great number in
China at that time. The Church seems to have disappeared during the disorders of the closing years of
the T'ang Empire, and may have suffered as Buddhism
did from the persecution of the Taoist Emperor, Wu
Tsung (845). The problem of why Buddhism survived
while Christianity failed requires a longer discussion of
the changes which Buddhism underwent than can be
entered into here. It is true that contact with India was
closely maintained, and that Buddhism flourished
there, whereas contact with Syria was interrupted and
eventually the mother church of Nestorianism itself
weakened and died. But that is not all; Buddhism
adapted itself to Chinese thought, especially Taoist
thought, and developed peculiarly Chinese forms in a
way that Christianity has not yet done.

The second missionary effort, that of the Franciscans
at the end of the thirteenth century, has already been referred to in its historical setting as part of the movement of Europe towards China begun by the journeys
of the Polos. The Franciscan Church was in China for
a shorter time than the Nestorian, not more than a
century, but it penetrated further, and its adherents
were probably more purely Chinese. Yet it too faded
away without leaving any permanent traces. As before,
failure may be assigned to the distance from the base
and the difficulties which the mother church itself
was encountering, preventing adequate support being
given, and to the collapse of the dynasty which had
favoured it. Though neither Nestorians nor Franciscans
succeeded in establishing themselves in China, these
episodes are significant, because in neither case were

there the political implications which complicated later missionary efforts. Those who sent these early missionaries may have had a political motive. It is clear that thirteenth century Byzantium hoped to enlist the Mongols in a united Christian effort to crush the power of Islam. But when both Nestorians and Franciscans arrived in China they were only small groups among many other foreigners, accepted at the court of strong empires which acknowledged no superior or even equal power. The great expansion of the white race had not yet begun. The missionaries were in a position to say with the first missionary, St. Paul: 'We preach not ourselves but Christ Jesus the Lord, and ourselves your servants for Jesus' sake'.

With the sixteenth century came the age of exploration and the arrival of Portuguese in Chinese waters. By that time the Church was in schism, and religious fanaticism was making a fatal alliance with nationalist animosity. Men were ready to kill their fellow Christians for a clause in a creed, and all the more ready to do it if there was some worldly advantage at stake. Of this generation was Ignatius Loyola with his vision of his spiritual sovereign the Pope needing tools of tempered steel for his use and of a world to be won by organised corporate devotion. From his vision came the Society of Jesus and plans for the evangelisation of the East. The saintly Francis Xavier was appointed in 1542, and worked his way by India and Japan to the gates of China. He never set foot as he had hoped in the imperial capital, but died, alone with one Chinese convert, on an island near Canton. But the Society, with a view to the known reverence of the Chinese for learning, was training other agents in the advancing sciences of the West, notably mathematics and astronomy. Two priests were sent out in 1583, one of them being Matteo Ricci, destined to be known to scholarship in China from the seventeenth century to the present day. Landing in the south, Ricci slowly made his way northward and finally achieved entry into Peking, where he gained the imperial favour. The Jesuit mission was allowed to establish itself. It held the privilege of practising and teaching its religion and of building churches. With their gifts of learning the fathers attracted attention among the *literati*; one of the Hanlin doctors, a high official, became a devout Catholic, and collaborated with the fathers in writing learned works. This was Hsü Kuang-chi, who dedicated some of his family land in Chekiang province, the spot which has since become a great centre of Catholic training and the home of the famous Siccawei Observatory. The Italian Jesuits were joined by Germans and Spaniards, and moved out to other parts of China. In Peking they continued in imperial favour, so much so that in 1611 the Emperor commissioned them to reform the Imperial Calendar: a sign of high confidence, since from time immemorial the rectification of the calendar had been one of the chief symbols of the authority exercised by the Son of Heaven.

The conquest of China by the Manchus meant years of purgatory for the Chinese, and as in earlier centuries with Buddhism these troubles brought a readiness to consider the claims of a foreign religion. The Jesuits went into most of the eighteen provinces and found ready listeners. The great Manchu Emperor, K'ang Hsi, gave them his patronage, and in spite of some jealousies, scholars were friendly. As also had happened with Buddhism, some slight persecutions took place, but on the whole missionaries had a right to claim that

Catholic Christianity had found a need in the country for its particular services.

A new factor, however, emerged to prejudice the situation, and eventually to turn success into failure. The Jesuit policy had consistently followed the teaching of the Scriptural injunction, 'Let every soul be subject unto the higher powers, for . . . the powers that be are ordained of God . . . for rulers are not a terror unto good works but to evil'. In addition the fathers paid 'custom to whom custom is due'. They accommodated themselves to such deep Chinese obsessions as the sacrifices to Confucius and the worship of ancestors. On this ground their enemies were able to make a case against them, and these enemies were not Chinese but their fellow missionaries in the south, in particular the Spanish Dominicans who had a mission in Fukien, and the Portuguese officials who saw in the whole Jesuit venture an infringement of their 'special position in the East'. They denounced the Jesuits at Rome, and thus brought about the Rites Controversy which raged for a hundred years. Decision after decision was wrested from one Pope after another, first in favour of one party then of the other. The proceedings were characterised by strong personal rancour, and as the decisions became known in Chinese circles the unedifying spirit of the controversy was equally clear. The Emperor became weary of the whole business, and when in 1706 Monsignor de Tournon arrived as a special legate with instructions to bring the controversy to a close, K'ang Hsi immediately resented the assumption of the authority of the Pope to deal with matters within the Empire. The Son of Heaven recognised no spiritual authority over his Chinese subjects except his own. The legate was dismissed from the country, and an edict was issued ordering all missionaries to leave China, unless they agreed to abide by the Jesuit practice. Rome's reply was a Papal Bull ordering everyone on pain of excommunication to do the contrary. From that date Christianity lost its standing as a universal religion and became suspect as an essentially alien force masking political aims.

For the next hundred and fifty years, until 1860, the practice of Catholicism was against the law. Throughout the eighteenth century and the early part of the nineteenth there was a continual succession of persecutions in which both missionaries and converts suffered for their faith. In spite of this fresh missionary recruits still contrived to smuggle themselves into the country, and the service of the Mass was maintained, though not for the most part with any regularity. When the foreigners were discovered by the officials they were sometimes quietly left alone, but sometimes they were arrested and deported to Macao: in a few cases they were executed. The result was a Church which survived and which in some places had even grown. There is no evidence to show what it was precisely in the Church's life and message which attracted converts, but the impression left by the records is that the Christians were to a very large extent men and women of simple piety and uneducated habits of thought.

The first Protestant missionary to arrive in China was Robert Morrison, sent out by the London Missionary Society, an interdenominational body founded in 1795. He landed in Canton in 1807, but found he had no means of remaining there as a missionary. Sir George Staunton, President of the Select Committee of the East India Company, at that time the only Englishman who had troubled to learn the Chinese language, befriended him and secured for him the post of Translator to the Company. This gave Morrison a position where he could work at the language, but it also made it difficult for the Chinese to differentiate between his aims and those of the merchants for whom he worked. This was even more the case when he accompanied Lord Amherst's embassy to Peking in 1816.

Morrison spent his twenty-seven years of service between Canton, Malacca, and Macao, where he is buried. During those years he and his colleagues baptised only ten Chinese, but he founded a school and printing press in Malacca and left to his successors a translation of the Bible and a dictionary. He was joined by other English missionaries, notably by Gutzlaff, who was sent by the Netherlands Missionary Society, and succeeded Morrison as Chinese secretary to the British authorities in Canton. Gutzlaff helped to negotiate the Treaty of Nanking in 1842. An ardent evangelist, he was fired with the idea of covering the whole of China with Scripture portions and tracts. To this end he gathered a band of Chinese who professed their willingness to help him and brought him reports of successful work 'in every province except Kansu'. But, not for the last time, a trusting foreigner was deceived. It was later discovered that the majority of these 'preachers' had never got further than the opium dens of Hongkong and had sold their literature back to the printer.

The small body of pioneers was also reinforced from America, the first-comers being Bridgman and Parker, the latter the first medical missionary to China. By 1840 there were about twenty-five all told. So far they had not got beyond Canton and Macao, and the converts were less than one hundred.

With the opening of the five specified Treaty Ports, Canton, Amoy, Foochow, Ningpo, Shanghai, missionaries were able to settle in these cities. The new British colony of Hongkong also made a good centre, and Americans as well as British carried on their work there. Within the area of these cities they were free to build churches, houses, schools, and hospitals, and to preach freely to those who would listen. They were, however, not content to remain in the Ports; their zeal carried them, in spite of treaty restrictions, into the surrounding country. Ardent souls like William Burns made extensive trips disguised in Chinese clothes. On occasion their disguise was penetrated, they were seized and returned to the Ports by indignant officials. Sometimes they suffered indignities and ill-treatment, but there were no cases of death by violence.

One of the terms of the 1842 treaty was the establishment of extra-territoriality, by which a foreigner did not come under the jurisdiction of Chinese law but was dealt with by the consular court of his own nation. The missionary caught travelling beyond legal limits was in the same position as the trader caught smuggling opium, or the even less reputable members of the foreign community who might offend in other ways. It was difficult for the Chinese to distinguish one from the other. Those who took the trouble to talk with the missionaries or read their tracts might get some idea that they were seeking to teach 'good doctrine'; but to most people, especially to the officials, they were suspect. If they were not political spies, they must be connected with the kidnapping of coolies, or, since schools, orphanages and hospitals were started, they might be seeking to entice away children, or to procure eyes or internal organs for the making of medicines, or to transmute lead into silver. This last was a very popular belief and arose from the idea that the black eyes of Chinese were particularly effectual for the purpose.

We must turn for a moment to the background from which the missionaries came. The England and America which sent out the early pioneers were the England and America of the Evangelical Revival. From this movement grew the great missionary societies, founded in the last decade of the eighteenth century. To men of this outlook, whether Anglicans, Presbyterians, Baptists, Congregationalists or Methodists, there was only one possible view of mankind. Either a man had a personal faith in Jesus Christ and the atoning power of His death and by this faith was freed from sin and saved for the life to come, or else he was a child of wrath and destruction sunk in misery and sin. The call of foreign missions, as is very vividly seen in the missionary appeals of those days, was that myriads of one's fellow men were standing on the brink of hell, and it was only the preacher of the gospel with his message of grace who could save them. The pure altruism in this is very clear. It was a determination at whatever cost to the missionary and his supporters to bring life where there was death, light where there was darkness. But there was hardly any thought given to the question of whether it was consistent with the universality of God's love to assume that all was sin and misery where a particular evangelical experience did not exist. Hardly anyone could be found so bold as to suggest that the Holy Spirit could have been at work in China throughout the dark ages. There is something in the accusation sometimes brought that the missionaries expected to find depravity and so found what they were looking for. Thus Robert Morrison summed up his view of the Chinese nation as 'ignorant, deluded, guilty men'. And Wells Williams (American) wrote in a letter in 1850: 'It is much easier loving the souls of the heathen in the abstract in America than it is in the concrete, encompassed as they are with such dirty bodies, speaking forth their foul language and vile natures'. It must be remembered that at the time he said this he had seen a great deal of the riff-raff of the Ports and very little of the decent, honest people, scholars and farmers, who corresponded to the people of his home town in New England.

It was an age of deep personal piety but also of narrow intolerance. In England, recently enough, there had been the bullying of Methodists, riots winked at by the authorities if these 'pestilent sectaries' might so be suppressed. It was an age in which feeling ran high over the Tractarian Movement, and a man like John Keble could be banned from preaching in his university, while the chaplain of an evangelical college seeing a cross set up in Newman's church near Oxford, mused darkly on the 'man of sin' and the 'depravity' of the deed. But it was also an age which knew about the India of Clive and Warren Hastings and the whole tribe of Jos Sedleys with their fantastic wealth gained from the 'natives', and had seen British administration there improved under the Lawrences with their sense of Christian trusteeship. Commercial intercourse with China involved scandals and abuses, opium and war, but after all England and America were Christian countries. It stood to reason that a greater good would come out of a smaller evil. As was said in 1858, when the Chinese Peace Commissioners were forced to accept dictated terms, we trust 'to a further knowledge to show them that we know their interests better than they do'. The same man had said in 1842, 'The ways of God's dealings with this people began to open, and He entered into judgment with them that He might show them His mercy'.

In most respects the Roman Catholic missionary movement did not differ from the Protestant. There were differences as to the actual means by which the personal salvation could come to the convert, an emphasis on the Church and her sacraments which was not in the Protestant gospel. But to all intents and purposes the heathen were to the Catholic in the same predicament of darkness and misery. The strength of the appeal to rescue them was enhanced by the fact that there were already some hundreds of thousands of Christians in different parts of the country, little congregations liable to be swamped by heathenism. To Matteo Ricci and his fellow Jesuits the situation admitted of an open mind. The teaching of the great Jesuit Cardinal, John de Lugo, had visualised a grace of God already at work in non-Christian lands, working through religious and philosophical systems in which God had revealed Himself. But the nineteenth-century Catholic mind was different. The Papacy had condemned the Jesuit attitude, and the persecution of Catholics, intermittent though it had been, tended to give the new missionary Orders a feeling of repulsion against the political authorities.

An interesting development of the nineteenth century was the rise of French enthusiasm for missions. The Church in France was suffering from the Gallican controversy. The State would have the Church under her control and serving her ends. The reaction to this among the devout was the stern temper of the Ultra-montanes. Catholic missionaries therefore could hardly feel anything but impatience with the temporal power of a pagan State. It was anti-Christ and must be beaten down by the forces of Christendom; and if the French Government made itself defender of the faith in China, so much the more hope for the soul of the French Government as well as the souls of the Chinese people.

There is a dearth of materials from which the minds of the early converts can be ascertained. It is easy to point to an experience like that of Gutzlaff's and pass the obvious jibe about 'rice-Christians'. Doubtless the Ports contained a number of unsuccessful men, cut off from their families and glad to put themselves under the protection of the missionaries and so find an easy way of livelihood. But this line of argument does not explain the growth of the Catholic communities in the far interior, nor the genuine devotion which was later proved to exist in the Protestant communities at the coast. A seedy scholar who had lost caste among his fellows might deceive an ingenuous foreigner, but real holiness of mind and purity of friendly purpose had a way of winning in the end. In spite of the barriers of language and tradition, the essence of Christ's religion found its way into some hearts.

The only evidence we have of anything like a 'mass movement' or a deep intrusion into the life of the nation is the Taiping Rebellion. The early history of its leader's activities are conflicting at some points, but there can be no doubt that Hung Hsiu-ch'üan went through a deep religious experience from which he emerged convinced that he had had a vision of the Christian's God by whom he was commanded to fight idolatry and bring his people to the knowledge of God the Father and His Son, Jesus Christ. His first knowledge of these matters had come to him through the reading of

Protestant tracts and some contact with missionaries. Hung and his associates certainly believed that they were setting up a Christian state and ordering a Christian society. There has been of recent years among some sections of missionary supporters an appeal for the indigenisation of Christianity among the peoples to whom it is preached. This Taiping movement would appear to be exactly what is meant by indigenisation; namely, a wholly spontaneous response coming from the depths of a man's soul and containing native elements of thought which the man has instinctively incorporated with the new message.

The missionary community was entirely unprepared for this miracle which was sprung on them. To the Catholics Hung and his friends were suspect, since they were known to have been inspired by Protestant teaching. To the majority of the Protestants the movement was a source of pure bewilderment, the more so because the Taipings came to have 100,000 men under arms for the liberation of China. It passed men's imaginations that the Christian message could fit in with a nationalist uprising on so immense a scale. Nevertheless some missionaries were so aroused by the spiritual possibility of what they heard that they made special journeys to see the Taipings in Nanking, their capital. Their reports varied considerably, a few being greatly impressed with what they saw, others feeling that it was all rather heretical. The main theological scandal was that the Taiping Emperor (*i.e.* Hung Hsiu-ch'üan) spoke of Jesus Christ as his elder brother who gave him, the younger brother, help and direction. There would seem to have been a failure here on the part of the heresy-hunters to realise the very marked distinction there is between the elder and the younger brother in the traditional Chinese ethical code. The elder brother practically occupies the position of the father in the West, whilst the Chinese father occupies a higher, almost a divine, position. Again, when the Taiping educational department made a revised version of the Three Character Classic for use in training children, it contained, among much teaching taken from the Old and New Testaments, an account of the Emperor's relation to God. Since the traditional title of the Emperor was Son of Heaven, he was described as 'Son of God', Jesus being distinguished as the First-born Son.

Whilst men's minds were wavering and some bolder spirits were urging that the missionary community should launch out in support of their Taiping fellow Christians, the political situation suddenly changed. The Powers decided that they were in support of the Manchu throne, and foreign officials immediately warned all their nationals against having anything to do with the 'savage rebels'. Not for the first or last time missionaries of all denominations took their colour from official suggestion and believed the propaganda which was passed on to them from Manchu sources. One cannot but deplore the failure of a movement which with better guidance might have proved the real thing and have established an empire in China which would have been at least as Christian as that of Constantine. It is particularly to be regretted that England, represented by that noble Christian, Charles Gordon, was responsible for the defeat of the Taiping armies. It was the more a tragedy in that the iconoclastic fervour of the Taipings alienated the common people from the name of Christianity, whilst their dogmatic Bible teaching offended the scholars.

The opening-up of the interior of China after 1860

gave the longed-for opportunity for a great increase in missionary work. It was a time of missionary enthusiasm in Europe and America, and the same kind of expansion was taking place in India, Africa, and the South Seas. In these other fields political control came more and more into the hands of the white race, and missionaries went forward in the company of their national flag. The main bulk of missionary support in England came from the class which was profiting most by commercial expansion, and while there is no ground for regarding their support as dictated by any other motive than the religious, the business mind would appreciate that its money should be invested in enterprises which could, if need be, be protected by the British Government. A new note began to appear in missionary appeals. Thus in 1863 a controversy sprang up in *The Times* as to whether missionary work should not rightly consist of introducing western civilisation in the first place, and only go on to religious teaching when that civilisation was making its way. The controversy spread to the American press and there, as well as in England, sturdy advocates came forward urging that civilisation should come first. Patriotic Americans and earnest Christians among them began to think in terms of 'our great universal Yankee nation'.[1] The feeling grew that the white nations had the solution to all problems in their hands, and in religious circles one of the chief grounds for this conviction was the Christian gospel with all that it had meant in the life of these nations. Victorian England was immensely taken with the story of the Queen offering to some dusky potentate a copy of the Bible with the assurance that the secret of her power

[1] On the accession of Hsien Feng (1851), the President wrote to congratulate him and addressed him as 'Great and good brother'.

lay there. It was indeed difficult for religious people to be quite clear as to what was religious faith and what national ambition. The Chinese Government had proved itself completely incompetent according to western standards, therefore the true welfare of the Chinese people must depend on a victorious campaign of western civilisation and western Christianity. There were very few who sympathised with Lord Elgin's doubts when he wrote in 1858, 'God grant that in opening this country to the West we may not be bringing upon them misery and ruin'. There were many to applaud the eminent divine who, speaking at the International Missionary Conference at Exeter Hall in 1888, said: 'Doors have been opened within fifty years that no human power could have unbarred. The mighty moving of God can be traced back through the centuries, long since giving Protestant England a foothold in the very critical centre, the pivotal centre of oriental empires and religions . . . and the wide door was opened not by the vermilion pencil of the Emperor, but by the decree of the Eternal.'

In this spirit the missionary societies moved in to stake out new claims for righteousness in the heart of the kingdom of evil. The new treaties removed the ban from evangelistic journeys outside the Ports and guaranteed freedom to Chinese subjects to practise Christianity. The British and American Governments were at first very dubious about the advisability of any such practice. Their Consuls tried to discourage missionaries from getting too far from the Ports, and warned them against buying land. But the Protestants could not be restrained from exercising the same freedom which the Catholics had claimed. During the forty years from 1860 to 1900 the number of Protestant residential stations went up to 498, and missionaries were to be found in nearly all the eighteen provinces. They even began to try to storm the fastnesses of Tibet.

The Society which above all displayed this pioneering spirit was the China Inland Mission, founded in 1865 by James Hudson Taylor. He was a man with an intense prayer-life and from that he derived an exceptionally strong sense of divine direction. Having decided that a certain course of action should be taken, he made arrangements to take it, however impossible it might seem. It is the boast of the Society which he founded that its work is planned and carried out entirely by faith. Hudson Taylor made a public appeal for men and women to go out to do the purest pioneer work on the principle that there were elect souls in all parts of China waiting for the gospel, and that the Christian's duty was to find them and save them without delay. The building up of a church or the training of ministers was not their business but solely to cover all China with the 'call of Christ', and when they met with response, to instruct believers to the point of baptism. Hudson Taylor's challenge found response all over the Protestant world: in Scandinavia, Finland, Germany, as well as England and the United States. After forty years the Mission had nearly 700 missionaries in China; many of them living in places which could only be reached by weeks of travel from the coast. Unmarried women were as daring as the men, some of them travelling from place to place and being homeless for years.

While these triumphs of the gospel were very gratifying to the missionaries and their supporters at home, they were a source of considerable embarrassment to both the foreign and Chinese Governments. It might

71

prove politically and commercially convenient to have one's nationals in a certain area. But on the whole, in the eyes of British and American officials, the disadvantages outweighed the advantages. As for Chinese officials they felt themselves between the devil and the deep sea. Thus at the Cheefoo Convention (1875) the Chinese Government was pressed into more positive declarations of responsibility for missionary safety. The Commissioners pleaded almost piteously for a relaxation of terms rather than the reverse, and one of them is recorded to have said that they would yield anything if only the Powers would keep out their opium and their Bibles. Throughout the country zealous officials knew perfectly well that the more they could keep the foreigners out the better Peking would be pleased; only they must avoid action which might implicate the Government.

Under these conditions it is not surprising that the missionary and consular records of these years are a continual tale of petty outrage. Either a missionary found he could not rent a building or piece of land, or if he had made his agreement the roughs of the place turned out and made things too hot for him; or a patient died in hospital; or a child's parents removed it from school after having signed an agreement. Whatever the alleged reason might be, there was trouble, and property was damaged and lives endangered. In some cases the official in charge might be responsible, though this could seldom be proved. If he was not inclined to bestir himself, some fanatical scholar would come forward, strong in the conviction that this new teaching was subversive of all morals. On the other hand the cause might be mere panic laying hold of a mob.

Altogether in these forty years there were some 150 riots of one sort or another which had to be dealt with by the authorities, with efforts on the Chinese side to minimise the occurrence, and on the foreign side to put on the screw and make the occasion a lesson in treaty observance. In 1870 there was a horrible incident in Tientsin when a number of French Catholics, including the Consul and ten Sisters of Charity, were murdered, and the orphanage, church, and consulate were destroyed by a mob incensed with rumours of the deaths of babies taken into the orphanage. The Tientsin massacre was the only incident on so large a scale, and—one is tempted to say—the marvel is that there was so little loss of life. The damage to property, on the other hand, was extensive, and indemnities were constantly imposed. At some conferences of missionaries it was urged that these indemnities should be deliberately made heavy in order that they might act as deterrents. Thus a vicious circle was created. The more the Chinese community suffered in their pockets the more bitter their feelings against the Christian religion.

There was also the animosity aroused by converts' appeals for protection. Under the treaties of 1858–60 'any person who according to these tenets shall peaceably teach and practise the principles of Christianity shall in no case be interfered with or molested'. From the standpoint of after the event, nothing more provocative of trouble could have been devised, and the historian can only feel profoundly sorry for all the parties concerned, whether Chinese or foreign, official or private citizen. In case of trouble arising there was no machinery for carrying out this clause except that of appeal to a missionary, who appealed to his Consul, who brought the matter to the notice of the intendant of foreign affairs in the Port, who referred it to the local magistrate, who instituted enquiries on the spot. There was every possibility for divergence of opinion as to what 'peaceably teach and practise' might mean. To the magistrate it might well mean not teach at all, since that inevitably aroused opposition: to the missionary it meant the exact reverse. There was also the thorny question of subscriptions to idol festivals. These were included in a local rate, and a Christian's neighbours saw no reason why he should not pay his share. To a convert in poor circumstances, as most of them were, it seemed a convenient economy. To a missionary, specially an inexperienced one, insistence on payment was pure persecution. Consular officials, if they were unsympathetic to missions, suspected that most of the converts had an eye to the main chance and deceived their credulous missionary friends. Such officials were intolerably irritated by being called on to protect people whom they so mistrusted. Of the Chinese Government it must in justice be said that after the Tientsin Incident it made a series of statesmanlike proposals to the Powers designed to regularise the whole situation. These proposals would, however, have hampered the work of the missionaries, particularly as regards women and children, and they were rejected.[1]

As a religious movement aimed at inspiring the Chinese to honour and love the Christian's God and the Christian's Saviour, the missionary enterprise would appear to have been ill-advised in some of its methods. Both Catholics and Protestants were inconsiderate of what were after all quite reasonable susceptibilities in a people with so long and cultured a tradition. Alexander Michie, a careful observer with

[1] See Latourette, *History of Christian Missions in China*, pp. 351–2.

a markedly impartial mind, wrote in 1891:[1] 'The Christianisation of China is waiting for men of simple faith little concerned about themselves or their systems, ready to honour the good wherever found; who will leave the windmills called "strongholds of Satan" severely alone and unobtrusively seek entrance to the hearts of living men, waiting in short for the time when Christianity can be introduced to the great Chinese people in a form that will be permanent in proportion as it is pure.'

The question arises how missionaries succeeded in getting any converts at all. To this an answer—inadequate as must inevitably be the case with so complex a problem—can be given along three lines of approach. One is that there was all over China a deep sense of dissatisfaction with the existing régime and a growing suspicion that the Manchu Dynasty had lost the divine mandate to rule. Since K'ang Hsi and his immediate successors had made studied efforts to get their sovereignty recognised on the basis of traditional religious principles, the feelings of dissatisfaction which were aroused were as much religious as political. Such feelings were not dominant in men's minds until after the Boxer troubles, but they were alive earlier. Few scholars joined the Christian Church, but many merchants and farmers did, seeing in it a religion which claimed to redeem the world and build up society on a new spiritual basis.

The second line of approach is to be found in the facts and interpretations given at the beginning of this chapter. Confucianism was all true, but a man, especially a non-scholar, required more, something which would relieve the burden of this world and meet his needs

[1] Alexander Michie, *Missionaries in China*.

75

more as an individual than as a servant of his family. Especially did he need this when times were bad and the world was plainly out of gear. He then required a religious hobby, so to speak, to keep his mind comfortably occupied. Since Confucianism had created a mistrust of plainly superstitious practices, here was an opportunity for Christianity, the great religion of the West, calling men to abandon the illogicalities of polytheism, exalting the one true God and His Son, an all-beneficent Saviour, above all extending the scope of goodness and raising it to a higher power by emphasising self-sacrificing love beyond the family and the clan. This might be regarded as Confucianism with a richer content for the individual in his troubles. Then also Christian worship had its attraction: to some the richness of the Catholic Mass with its dominating suggestion of a supernatural power being mediated, to others the austerity of a Presbyterian Service with its insistence on the minimum of form and the maximum of ethical aspiration. It has been one of the greatest possible mistakes to regard the Chinese as all cut to a pattern, and showing but little individuality of religious temper. Almost every century has produced its new sects of one sort or another, and in many of these there is clear evidence of the nonconformist, not to speak of the puritan, spirit with its revolt against the shams of traditional ritual.

The third line of approach is to be found in those special agencies which the missions used to commend their teaching: the schools, hospitals, orphanages, schemes of famine relief, and along with them the more general introduction of western culture. Schools will be dealt with more particularly in the educational chapter, so also medical work in its place. But it needs to be emphasised that in founding schools and hospitals the

missionaries appealed not only to the Chinese traditional veneration for learning but also to their traditional association of schooling and doctoring with
philanthropy. There were many, of course, who traduced
these ventures, pointing out the cunning of the
foreigners and the opportunity these institutions gave
them for carrying out the vilest designs. But the base-
lessness of these aspersions was bound to be known in
time, and doctors in particular proved to be great
openers of doors. So also did the women missionaries
with the opportunities they brought to middle-class and
peasant families for girls' education. Again, it has been
a great mistake to regard all women in China as downtrodden slaves, and daughters and daughters-in-law as
receiving no affection and care. The Chinese generally
have a great love of children, and though poverty has
acted there as elsewhere and been responsible for callous
institutions and customs, above the poverty line parents
have unmistakable affection for their daughters.

With regard to western culture generally, some mention of it comes in other chapters, but something needs
to be said here about the attitude taken up by the
missionaries. Most of them, whether Catholic. or
Protestant, agreed with the pioneering stalwart who
said on one occasion, 'We are here, not to develop the
resources of the country, not for the advancement of
commerce, not for the mere promotion of civilisation;
but to do battle with the powers of darkness, to save
men from sin and conquer China for Christ'.[1] But there
were a few who visualised their task from a wider point
of view. They conceived the civilisation of the West, its
political institutions, its philosophy, arts, and sciences
as the products of the Christian religion, and equally

[1] Griffith John speaking at the Missionary Conference in Shanghai, 1877.

77

needed by the Chinese. They proceeded, therefore, with schemes of translation of works dealing with these subjects. From the 'eighties on, one of the mission presses in China was used by an American, Dr. Young Allen, for the publication of a monthly periodical in which general information was given, whilst a fervent Welsh Baptist, Timothy Richard, boldly took the line followed by Matteo Ricci and the Jesuits of the seventeenth century. He was profoundly convinced that not only should all western learning be laid open to the Chinese but also that every effort should be made to emphasise in Chinese culture those essentials of wisdom which could be compared with Christianity. He gave himself untiringly to these spiritual adventures, lived on rice and vegetables in order to buy astronomical telescopes, claimed viceroys and coolies equally as his friends, dreamt more of a China reforming herself in her own way than of a China studded with Churches after the western pattern. He maintained that the scholars were the leaders of the nation and Christianity must commend itself by its ability to get inside their minds, and so lead them to a new sense of the value of their own culture. He won an extraordinary reputation in official and scholarly circles. 'Li Ti-mo-tai' came to be known all over China and honoured as a man of learning and a friend devoted to China's true welfare.

There was only one Timothy Richard, but there were a few other men with the same breadth of vision and intellectual urbanity; for instance, W. A. P. Martin, who became head of the Tung Wen College in Peking, and Alexander Wylie, the British Bible Society's agent and friend of Chinese mathematicians, whose Chinese library now in the Bodleian Library testifies to his catholic interests. Their influence went much further and became other than they knew.[1]

The Boxer troubles do not concern us in this chapter so much as might at first sight appear. This is not to minimise the fact that after seventy years of close intercourse between China and the representatives of western power and culture, the outcome was a major disaster of this nature. But it is easy to overestimate the significance of these troubles. There is, of course, no question as to there having been an outbreak of fierce xenophobia among the people of north China, no question but that this was the culmination of a long series of petty incidents denoting suspicion and dislike, particularly of missionaries. These feelings had been repressed because Peking had become increasingly alarmed by the foreigners' resentment against outrages and had given frequent injunctions that missionaries were to be treated properly. In the end there came an apparently inevitable explosion of popular feeling. This might easily have been turned against the Court and its sycophants but, largely owing to the 'Old Buddha's' statecraft, it was directed against the foreigners.

What concerns us here is that it was not primarily an anti-religious movement, nor anything like as nation-wide as has sometimes been supposed. There were missionaries scattered all over the country at the mercy of the people among whom they were living, yet it was only in the two provinces of Chihli and Shansi and in Manchuria that there were widespread or even serious attacks on missionaries. The rest of the country hardly moved, though news of what was happening spread rapidly and caused a panic among foreigners. In a

[1] Vide Chaps. V, VI.

number of places there was looting of mission property, and where Church people were unpopular they suffered some persecution. But many of the refugee missionaries found friends to help them on their journeys to the coast. In the bad areas some Catholic communities, Chinese and foreign, gathered together and defended themselves for weeks until they were relieved. A number of instances are on record of Chinese men and women who preferred death to recanting.

The real importance of the Boxer Year lies in its results. In Europe and America the modern popular press was then in the floodtide of its initial success, and the Boxers and their doings became front-page news. Thus the attention of the world was centred on China, and what with 'Shanghai rumours' about the Legations in Peking and then the sensational reassertion of western military power, the deepest impression was made. The vast majority of people regarded the revolt against western penetration as a challenge which must be taken up with the utmost dispatch. So to all missionary enthusiasts here was a clear call of God to see to it that the blood of the martyrs should be the seed of the Church.

From 1902 right away through the Revolution of 1911 down to about 1922 was the period of real expansion in missionary influence as distinct from pioneering occupation of unknown territory. Not only did the number of missionaries increase continuously,[1] especially of those from America, but the nature and form of missionary work changed in all sorts of ways. Above

[1] The number of Protestant missionaries in 1889 was reported as being 1296, in 1914 as 5462, in 1925 as 8158. In Roman Catholic missions the increase was most marked among Chinese priests and sisters.

all, the Chinese churches grew in size and importance.

Heavy indemnities were levied by the Boxer Protocol, and these, proportionate to the property losses which they had sustained, were paid to the missionary societies concerned. Old stations were reoccupied and new ones opened; the opportunity was taken to get bigger and better premises. The old missionaries therefore were re-equipped to go back, and a number of new volunteers went with them. Amongst them were men and women of the old zealot type, burning with ardour to set up the Cross of Christ in the country which had spurned Him. But there was a new type of Protestant missionary emerging at this time, men and women from universities such as Oxford and Cambridge, Harvard and Yale. Actually the movement among students had begun in America in the early 'nineties, and from there it had spread to England. Ten years later the Student Christian Movements in both lands were a force in undergraduate life, and an increasing number of university graduates went out to the mission field, highly qualified doctors, richly endowed educators, and evangelists who had had the best that university education could supply. Also there was a new type of missions leader coming to the front. Responsible people in the Churches had begun to see that this missionary enterprise was a vastly more complicated affair than had been realised, and required much more statesmanship in planning.

The new type of missionary was affected by the changes in thought which were taking place particularly in the universities. There was first the development in the critical studies of the Bible and of Church history, a reflection of the great developments in the whole study of history and religion. The fields of

anthropological enquiry had been enriched by missionary observation, and on this had followed expert
investigation. Tylor's *Primitive Culture*, published in
1871, was an epoch-making work, and by the 'nineties
James Frazer was at work on the materials for his
Golden Bough. In the study of eastern religions, Oxford
in the 'eighties was publishing Max Muller's *Sacred
Books of the East*. In 1893 it republished James
Legge's translations and commentaries on the Chinese
Classics. In Leyden De Groot also was publishing his
researches. There were professors and schools of
Chinese studies in France, Germany, Austria, and
Russia, as well as in England and America. But above
all, Darwin's results, followed by Herbert Spencer's
adaptation, had permeated the minds of educated
people, and the time had come for purely secular
philosophies of history of which the most striking was
that propounded by Marx and Engels. In France
Durkheim was perfecting his sociological interpretation of the phenomena of religion.

The main circles of Protestant missionary support
were still outside the scope of these influences. They
knew about them but only as evil signs of the times,
tendencies to be combated. But to university students
they were part of the air they breathed, and by 1910
nearly all the theological colleges in England and a
good many in America were training men in critical
studies. Thus the new type of missionary came to
China with a sense of the relativity in some aspects of
western Christianity. He had, for example, a knowledge
of Harnack's work on the expansion of the Church[1] and
saw China as a problem for study. The words which
Timothy Richard had spoken began to bear fruit, and

[1] *The Mission and Expansion of Christianity in the First Three Centuries.*

by the second decade there were a number of missionaries who were trying to see at what points the Christianity which they brought was purely western and so not necessarily part of the fundamental message for China. Most, though not all, of these men gravitated to educational work, and it is safe to say that their teaching on religion was less dogmatically assured than that of their more conservative colleagues. This applies especially to the young and vigorous men and women who went to China under the auspices of the Y.M.C.A. and the Y.W.C.A. They were almost entirely from the United States, and for all their religious earnestness they were alive to the fact that Young China was calling out for western science and democracy. For youth in the Protestant countries the moral problems of industry and commerce had brought about a revulsion against a certain other-worldly pietism associated with evangelical Christianity. From this revulsion sprang what came to be called 'the Social Gospel', a movement in religion which had its repercussions in China, particularly in Y.M.C.A. circles.

On the Chinese side the Boxer year was as a black cloud receding over the horizon while a new day was beginning to dawn. In many parts of the country, groups of *literati* got together to consider ways of reform; and where missionaries proved friendly and interested in discussing western institutions and culture generally, these reformers were more prepared to listen sympathetically to their religious appeal. They were realising that there were two sides to this western civilisation, a lower and a higher, and that the missionaries stressed the latter. It was a deep-lying habit of mind in the Chinese to regard civilisation as essentially

83

a moral phenomenon; and now they were prepared to find moral greatness behind the material power they had been facing for so long. To some therefore, indeed after 1911 to many, there was an attraction about the noble idealism of the Christian faith. It claimed to achieve, to produce practical results in society. Students returning from abroad, especially those who had found good friends and lived in cultured Christian homes, acclaimed the force of this in ways which made their hearers feel the ineffectiveness of their own cultural ethic. It was after 1902 that the cry began to be heard 'a new people', and the cry grew as the years went on. How far enquiring people of this kind took pains really to investigate Christianity on its own merits is another question, as also whether they found in it the secret of power which they sought. The Chinese tendency to make a hobby of personal religion is visible here: undoubtedly a much larger number of *literati* than actually stayed by the Church had at one time or another some contact with it. They were not prepared to pay the price of exclusive allegiance.

The post-Boxer situation also produced another class of people who, although they came right into the Church, were in some ways less satisfactory. The demonstration of the power of the foreigner acted on the peasant mind even more than on that of the scholar. Many Christians were reimbursed for their losses during the troubles, and the idea spread that it paid to be a member of the Church. The missionary was now a person of some importance whom the officials dared not offend, and who could therefore be of considerable help to converts involved in law-suits with their neighbours. This attitude had been at work in the pre-Boxer years. It inevitably was more so after, and the Church, Roman and Protestant, expanded largely but at considerable expense to its purity, specially in the north. The Catholic priests tended to think that in any case no Christian of the first generation could really be a sound Catholic, and many of them accordingly saw no harm in exploiting their political prestige in local *yamens* and taking in to the Church all those who came to them in consequence. Once get a man, whatever his motives, under the authority of Mother Church, instruction might improve him, and anyhow his children would produce the real fruit in the next generation. Protestants for the most part did not formulate any such clearcut policy, but they were often at the mercy of their local Chinese workers, many of whom were concerned for the numerical growth of their group and thought a judicious exercise of political prestige a legitimate means to that end. The result of this and of all the other forces at work was thousands of congregations of a strangely patchy and uneven temper where undesirables and curious enquirers mixed with men and women of real piety.

In this situation much depended on what attitude the reformers and anti-Manchu revolutionaries took to the Christian religion. In them above all the impact of western civilisation was producing the most striking results. It did for them what it was doing for a large number of thoughtful but more conservatively minded men in the country: it made them doubt whether the old faith was of any avail in this new world in which material non-moral forces were so powerful. For conservatives and liberals alike the effect was spiritually disruptive; and it was inevitable that Christianity should have the same effect. The great question was whether the liberal spirits would find in the new religion the basis of a new faith in the moral order of the universe. We cannot here consider whether they could find it there or, also, whether any failure to do so was due to an inherent religious blindness on their part. What has to be recorded is the fact that though on a small scale there was a turning in the direction of Christianity, on a large scale there was not. Sun Yat-sen, now rapidly extending his sphere of influence, was at that time an ardent Christian, and to him Christianity was an integral part of the whole western civilisation which he wished to see China adopt. The God of that civilisation would surely inspire his fellow countrymen to overthrow the Manchu tyranny and help them, as He had helped England and America, to become powerful and wealthy nations. It is significant that about 1903 a hundred students in Tokyo were baptized as Christians. But to the more learned and, it must be noted, more thoughtful minds of K'ang Yiu-wei and Liang Ch'ich'ao the answer to China's problems was not to be found in this direction. They were passionately concerned that in the spiritual readjustment which they visualised as necessary, the best of China's past should be preserved. From their studies of western history and western science as well as western Christianity, they came to the conclusion that the spiritual power of the West lay more in science than in religion. Strong traces of Christian influence can be found in their writings but to Liang Ch'i-ch'ao, whose popularity and influence grew by leaps and bounds during his years of exile (1898–1911), religion in general, and Christianity in particular, was the tool of State policy. From the point of view of missionary influence the irony of this rejection of Christianity was that in the Protestant West the old narrower concept of the Christian faith was at the same time giving place to a new and broader concept. Alongside of this was a consciousness of science as facing both ways, able to contribute enormously to man's spiritual welfare and at the same time able to do irreparable harm. The very hopes and fears which K'ang Yiu-wei had for the world were what Christian leaders had come to have. Unfortunately, the mischief was done: many, if not most, of present-day Chinese intelligentsia still think of Christianity only as it was preached in the nineteenth century.

The great missionary Conference held in Edinburgh in 1910 clearly illustrated both this new outlook and a new determination to carry on the missionary enterprise under the best auspices. John R. Mott and the other promoters of the Conference, as also the delegates who came from all the Protestant churches in the world, recognised the penetration of western civilisation and the great colonial empires as being indicative both of the providence of God and of an inevitable overpowering of weakness by strength. The condition of the world was therefore a challenge to the Church to see to it that Christianity gave of its best to the non-white parts of the earth. But the Conference was called not only to arouse the Church but to face the spiritual dangers and difficulties of the missionary enterprise. It was frankly recognised that, for example in China, the existence of the treaties and the political conditions generally had resulted in a number of 'lamentable features' in the Christian movement. Stress was laid on the necessity for missionaries 'gaining an adequate knowledge and understanding of the existing civilisation of China'. For the first time a generous tribute was

paid by a great missionary-minded assembly to the
high moral quality of that civilisation, though Arch-
bishop Lang undoubtedly expressed the mind of the
Conference when he said: 'It cannot be too often re-
peated that it is not the missionary who breaks up the
national life, the traditional religion and morals of the
people, it is the white man himself . . . what we have to
see to is this: that a Christian nation is not, so to say,
allowed to begin a work which cannot but be of the
gravest moral danger, unless it is carried on in the way
of securing that there shall be a constructive work re-
storing and re-establishing the moral and spiritual bases
of national life.'[1] This was to go much further than any
controversialist on missions and civilisation in 1863.
The missionary was called to be a socially constructive
force. It was assumed that the force of Christianity in
the 'Christian' nations was so pure and strong that by
the direct influence of those nations a disrupted national
life in China could be reintegrated: an assumption the
magnitude of which was not realised as it is to-day.

With the establishment of the Republic there came
what the Edinburgh Conference had called 'an un-
paralleled opportunity'. The Chinese people to an
almost naïve extent adopted the attitude of bygones
being bygones, and whether in Treaty Ports or in the
far interior, the barriers of suspicion and dislike were
very largely broken down. The Church in any particular place quickly came to be recognised as a legitimate institution and even as a centre of much-needed
light. Missionaries and Chinese clergy were sought out,
not avoided. High schools and colleges, hospitals and
orphanages, were no longer libelled but applauded as
demonstrating love for the Chinese people. How the

[1] Edinburgh Conference Report, vol. vii.

Protestant societies, the American above all, took the opportunity in the field of education will appear in the next chapter. Here it is enough to note that schools, almost without exception, were carried on with two aims, one of being centres of evangelism, the other of training the sons and daughters of Christians; and of the two aims the first was undoubtedly the one which appealed most to the supporters of missions in the West. From the vantage-point of to-day we look back with surprise at the naïvety which characterised this use of the opportunity for penetration. It apparently did not occur to people that the Church was utilizing the demand for western education for ends which, to the Chinese, were ulterior ends and therefore might be open to question. Neither, apparently, did it occur that a generous approach might well have been made to the Chinese Government with an offer to put the Church's resources at their disposal to help on the reorganisation of education.

This aspect of the Christian educational expansion is the more interesting and indicative of a particular attitude towards China, because Church schools in England were the source of so much dissatisfaction among Nonconformists. In Germany also, Bismarck had demonstrated how marvellously the whole educational machine could be made subservient to defined socio-political ends, whilst in America the school was recognised as the supreme means of turning the alien population into good American citizens. Further, in America the attempt of the Mormons to evangelise by schools had aroused indignation to the pitch of rioting. In France the Church was looked upon with grave suspicion by the secularist Government and had the greatest difficulty in getting permission to start schools. In

China these principles and natural prejudices were thought not to apply. For the time being the assumption appeared to be warranted. During the first ten years of the Republic Chinese educational opinion had nothing to say but commendation, and the Christian schools and colleges not only became larger and more numerous but they also proved on the whole to be successful centres of evangelism.

A number of hospitals were also founded with this same object in view, and here also the special approach to the people in their need proved a great source of increase to the Church now that the old superstitious fear of foreign medicine was passing away. The devoted concern of doctors and nurses for the patients' welfare made the deepest impression, but where the popularity of the hospital made a mechanisation of work inevitable and evangelising was done on a larger scale and more professional lines, the results were not so profitable to the Church. One curious quirk in popular appreciation showed itself in relation to hospitals and schools and, indeed, all works of an outstandingly benevolent nature. The Chinese understand the doing of works of charity, with the motive of either attaining reputation in this life or merit in the next. That being so, they do not expect the philanthropist to carry on his activities on a business-like basis. Free treatment of patients, grants to needy scholars, are what they understand and appreciate. Missionary institutions which had to be conducted with strict economy did not always pass this test, and later it became a favourite criticism against mission schools.

As time went on, there came a marked change in the tone of the great majority of both the schools and medical colleges. Their very success made it necessary for the societies at the back of them to engage trained teachers. The result was that education became something more than the handmaid of evangelisation. It was more liberal and more efficient, and the evidence goes to show that the converts who came from these institutions were of a high order, young men and women with a fine sense of what Christianity means for society as well as for the individual. But the objection which came to be raised by the older type of missionary that schools did not make Christians in proportion to the money spent on them was in the main true. As in the West, training in the natural sciences and the science of history sowed doubts as to the existence and overruling providence of God.

This period was one in which the training of Chinese ministers and priests was undertaken with much greater care and attention to intellectual qualifications. Fairly well-equipped theological colleges were founded by Protestant missions. The Edinburgh Conference had had some strong advice to give on this matter of the ministry of the Church, as also on the medley of competing interests resulting from the forty-odd denominations which had missions in China. In this last respect the bitter sectarianism of Protestant Europe and America had become considerably less acute, and missions tended to pool their resources, more particularly in connection with universities and hospitals, and plans began to be put in train for achieving sectional reunion among Churches. The Episcopalians drew together in one body, and two other nation-wide Churches came into being, one of Methodists, the other of Presbyterians and Congregationalists, together with some Baptists. Thus union seminaries for theological training became more feasible, and through these and the ecclesiastical reunions the feeling began to grow that sectarian competition was in the nature of a scandal. It is important to note that where difficulties and hindrances came, it was as a rule from the side of the missionaries and the societies and not from the Chinese, to whom the historical background of sectarianism meant nothing. The Roman Church, of course, remained outside these movements. On the other hand, there was a new cause of offence and division which came in from the West and affected both Chinese Church and missionary body, namely, the controversy between those who were conservative in their theology, the so-called fundamentalists, and those whom they described as 'modernists'.

The year 1922 may be taken as the peak in mission success. In that year a great Protestant conference was held in Shanghai in which, almost without exception, representatives of every missionary society and of every organised regional Church were present. Chinese took part on a position of equality with foreign missionaries, the number of Chinese being slightly more than the number of foreigners. It was an impressive gathering, not only by the actual numbers there and the feeling it gave of an oecumenical Christianity overleaping all national as well as denominational barriers, but also because it represented 402,599 baptized Christians with some 400,000 others under instruction, ordained Chinese clergy numbering 1745, and a missionary body of some 6000 men and women of whom nearly 1100 were ordained.

It was 115 years since Robert Morrison had landed in Canton and could find no way of staying there except as an interpreter to the East India Company. It was 370

years since Francis Xavier had died looking longingly
at the land he never entered; 340 years since Matteo
Ricci had arrived at Macao. For Catholics as well as
Protestants the years had brought the same super-
human difficulties and in the end the same opportunities for expansion. In the Catholic Church there
were at this time nearly 2,000,000 converts and nearly
1100 Chinese priests. Since Chinese were seldom
ordained priests unless they were third-generation
Christians, the number is significant of the Church's
far-sighted planning. The number of foreign priests
was about 2650, and by this time included not only
continentals (European) of all nationalities but also
English-speaking priests from Ireland and America.
After the War the Pope paid close attention to missions
in China, making conspicuous efforts to consummate a
national organisation for the Church and at the same
time to overcome a certain conservative reluctance on
the part of the missionaries to allow the Chinese priests
to advance to the higher offices. He went forward with
plans for the immediate raising of Chinese to the
episcopate.

This development coincided with the same kind of
movement in the Protestant Churches. The Shanghai
Conference created a National Christian Council with
a permanent staff of a Chinese general secretary and
Chinese and foreign secretaries on an equal footing.
Chinese ministers came more and more to be elected as
presidents in Church assemblies, whilst some missionary
councils decided to give control of missionary funds
to Church courts. A Home Missionary Society was
founded to be managed entirely by Chinese and
supported by Chinese funds. Altogether, in both
Protestant and Catholic circles, the feeling was pre-

dominant that in spite of the grave political, social, and
economic situation in China generally, the Christian
movement was going to go from strength to strength
and reach a position of great prestige and importance
in the Chinese nation. The Shanghai Conference had
adopted the watchword of 'China for Christ'. It was
felt that China was in desperate need and could not
achieve her own salvation politically, socially, or economically. The followers of Jesus Christ as individuals
and in great organisations were called to a nation-
wide task of supreme urgency. The early missionary
objective of saving individual souls from damnation
without regard to the temporal order of society had
gradually given place to much wider ambitions. The
War had changed missionary mentality just as it had
changed the mentality of so many in the West. The old
late-Victorian belief in a world which, through the
dominance of the white race, was set on a course of continual and inevitable progress was now seen to be a
delusion. A start in industrialisation had been made in
China during the War, and people were horrified to
see the ease with which the worst evils of large-scale
industry were reproducible in China. This state of affairs
gave missionary supporters and workers a sense of a
race against time with God calling His people to expect
miracles in China: there society generally was in the
melting-pot and there a kind of world progress might
yet be achieved, if the Christian Church were active
enough to seize the opportunity.

In the same year as the Shanghai Conference the
anti-Christian movement began its attacks on missions
generally. Three years later the Nationalist agitation
which swept the country proved with unmistakable
force that the Churches had by no means the general

esteem on which they were counting. Indeed, the Renaissance movement had already given clear indication that Young China was looking for spiritual inspiration from other than Christian sources. Professor Dewey and Bertrand Russell were the prophets to whom university students and the new liberals were ready to listen. The real power of the West was regarded as having nothing to do with the Christian religion. Any sort of religion was a mere survival from a superstitious and semi-barbarous past and was rapidly being discarded by intelligent men in the West. In the light of modern science society would go forward and solve its problems without needing to trouble about religion except to tear away the meshes of irrationalism with which it clogged man's genuine advance.

The critics of Christianity brought definite accusations against missionaries and the Church. Communist propaganda, at this time making advances in student circles in the north and destined soon to be legitimised in the south, had made the intelligentsia entirely conversant with the Communist attitude to religion. A whole new vocabulary was thereby put at the disposal of the critics. Missionaries were reviled as the spies of imperialist and capitalist forces; and Christians as their 'running dogs'. Religion was spoken of as the 'opium' used for keeping the depressed classes content with existing conditions. The word 'opium' had a special barb to it, for the critics went to history and traced out the contemporaneous (more or less) arrival of opium and Protestant missionaries. All the motives of the missionary enterprise were traduced, and it was urged that if there were missionaries of a quiet, inoffensive temper they were just boobies who could not hope to earn a living in their home countries and so drifted out to China, where they lived on the fat of the land. Every little weakness and failing was exposed and placarded as common to all missionaries, but, most significant of all, there was revealed a very widespread resentment against Christian schools. The educational side of this belongs to another chapter, but there was also a very definite religious issue.

The main point of contention was whether foreigners could claim a right in equity to utilise the educational needs of a friendly State for the purpose of carrying out religious propaganda among the nation's youth. The Chinese authorities took up the position that any such utilisation was bad educationally for children of elementary school age and they would not allow it—this, of course, was a theory imbibed from the West. There was religious toleration under the Republic, but that meant that a child was free from pressure until he had reached an age when he could judge for himself whether he would observe this or that religion or none at all. To this the general response was given that as missionaries they wished to give the best education the West had to offer and that religion was an essential part of that education. It was also maintained that it was unfair to expect religious people who had invested so much money and energy in founding these institutions to carry them on without the teaching which was their very *raison d'être*. The authorities were unmoved by this plea. From their point of view it was better to be unfair to the missionaries than to the nation's youth. Moreover, national unity was at stake. It was at this time that cutting references to the disruptive effect of religion appeared in Chinese periodicals. It was pointed out that the Roman Catholics and Protestants were opposed to each other and that Protestantism was sown with competing sects. To this it was difficult to reply, even though among Protestants there was the strong recent tendency to co-operation.

With regard to the educational plea, Protestant missionaries were hampered in defending their theory by the relative failure of their practice. It had been so easy to make school worship and class teaching in religion compulsory that little had actually been accomplished in exalting that worship into something which was really spiritually effective. This weakness was partly a reflection of the poverty of worship in the Church, partly due to a failure in imagination. In so far as the child's approach to religion was considered, the reforms introduced were almost entirely reproductions of recent trends in this direction in America and England, as, for instance, in Sunday School teaching. There had been hardly any serious effort to study the child as a Chinese and to find out what the great spiritual dispositions were which had been built up in it as habitual channels of emotion. In class teaching in the majority of cases the Bible was the text-book, and after a laborious reading of the passage a long period of exposition was given. Examinations were held in this subject as in all others, and the marks were included in the total for the term. Thus the missionary educators might feel convinced that the authorities were wrong in divorcing the child from religion, but their technique in the matter had not proved their point. On the contrary there were numbers of non-Christians who had passed through mission schools and were ready to fulminate against 'the tyranny' they had suffered.

The authorities had their own substitute for religion to offer, and this was another difficulty for the missions and churches. The Nationalist Party, after 1927, proceeded to inculcate the religion of 'my country'. Class teaching on Dr. Sun's Three Principles of Democracy was made compulsory. They devised a religious service to be held every Monday morning at the same hour all over the country in all schools and Government offices. It was concentrated on Sun Yat-sen, the nation's dead hero, and it was no worship of a deified saint whose merit could bring protection and a mystical salvation, but communion with the soul of the man whose incredible labours had brought the country so far on the road to national salvation and who now laid on one and all the responsibility of following his example and bringing the revolution to a triumphant conclusion. The heart of the service was three bows to the Dead Leader's portrait and then three minutes' silence of commemoration, all standing rigidly to attention and making their vows of service; and finally a recital of his last appeal to his people. To those who are familiar with the elaboration of traditional Chinese ritual there is something particularly striking about the utter simplicity of this service. There was also something distinctly reminiscent of Protestant forms of worship, especially when a rousing hymn of revolution and an exhortation were added to the ceremonial.

The majority of Chinese Christians did not have the same suspicion and repugnance towards this service that many missionaries had, and it was largely owing to their persuasion that a policy of submission was almost universally adopted. Recent evidence goes to show that under the spur of the restrictions and owing to the voluntary nature of attendance at worship and Bible classes a more serious effort has been made by many churches and institutions to discover what Christian worship and Bible teaching are really suitable. The outcome is reported as a more genuine response though from smaller numbers.

On the political side of the missionary movement the Nationalist Revolution proved itself an illuminating experience in more ways than one. First there came the agitation caused by the anti-foreign outbreaks of 1925–27, together with the campaign of vilification carried out by the propaganda corps of the Nationalist Army. Naturally people wondered whether there would be a repetition of the Boxer time, and consuls called missionaries in to the Ports. All but about 500 left the interior. Actually, apart from the horrible twenty-four hours in Nanking (March 1927) and a certain ruthless fleecing of retreating missionaries, there was nothing serious in the way of violence offered. A good deal of house property was looted and some churches destroyed. Also a number of schools were taken over by ardent Nationalists. They used the specious plea that since the schools had been built for the good of the Chinese people and they, the Nationalists, knew better than any foreigner what was for the good of the Chinese, therefore they had the right to use these buildings.

The storm, however, blew over, and in a few months the missionaries were back at their stations except a small number who felt they could not return under the changed conditions. The change was great indeed. The whole position of foreigners and specially of missionaries was affected. Ever since the horror of the Great War had dawned on the Chinese, the moral prestige of the West had been seriously impaired. This gave more ground for suspicion as to Westerners' motives in pushing themselves into China; and on top of this came the Nationalist Revolution with its regiments of Russian-trained agitators penetrating the North as well as the South. One of their chief slogans was 'Down with the Unequal Treaties'. Since then missionaries had benefited from those treaties, they were equally suspect with the merchants, both being the agents of imperialist and capitalist nations which had oppressed China in the past and were still seeking to use her for their own advantage.

It came as a shock to most missionaries to realise how bitter the feeling was, but once they realised it, changes began to appear. Some Protestant missionaries disassociated themselves personally from the Treaties, some indeed of the missionary societies' headquarters notified their governments that they were prepared to see treaty privileges abrogated. The Pope also realised that the situation was open to objection and about this time warned all priests not to use the power of the Church on behalf of their people. There was a general recognition that the position of missionaries was essentially not one of right under the Treaties but of privilege as for guests of the country, and that it was the business of the missionary to behave as a guest with due regard to the susceptibilities of his host.

The change in the missionary attitude was brought about not only by the Nationalist Revolution. It was part of a movement throughout Protestant Christendom to restudy the missionary enterprise in the light of modern conditions. This found expression in the meeting of the International Missionary Council at Jerusalem in 1928, a second world conference in succession to that held in Edinburgh in 1910. That meeting placed on record 'its conviction that the protection of missionaries should only be by such methods as will promote goodwill in personal and official relations' and 'that since the foreign missionary enterprise is a spiritual and moral and not a political enterprise, its work should be carried on within two great human rights alone, the right of religious freedom for all men, and the maintenance by each nation of law and order for all within its bounds'. It also accepted a statement from a Chinese Christian that 'the type of missionary that is needed in China is the one that has a passion for China, real love for China . . . one who is willing to learn, willing to work with the Chinese'. The Government regulations requiring all schools and colleges to have Chinese principals gave the opportunity for educational missionaries to show whether they were or were not of the kind thus described. A few found the situation too irksome, but the majority settled in again to work under, as well as with, their Chinese colleagues. This happened also in other forms of Christian work.

This has had the best of effects inside the Church, but there remains a deep-rooted prejudice in the minds of the many outside. The Christian movement in China to-day is faced with the same difficulties and problems which confront the Church in all lands, and which arise on the one hand from the fact which is now recognised that whole tracts of the world's social and economic life are not Christianised, and on the other from the break-down of traditional faiths, Christianity among them, before the oncoming tide of scepticism and material-ism. But it is also hampered by this prejudice which regards the white man as essentially an exploiter and his religion as one of conquest. That there are grounds for this assumption is shown by a study of missionary hymnology, where military metaphors abound. Audiences at missionary meetings have been greatly stirred by these sentiments without realising that there was a curious affinity with the idea of the white man possessing the earth and remaking the nations to suit his ideas of what was best for them. For missionaries in China the idea was the more dangerous because they went to a people which long ago made a vital distinction between the way of conquest by force and the true kingly way (*pa tao* and *wang tao*). The kingly way was one which never used force but always made men agree with it by the sheer majesty of its spiritual excellence. It was so luminous in its rightness that it hardly had need to denounce evil: the evil man was abashed by its presence and slunk away of his own accord. There was also the Chinese belief that this would happen in Heaven's time when the opportunity was ripe, and that it was worse than useless to try to force the situation. Thus a missionary who was eager to seize every opportunity, who pursued his ends with restless busyness, and denounced those who differed from him, was not the Chinese ideal of a religious teacher. So there grew up a certain attitude to the Christian movement and more particularly the Christian Church, an attitude which fitted in with the tendency of which we have spoken to make a hobby of private religion. Scholars read the Bible and Christian apologetic works, would frankly express admiration of some of the teaching, and would even confess that China had need of the spirit which Jesus had shown; but they would not become members of the Church. There was something in them which revolted at the idea of being a captive of the missionary's bow and spear, and of pledging allegiance to what even after so many years was still a 'foreign' religion.

A certain group of philosophic minds in classical China had a very striking illumination with regard to the psychology of spiritual leadership in society. One of their sayings has been engraved on the hearts of the Chinese people:[1]

The Sage relies on actionless activity,
  Carries on wordless teaching,
But the myriad creatures are worked on by him; he does not disown
  them:
  He rears them but does not lay claim to them,
  Controls them but does not depend on them,
  Achieves his aim but does not call attention to what he does,
And for that very reason that he does not call attention to what he
  does
He is not ejected from fruition of what he has done.

[1] Arthur Waley's translation of the Tao Te Ching c2: vide *The Way and its Power*, p. 143.

CHAPTER III

THE INFLUENCE OF WESTERN POLITICAL
THOUGHT

WESTERN political thought is in some ways
the most revolutionary of all the revolutionary
influences which the white races have exercised in
China. The story of the outstanding events of our
period demonstrated in the first place the increasing
rigour of pressure exerted by the Powers, primarily
economic but by no means exclusively so; and in the
second place the increasing sense of division between
the Chinese people and their Manchu overlords. When
the foreign pressure reached such a pitch that there
was danger of China being partitioned, the Chinese,
despairing of their rulers, and taking the matter into
their own hands, abandoned their four-hundred-year-old
habit of isolation, and turned with an open mind to
anything and everything from the West. This brought
about the downfall of the Manchu Empire. Further-
more, the principle of monarchy was so discredited
that two subsequent attempts to restore that form of
government failed ignominiously.

The attempt to work on a republican basis has not
yet been completely successful. Some observers, including Chinese, maintain that the country has been
reduced to a state of anarchy, and that the Chinese
have demonstrated during the last twenty-five years
that they are incapable of government as understood in

the modern democratic state. And yet over some quite long periods of time and over a very wide area of the world's surface the Chinese have carried out a very successful system of government. This system compared with that of Rome—the only example on the same scale in the history of Europe—has been greatly productive of human happiness and cultural refinement, and at the same time has given good scope for local self-government as well as some other features of democracy. Also, whereas Rome, when attacked by barbarians, was rent in pieces and never regained its earlier unity, China, subjected to the same grinding test, nevertheless recovered herself again and again.

The question is what the invasion of western political ideas has done in destroying the old Chinese Empire. Has it merely abolished an illusion existing in the minds of the Chinese (and in those of western observers also from Marco Polo onwards) as to the greatness of their system of government? Or has it by unhappy chance killed something which had in it elements of real and lasting value for the West as well as for the East? From this a further question arises as to whether after all it is possible in one cataclysm to destroy the political wisdom of a race built up on the experience of centuries. Will not that which is of abiding value reassert itself as happened in Rome? The answer to these questions must rest with the historians of future generations. What we propose to do now is to piece together the story of the invasion of political ideas. The Chinese may prove not to have been merely weakminded imitators of the West, as some have thought them.

The story is concerned not only with the fact that certain new ideas broke upon the Chinese political consciousness but even more with the manner of the impact. The first Chinese observers of western political institutions and students of western political principles started with the rooted conviction that whatever other nations might excel in, the Chinese excelled in their knowledge of the high science and art of government. Trade relations, the manufacture of guns and the building of steamers, the opening of mines and the building of cotton mills, all these had been accepted as part of the national policy without disturbing this complacency. It was therefore a blow at the very heart of Chinese *amour propre* to find reason for doubt on this score. The key date is 1860, when, by the Second Treaty of Tientsin, the Powers extracted for their representatives the right of residence in the capital.

The establishment of the foreign legations in Peking was followed by the organisation of an *ad hoc* department of State to carry on negotiations with the foreign representatives. This necessitated an institution for training men for the service of this department. In 1862 W. A. P. Martin, an American missionary of twenty years' residence in China, was appointed head of the Tung Wen Kuan. Under him were nine foreign professors, English, French, German, and Russian. The students soon numbered over one hundred, at first all Manchus, later half Manchus, half Chinese. Martin organised a corps of translators, and among the translations issued were books dealing with international law, history, French and English codes of law, and diplomatic and consular guides. Here, then, was an insidious influence at work in the very capital itself, where thousands of picked scholars from all the provinces were preparing for the highest civil examinations.

Efforts of the legations to achieve social relations with Prince Kung and his associates in the Tsungli Yamen seem to have had little success. Anson Burlinghame, the American Minister, alone engaged their confidence. Sir Robert Hart, however, as head of the Chinese Maritime Customs, came more and more to be trusted by high officials both in Peking and Tientsin. It was he who persuaded the Grand Council to appoint representatives to the foreign Courts. This was the second way in which political ideas began to penetrate China. The Manchu Court realised that able and responsible men must be appointed to these posts. There came therefore to be a continuous succession of influential scholars living abroad and taking stock of what they saw, and in compliance with their instructions writing long reports on the customs of the countries in which they were living. The first Minister to the Court of St. James was Kuo Seng-tao, appointed in 1867, and he is a good example of others who served their country in London and the other capitals.

Minister Kuo was an excellent man for his post, a scholar and a gentleman and also a shrewd observer. Mr. Gladstone spoke of him as the most urbane man he had ever met. According to Ku Han-min, when Kuo came back he made the epoch-making remark: 'Confucius and Mencius have deceived us', by which he meant, not that he was converted to the adoption of western institutions, but that he now realised there was more than one way of governing a civilized country. A diary kept on his voyage to England shows how the leaven immediately began to work. He was not three days from Shanghai when the 'ritual of courtesy' displayed between his steamer and a passing man-of-war gave him his first idea of the civilization which might lie behind England's strength. In the Red Sea he wrote deploring the policy of seclusion which the Chinese Government had inaugurated at the end of the Sung Dynasty (thirteenth century), for 'Western States have been established for two thousand years, and their principles of government are entirely civilized and rational'. This was a little too much for the Court die-hards in Peking, and when after his return Kuo published his diary, the order went out for it to be banned. It is significant that the order was not universally obeyed.[1] Kuo was succeeded by Tseng Kuo-fan's son, who on his return after nine years' service in London was given a high post in the Tsungli Yamen. Things indeed were beginning to move.

By the beginning of the 'seventies there were three translation bureaus at work, one in Peking, one in Shanghai, and one in Canton. The two in Shanghai and Canton confined themselves at first to technical subjects, but later published books of general interest including textbooks on political organisation. Japanese versions of western books were in existence, and by their use the pace of production was greatly increased. People began to appreciate the difference between written and unwritten constitutions, and also the importance of coded laws. This latter was of special interest, as during the Manchu Dynasty there had been a marked trend in the direction of legalising the State and its relations with the people. There had appeared not only the Ta Ch'ing Legal Code with its periodic revisions but also the House Laws of the Imperial Clan. In addition there now arose an ever-increasing body of

[1] The copy of this diary which I possess was published in 1897 in Chengtu, the capital of the remote province of Szechwan.

binding regulations under the foreign treaties. It is not therefore to be wondered at that W. A. P. Martin's translation of Wheaton's International Law found serious readers.

By 1880 the first students sent to study abroad began to filter back into Chinese society. Some came from an America which was on its way to effective development of the whole of its territory. In that country there seemed nothing which government 'for the people and by the people' could not achieve. Some came from England where the governing classes were making the best of democracy and submitting to the call for universal education, public parks and libraries, and the whole gamut of municipal services. Wherever these students lived in the white man's West they found the idea that the old world must give place to the new. In this new world those who had learnt the way of it had both new Nature and old God on their side, and so were bound to prosper to an unimagined degree. Americans, generously enough, if somewhat patronisingly, thought that the Chinese might play their part in this great development, so the influence of America began at this early stage to be stronger than that of England or France.

Apart from the students there were the huge numbers of Chinese labourers who were attracted to the Straits Settlements, Java, Cuba, and the American continent. It is here worth noting that a certain prosperous merchant in Honolulu had his young brother sent out to him in 1879, and put him to school in the Bishop's school. That boy was Sun Yat-sen, destined to be the arch-exponent of western democratic principles and the first president of the Republic of China.

At this time also mission schools were being founded

up and down the coast, among them St. John's College (1879) in Shanghai, which became thirty years later the chief forcing-house for officials of the new stamp. In Shanghai also Chinese daily papers were founded during the 'seventies and flourished during the next decade. They printed not only foreign political news but also editorials, some of them radical enough. And last but not least in influence, there was the new Protestant missionary venture in journalism by Williamson, and later by Timothy Richard, the famous *Wan Kuo Kung Pao* (Intelligencer of all Nations), which was for years distributed at the imperial examinations. It is significant that Viceroy Chang Chih-tung and other semi-liberals began to give donations in aid of this paper. There was therefore a very definite turning of the tide. In all the coast provinces, and indeed wherever groups of scholars forgathered, there was talk and more than talk: keen minds began to study and compare.

The humiliations of the 1894–98 period intensified this feeling of unrest and dissatisfaction. Here is a quotation from one among the many memorials submitted to the Throne: 'Since the disgraceful defeat of our eastern forces, the Western Powers despise us and treat us like barbarians. . . . Formerly they regarded us as half civilized, now they compare us with the black slaves of Africa. Formerly they disliked us for our pride and self-complacency, now they insult us like irreclaimable dolts. According to their international law, their balance of power, and the provisions for protection, there is respect for civilized countries and not for barbarian tribes. What is more, they say, slice up the barbarian countries with their lack of government in order to save the people from destruction. Therefore ten years ago, when there was no trouble with us, the Western Powers concentrated on the partition of Africa. Now that that is finished they are talking these last three years of dividing up China. The newspapers discuss the matter, getting public opinion . . . with detailed plans and no concealment about it.'[1] Here is a new note struck by one of the official class. He pays attention to what the foreign press is saying, and what has been happening in other parts of the world. That he was not exaggerating the trend of foreign policy towards China may be seen from an article by a competent observer in *Blackwood's Magazine*: 'The scramble which moderate men hoped to see indefinitely postponed was entered into with the zest of a Cornish wrecking raid. The officious interference of quasi-friendly Powers to save the derelict empire from mutilation proved according to unvarying experience a remedy which was worse than the disease. Russia, Germany, and France proceeded to treat China as a No-Man's-Land: disintegration was the order of the day.'[2]

Arousing out of this situation, illiterate farmers in the north began to band themselves into secret societies and make their Boxer ritual. But another and very different movement started among scholars, mostly in the south. The leader was K'ang Yiu-wei, who brought about the Hundred Days of Reform in 1898. He and his disciples, T'an Ssu-tung, Liang Ch'i-ch'ao and others, show to a remarkable degree how far the new spirit had penetrated. Most of them came from country families, half farmer half scholar. K'ang himself came from a village near Canton; it was not until he

[1] Chang Pai-cheng, *Nan Hai K'ang Hsien Sheng Ch'uan*.
[2] Alexander Michie.

went to Peking for his third-degree examination that he saw Hongkong and Shanghai. These cities so impressed him that he bought every book on western countries and western learning that he could lay hands on, went back to his village home, and there buried himself in study. He was already distinguished for his scholarship and profound knowledge of classical history and for the radical theories which he held with regard to the mind of Confucius and the authenticity of the Confucian Canon. Learning for him was not mumbling of old saws and trifling with elegant verse, but stern attention to the real lessons of history. In this he was a Confucianist of the best tradition. Also he had for a time made a close study of Buddhism, and thereby come to see the world as caught in the net of pain and suffering. It was with this type of mind, humanist in the full Confucian sense and touched with the noble Buddhist power of compassion, that he absorbed the science and political thought of the West. It was born in on him with the force of an apocalyptic vision that a day of salvation for mankind was dawning, and that he had a leading part to play. First 'a new China must be made' in which the full force of Chinese universalism and glorification of social harmony might shine forth, and then he and his fellow scholars must 'take responsibility for the whole world'.

Again, in the best tradition of Confucianism, he saw that the first step must be education. At the age of thirty-three (1891), he came out of his retirement and settled down in a suburb of Canton city to teach any who wished to listen: one is reminded of Plato and his academy. K'ang's famous disciple, Liang Ch'i-ch'ao, has left on record an account of the amazing, electrifying influence of the master upon those who gathered round him: 'He made Confucianism and Buddhism, and Sung and Ming Philosophy the essence, and history and western learning the application. What he aimed at was the inspiration of men's souls and the widening of their wisdom. . . . Every day he would be in the class room for four or five hours, discussing one branch of learning or one particular matter; tracing its development and success or failure, looking at every side from the past to the present and illustrating it by comparisons with Europe and America. Also he went to the full lengths of his idealism, holding up some noble standard with its advance and decline, in the past and the present, in China and abroad: all in order that the learner might grow in the freedom of idealism, and the power of intelligent discrimination be born.'[1] This went on for four years during which K'ang worked out his famous *Ta Tung* philosophy of politics, society, and life. The two characters *Ta* and *Tung* are a phrase in the Classic of Rites denoting the glorious consummation of world peace and world unity. Before ever he had started on western learning K'ang had been attracted by the concept, and it figured prominently in his revision of Confucius's original teaching. Now, with an impulse in which the teaching of Christianity can be traced, he made it the centre of his philosophy. Always he came back to world unity with love as the binding force.

His great book, which he published after the foundation of the Republic,[2] is entitled the *Ta Tung Shu*. Analysing the different kinds of suffering in the world, he urges the necessity for the abolition of national

[1] Liang Ch'i-ch'ao, *Yin Ping Shih Wen Chi Lei Pien* (1902 ed.), vol. ii, p. 388. The other quotations in this chapter are also taken from these two volumes.

[2] For political reasons it could not have been published in China during the Manchu régimes.

barriers. He details the wars in which the Chinese people have engaged since the beginning of their history, and follows this up by an account of the main wars in the West 'from the days of Rome a total of eight hundred odd great wars, not to speak of small ones', culminating in the battle of Sedan and the siege of Paris. He draws the moral that as civilization advances in the West so the virus of nationalism becomes worse and the ability to slaughter more infamous. Therefore the barriers between the nations must be broken down, and all peoples come under the authority of a World Council composed of representatives from all countries.

Looking at this development all round, we see that K'ang had not only read the story of other nations and realised that China was 'only an eighty-oneth part of the world'; he had also made this story part of his own experience as a Chinese. He was neither crushed nor dazzled by what he read. On the contrary, his mind was stimulated and invigorated, and the measure of this is found in the easy, natural way in which he turns from Chinese history to western and vice versa. There is no discounting of foreign history in favour of Chinese, just as there is no sign of indiscriminate admiration of the West. He grants that to the West the modern awakening of its peoples has brought with it a new understanding of the common people; but he turns to passages in the Classics which show that this is no new discovery for China. Both Confucius and Mencius had something to say about this over 2000 years ago, emphasizing it as an essential part of true government. What he finds really significant in the West is that it has devised machinery for making the wishes of the people effective in the councils of state: parliaments with upper

and lower chambers, ballot-boxes, and the other con-
trivances of democratic government. To these, he felt,
the governing class in China would do well to give close
attention. Machinery already existed whereby responsible people could urge their views on Peking; but
under the pressure of new needs it was plainly inadequate. The Empress Dowager had built her Summer
Palace with the money raised by special tax for a fleet
and thus the country had been exposed to the humiliation of Japan's victory. In one of the memorials presented by K'ang to the Throne he speaks of sitting in
his room meditating on the desperate perils of the
country and 'weeping tears of blood'—the expression consecrated by sons mourning their parents lately
dead. It was this intensity of feeling which drove him
from his study to agitate for radical reforms, and when
he did so he was a true disciple of Wang Yang-ming,
the great Ming philosopher, whom his tutor had taught
him to revere. The essence of Wang's philosophy was
that 'to know is to act'.

In K'ang Yiu-wei we can see an instance, not of a
struggle between East and West, but of the way in
which the Chinese mind when presented with a whole
new world of political experience could retain its
initiative and derive inspiration. There was stuff already there in the race's tradition which could and did
respond in the mind of a man who has been described
as having 'the three great qualities of leadership:
idealistic thought, sincerity, and courage', and 'the
man who turned the first page for the new China
of the twentieth century'. After 1898 he was an exile,
and he never again achieved the same prominence as a
political leader. He did not approve of republican
principles, so that when his world turned in that direc-

tion under Sun Yat-sen's influence he was left behind. Nevertheless he continued to exert a spiritual influence, and through the stormy years after 1911 there was always a *Ta Tung* group which looked to a world re-united according to K'ang's ideas.

It will be remembered how in the first chapter reference was made to Jesuit works on China and the influence which Chinese humanist and naturalist philosophy came to exercise in Western Europe, particularly in France of the eighteenth century. Amongst others, Montesquieu, and then later Rousseau, betray this influence. In the latter it shows itself as fitting in with his romanticism and leading him to his theories on natural rights. Now through the translation of the *Contrat Social* these ideas were to reach China. They were highly attractive to those who felt the Manchu sway as a tyranny. Thus political romanticism began in China, a temper of mind destined to go to great lengths in the twentieth century. It did not appeal particularly to K'ang Yiu-wei, his mind was too classical. More in keeping with his outlook was Montesquieu, as he showed himself in his famous *L'Esprit des lois* with its universal approach to questions of polity and its emphasis on the necessity of constitutional law. This too was among the early translations and along with it Bluntschli's *Allgemeine Staatslehre*, in which was set forth, with all the diligent cogency of a good Swiss-German mind, the necessity for constitutions being drawn up methodically. It is the influence of these legal ideas which must now be considered.

L'Esprit des lois was exactly calculated to excite admiration. To begin with there were references, partly appreciative though mainly critical, to China and her form of government. The Chinese were made part of world history, which was capable of being patternised with the help of classified evidence drawn from all ages and all countries. To a good Confucianist mind with its own predilection for systematisation this was immensely impressive. The way was thus open for Montesquieu's argument that without a constitution of some sort the essential liberties of the people were at the mercy of the supreme authority. The idea that law existed primarily not to strengthen the arm of the government but to protect the governed came as a revelation, as also did Montesquieu's sections on the types of perversion to be found in the various forms of government. Take the following statement as coming from the pen of a Westerner, famous through two centuries: 'The emperor of China is not taught like our princes that if he governs ill he will be less happy in the other life, less powerful and less opulent in this. He knows that if his government be not just, he will be stripped of both empire and life.' Liang Ch'i-ch'ao, writing in exile after 1898, quoted: 'Montesquieu also says, "All autocratic rulers misleadingly say that they unify the people. Actually they cannot do this for the reason that they steal the people's right of liberty and make them afraid. . . . What is called Great Peace in countries under an autocracy always contains in it the seed of disorder." ' Liang also described the American system of government, the abolition of slavery, and the movement for penal reform, winding up each paragraph with the words, 'Who is the creator of this blessed state of affairs? Montesquieu!'

Bluntschli was translated by W. A. P. Martin and published through the Tung Wen Kuan, and, as was customary with that institution, copies were presented to high officials in Peking and the provinces. Here the Chinese scholars found the distinction of the world's races into white, yellow, red, and black, with the yellow race in a class above the black and red but definitely below the white. Bluntschli had some complimentary things to say about the Chinese form of government as a benevolent despotism, but in the last resort he claimed for the Caucasian and Iranian nations the sole power of determining the history of the world. Since he also emphasised that diversity of races was due to the creative energy of Nature, the Chinese reader would make allowances for the inevitable prejudices of the foreign thinker and fasten on his more universal ideas. Further, Bluntschli had no sympathy with a proletarian movement. The power to influence a nation's executive must be in the hands of the solid people, the men who can read and judge on the national problems. That was precisely what Chinese scholars felt themselves to be. They were therefore impressed by what appeared in Bluntschli's pages as a great world movement in the direction of parliamentary government with definite powers guaranteed by precisely worded legal instruments.

Reformers were urgent that China should align herself with this movement, but there were others, in some ways liberal minded men, who viewed it with doubt and even fear. The great Viceroy Chang Chih-tung wrote his *Ch'uan Hsüeh Pien* (Exhortation to Learn) as a tract for the times. In it he is not at all carried away by all that he hears of western political progress. He is persuaded that in all this talk about democracy and parliamentary government there is a fundamental misunderstanding as to the legitimate, or even possible, powers of the people in the government of the country.

He says: 'Formerly France after rebelling against its monarch and exercising oppressive government excited the whole country to hatred, with all ranks attacking each other. This was the beginning of the change to a "people-lord" (*min-chu*) country. Our Throne has deep humanity and rich mercy. Its administration is in no way harsh. Why all this trouble to stir up class confusion? . . . Examine the way in which the western theory of democracy came. Its meaning is no more than that with a parliament public opinion has a means of expression and the wishes of the whole people may be brought to prevail. But the desire for this is not a desire to arrogate authority. Translators have made a mistake over the meaning of the democratic idea. The countries in the west, whether they are monarchies or republics, have the ruler and people together as lord. A country has to be governed, and that government has to be by law. . . . Neither ruler nor people are at liberty to break the law. The members of parliament have the opportunity to criticise, but the Executive decrees. The Throne has the right to dissolve a parliament, if it has come to a decision [of which the Throne disapproves].' Chang's book received the imperial imprimatur during the Hundred Days of Reform and is said to have had a circulation of a million. In spite of some liberal ideas, he was a conservative at heart. His mind never moved beyond 'making our holy faith the essence and western learning the means of application'. He realised that western government must be studied and, if necessary, cautiously applied. He made the mistake, however, as did many others of his day, of thinking that this was merely a matter of adding on a little suitable machinery, leaving the traditional government unaltered in all essentials.

The other great Viceroy of the time, Li Hung-chang, was for thirty years and more *the* outstanding man in the eyes of diplomats and other foreign residents in China. They had a very high opinion of his ability and shrewd grasp of the real forces of the modern world, and there is reason to suppose that at one point in his career some of them thought that he should make himself Emperor. Whether he could have done so is doubtful, for his fellow countrymen maintained a cynical attitude towards him. We are not very far wrong if we say of him that the one fixed star in his firmament was the Empress Dowager and her favour. The only ideas he was concerned with were those of military and naval and industrial strength into which he had been forced in his early days and which had brought him place and power. In spite then of his political prominence he counted very little, if at all, in the movement we are trying to portray.

In 1899 Liang Ch'i-ch'ao wrote the following words: 'The Japanese are constantly speaking of what they call the Soul of Japan . . . it is by reason of this that they are able to re-establish their country on a new basis. I therefore am searching for what is to be called the Soul of China. I look for it everywhere throughout the 400 districts, and I cannot find it. I am distressed beyond measure. Is it that nowhere there is a Soul of China? This frightens me.' Liang stresses the fact that this 'Soul of Japan' was a martial spirit and refers to the Chinese people as discounting the value of this quality. There was, however, one province in which this martial spirit came to conscious expression in a way in which it did nowhere else in China. This was the province of Hunan, the home of Tseng Kuo-fan and the army which saved the Manchu Dynasty from the Taipings, the province which had a long tradition of producing China's fighting men. Its people were well known all over China as having a passion for red peppers, a symbol of the peppery temper to be found in so many of them. Up to this time Hunan had been fiercely anti-foreign. In 1898 a group of Hunanese scholars published *A Collection of Essays in Defence of the Faith.*[1]

In these three volumes we have one side at any rate of the 'Soul of China', an expression of convictions deeply and proudly held. Their great fellow provincial, Tseng Kuo-fan, had led the way in making use of foreign inventions to protect China against foreign invasion. In the pages of this book we can see that to the true Chinese this was no concession at all. It was something entirely at the circumference of their life. When, however, K'ang Yiu-wei and his disciples began to let the poison of Westernism creep into the holy centre of their semi-religious, semi-political faith, then they were roused. Their fiery invectives were not in defence of any Manchu Court or Dynasty: Hunan had long been a happy hunting-ground for the secret societies, and Tseng's Hunanese army had fought the Taipings because they were heretics and not because they were rebels against the Manchu Throne. So now with their pens these scholars were defending holy China. They ransacked their own history for precedents of how to deal with these wild and erroneous ideas which were beginning to sap the Chinese morale. Here then we have in all its grandeur, as in all its self-complacency, the consciousness of being a great race with the roots

[1] These included violent and even scurrilous attacks on missionaries which roused much indignation in the foreign communities, where they were regarded as instigating much of the anti-foreign feeling which the mob vented in rioting.

of its social and political system deep in the laws of heaven and earth.

Hunan is a great agricultural province, self-supporting, giving of its surplus to the needs of other provinces. It was, therefore, with a proud sense of being both Hunanese and Chinese, of being able to speak as representatives of the whole nation, that they denounced the new idea of the individual having the right to be his own lord. For them, as for Chang Chih-tung, it was not common sense. Life was to be construed in terms of three great bonds: the bond between ruler and subject, the bond between father and son, and the bond between husband and wife. The new individualism could not but bring the destruction of the very foundations of society; witness the course which the Revolution in France had taken. As Confucius, and every sage since, had insisted, government can only be by those with knowledge: and in time the much-vaunted Westerners would discover the truth of this. Thus they arrived at the triumphant conclusion that 'western learning in the field of politics is wildly misleading and cannot endure for long'.

The reason for the publication of these essays was that the virus of Westernism was not merely spreading in China generally, but also in Hunan itself. One of K'ang Yiu-wei's chief disciples was a Hunanese, T'an Ssu-tung, who came back to the provincial capital in 1895, burning with the gospel of universal love which he had to proclaim. He sprang from a good official family and had friends everywhere, men who were attracted by his typically Hunanese courage and zeal. In an amazingly short time he captured the hearts of the younger scholars, and they flocked to Changsha to listen to him and join his society, the Nan Hsüeh Hui (Southern

Association of Learning). Meetings of over a thousand people would gather to listen to his addresses on the nation's affairs, and of those who listened 'not one but was stirred'. Thus in the very citadel of conservatism people came to be drawn away from their bigotry. They saw their Chinese world from an entirely new angle.

T'an was not destined to lead this movement for more than two years. In the spring of 1898 he went to Peking to join the agitation for reform. When he saw that the reformers were in great danger of their lives, he refused to seek his own safety. To his friends' urgent appeals he replied: 'No country has achieved reform without the shedding of blood. I have not heard of anyone doing this for the cause to-day.' With five others of the band he was arrested and executed; a gentleman of Hunan who cherished within him the 'Soul of China', and radical though he was, died a true Chinese to establish a precedent and engrave it on the hearts of his country-men.

We pass on to the Boxer Year 1900 and the following decade. It is important to realise the effect which the flight of the Court and its return later had on Chinese opinion. There was something shocking to the best minds that after such a signal defeat the rulers should be reinstated, particularly when the real ruler was a woman and held the titular Emperor a prisoner. From K'ang Yiu-wei had come the warning 'the Heavenly commission is not permanent', and the idea now spread all over the country. In true Chinese fashion the man in the street took no action himself but watched for where and when the *coup de grâce* would be given. Nobody was deceived into regarding as signs of a real change of heart the abolition of the State Examinations, or the promise of national and provincial assemblies. There was no rallying of loyalty to the Manchu Throne; the centre of political initiative shifted from Peking to Japan and Shanghai.

Of the survivors of the '98 reformers, K'ang Yiu-wei remained faithful to the Manchu Throne and the idea of constitutional monarchy. Liang Ch'i-ch'ao, how-ever, broke away and joined the new republican party, using all the power of his pen in its support. The moving influence in this party was a little, quiet, shabby man dressed in foreign clothes who for ten years had been going about from one country to another, where-ever there were Chinese. He was the Cantonese doctor, Sun Yat-sen, who had been exiled in 1894 after the discovery of his plot, and had since then been working ceaselessly towards the formation of 'a people's govern-ment'. This invasion of the republican idea was wholly from the West. The study of its development falls naturally into three parts: the way in which the idea grew in the mind of Sun himself, the way in which it laid hold of a number of ardent young Chinese, and the curious irrelevance of it in the Revolution of 1911.

Sun Yat-sen was born in 1866 of simple folk in Kwangtung (Canton) province. He had hardly begun his education when his brother sent for him. After three years in Honolulu he returned and went to school in Hongkong. It was then that he came under the influence of an American missionary and was baptized into the Christian Church. This brought him into difficulties with his family, but he stood by his convictions and with the help of his missionary friends was trained as a doctor, first in the American hospital in Canton and then in the medical school in connection with the London Missionary Society's hospital in Hongkong. In all this we see a young and ardent boy being subjected to an education quite other than that given to the ordinary Chinese youngster. What he picked up of the national tradition was through family and village influence, vitally interrupted by his three years abroad. He became a man of the world before he was twenty, able to find his way anywhere and to converse with foreigners in their own tongue. His five years of medical studies gave him a good approach to western science, and, according to Dr. Cantlie, his teacher and lifelong friend, this planted in him a great contempt for the time-honoured round of Chinese studies. There was, therefore, almost everything to make him an iconoclast and even a deracinated man. That he was the first, at any rate in his young days, is perfectly clear; at the age of sixteen, on his first return from abroad, he and a friend mutilated the images in the village temple to prove the powerlessness of the spirits. That he was the second is true only up to a certain point, for he did not settle down, as many Chinese have done, to make their living in a foreign country. There was every inducement for him to do this, and that he did not must be put down to the patriotic zeal which grew in him. But it must also be borne in mind that by the time he was thirty he was an exile, and that for over fifteen years he was at home not in China but in Britain, America, Japan, and other countries, where western thought and institutions were taken as a matter of course. It was inevitable that he should hardly realise how alienised he was becoming. At certain periods he read widely in western history, economics, and political philosophy. He was one among those many revolutionaries to whom the Reading Room at the British Museum came to be almost a home.

The upshot was a rooted conviction that China should and could become a republic. With true Chinese admiration for learning he decided that he must make an exhaustive study of the whole field of republican institutions and constitutional government. One can see him addressing himself to the task with that quiet sustained ardour which was one of the great qualities of his soul. But what he did not realise was the extent to which his search was affected by the idealism of his temperament. He was more than an idealist: he was a romantic, unquenchably so, and able, as all romantics are, to deceive himself about what he wanted to believe. Thus his adoption of western history was very different from that of K'ang Yiu-wei. For Dr. Sun it was not *part* of the relevant history of mankind, in which China also had a share, but the *only* really pertinent history. In that sense he had not the good Chinese catholic mind and was to a very real sense deracinated. Thus as a politician he may be said to have capitulated to the West, and to have suffered from what can be traced in the psychology of all those who plot revolution from outside their native land: their doctrines emerge as something quite inhumanly logical, faultlessly true to theory but dangerously out of relation to facts.

When China was being urged to appoint diplomatic representatives abroad, one argument used was that she could thereby protect her emigrant subjects. A certain official is said to have replied that his master, the Emperor, had so many millions of subjects that it was immaterial to him what happened to a few hundreds who went abroad. That might be so, but in the first decade of the twentieth century the total ran into millions, and it was among these that Dr. Sun found his first supporters. Peking's lordly disregard of her emigrants was to prove a costly mistake. They nearly all came from the south, where the feeling of loyalty to the Throne was notoriously less certain. Their feeling of nationality developed apart from and in contra-distinction to any feeling of loyalty. Coolies working on railways and in plantations, laundrymen and market gardeners, pedlars and shopkeepers were all imbibing a new nationalism from the atmosphere in which they lived. The same mistake was made at this time with the students who went abroad in large numbers. When they arrived in Japan or America or Europe, they found reform and revolutionary associations waiting for them in every city where there was a Chinese community. At first they and the more well-to-do merchants favoured K'ang Yiu-wei's programme of a constitutional monarchy. They were inspired partly by Japan's success along that line. But after 1905 Dr. Sun's republican gospel attracted more support, and this continued down to the fateful year of 1911. The question is whether there was in the minds of these ardent young men the same capitulation which we have traced in the mind of their leader.

The younger men who joined the Revolutionary Party had mostly a different background from that of their leader. They came from normal Chinese homes and had had their earlier education along the old lines. All of them were soaked in the tradition that learning made a man adequate for the technical business of government. Whatever the subject of their academic studies, they were all attracted by western political institutions, and they were eager to play their part in the new day which was to dawn in China. It was a thrilling time for youth and it was easy for them to be swept off their feet with enthusiasm for the new political gospel which was to save their country. So there was a capitulation to the West, but a more superficial one than that which took place in Dr. Sun's mind. It arose more from emotion than from deep conviction founded on prolonged study. Nor was there for any but a very few the deracinating experience which came to their leader.

The thoughts which were seething in men's minds can be found in the writings of Liang Ch'i-ch'ao, published for the most part in the Chinese *Min Pao* (People's Newspaper) at Tokyo during 1902. Dr. Hu Shih in his *Autobiography at the Age of Forty* has described how eagerly he and his school friends in Shanghai looked for the issues of this paper and how they gloried in Liang's 'theory of a new people.'[1] The first catchword half a century before had been *hsi hsüeh* (western learning), later *pien hwa* (change and reform), then *hsin hsüeh* (new learning). Now it was *hsin min* (a new people). Liang's contention was that this new world in which China found herself needed new methods of government; but without a new people alive to the real requirements of their national life no reforms in methods could be guaranteed to have lasting efficacy. 'Without a new people', he wrote, 'although you change a method to-day and change a man to-morrow, daub a bit on here and clean a bit off there, however you knit your brows in learning, I do not see that it can have any effect. We have been talking of new things for tens of years. Where is there any visible result?' He went on to bid his readers study the self-governing ability of the people in England, the United

---

[1] In the first great classic which the old Educators gave to boys to learn the opening sentence contained, according to the accepted rendering, the words, 'making a new people'.

States, Germany, and France. Their secret was the principle of nationalism which made the people of any area, being of the same blood, having the same language, the same religion, the same customs, regard each other as brothers and set themselves to be independent and self-governing. 'From this has come the principle of national imperialism by which they not only govern themselves but go out to govern other peoples. . . . Their strength abounds within their countries and so overflows outside . . . Whether by military force or by commerce or industry or the church, it is all one policy, to control the taming and saving of others.' This virile spirit is held up to the Chinese as an 'admirable' thing to be 'imitated'.

Liang reinforced his argument with an appeal to the biological view of politics. It is because the white races have learnt the secret of the struggle for existence and the survival of the fittest that they triumph in all quarters of the world. 'The other races love contemplation, the white races activity; the other races are in a net of peace, the white races never refuse a struggle of competition; the other races are conservative, the white races progressive.' This is definitely not a philosophy which came naturally to the Chinese mind. True it is implicit, and along a number of lines explicit, in the tenets held by the statesmen known as the Legalists in the third century b.c., and by the ruthless application of this principle the First Emperor had crushed all his opponents and unified China. But as a philosophy of life and politics it had soon become entirely discredited as immoral and unworthy of a people calling themselves civilised. Now it reappeared with the cogency attached to it of being not only Nature's law but the secret of western power.

There were, then, two main factors which went to make the 1911 Revolution a success; the ancient idea that no dynasty could continue to rule without a perpetuation of its heavenly commission and the hour for the overthrow of the Manchu Dynasty was long overdue; and the new idea of the 'new people'. It was easy to say that the Manchus must be overthrown, but not so easy to accomplish their downfall. The Emperor and his Court were entrenched in the Forbidden City surrounded by the Tartar city, and scattered around the capital were the Bannermen[1] villages, where dependants of the Government were kept to the number of some three million. Besides that there was the Bannermen garrison in every province as well as the whole hierarchy of officials who, whether they were loyal or not, were inclined to hang on to their posts. It was on the destruction of this solid fabric that the Manchus' enemies had to concentrate, and their task was so stupendous that it absorbed all their energies. Further, the psychology of a revolutionary time in China is, as has been already said, more passive than active. The majority are concerned with the drama of judgment, so that it is left for a very small minority to have definite opinions as to what power is to take the place of the old.

The 'new people' idea was common to the revolutionaries abroad and the students, and to their supporters and well-wishers in China. As a vague feeling it spread through all sections of the inarticulate common people, the peasant farmers, the craftsmen and shop-

---

[1] The Bannermen were mainly families of Manchu Blood, but also some Mongolian and Chinese families descended from supporters of the Manchu invasion in the 17th century. They all received pensions from the Government, so much rice, etc., year by year.

keepers in innumerable villages and small towns. They saw with their own eyes the changes in the schools, the new learning, new methods of transport, new industries. There was therefore a general willingness to accept the idea of a new people, whatever it might mean, particularly as its sponsors declared that it would make China rich and free.

Thus the 1911 Revolution was for the bulk of the people primarily the downfall of the Manchu Dynasty. But the removal of this incubus was also expected to open the way for the Chinese people to make a new path for themselves. Quite how this was to be done, no one knew. The revolution in one sense was too successful. When the end came the serried ranks of dynastic defence crumbled so quickly that the responsible people in the country generally were entirely unprepared to say what should be done next. There had never before been such a situation in China, where there was no victorious leader to assert that the heavenly commission had fallen to him. Yuan Shih-kai, as general in command of the western-armed forces in the north, was a power, but he was hated by all reformers for his part in the 1898 *coup d'état*. Apart from him there was no one person who could in any sense command or enforce loyalty. Then Dr. Sun and his followers came forward and insisted that the republican way was the world way, the way of progress and reform. This solution was accepted in the various provincial capitals with a feeling of relief. It was a peaceful solution and one which incidentally would commend the new régime to western peoples. To a large extent, therefore, in default of any other alternative but with the feeling that republicanism meant progress, the historic fabric of monarchism was discarded and a western form of government substituted. To this extent the revolution shows the power of western political ideas. It meant a sacrifice of their own political judgement in favour of the judgement of other races, and in that sense it was an imitation. Behind this was the feeling that what the western peoples had been able to do, that China could do. In this there was a proud, not a slavish, submission to the culture which they had been unable to keep at a distance.

Since the establishment of the Republic, it has become common to hear westerners exclaim over stories of faction and anarchy and to deplore that the relative peace and unity of the old empire have been sacrificed in an attempt to imitate western forms, which, it is maintained, are entirely unsuited to the Chinese temperament. The weak point in this argument lies in its failure to realise that no people can remain as they are in a changing world. It also ignores the fact that along certain lines there was considerable understanding of the democratic idea. In spite of the Emperor being in theory a benevolent autocrat, able to issue his personal fiats as ethical teaching, irresponsibility of rule was curbed by the censorship and the right of certain officials to memorialise the Throne. Besides this, some of the Confucian Classics had very much the force of an unwritten constitution to which the Emperor had to pay at least lip service. The Chinese people, therefore, were not slaves in any sense of the term. Further, class distinctions did not function in the way in which they did in feudal Europe. Thus the examinations for the public service were open to all except the sons of barbers, butchers, and actors. The son of the poorest peasant could become a viceroy or a censor, and there were such cases on record. The farmer or artisan knew himself to be a man with his rights and duties in society, and if he discounted half of what some ardent young revolutionary told him about democracy, it was because of his own shrewd experience of men and not because he could not grasp the ideas of liberty and equality. He had a very keen appreciation of the way in which his local affairs were run by his local elders, and could, through his clan organisation, make his voice heard. But taking life as a whole on its normal basis, he expected the duly established administrators to do their work and let him go on with his.

For the ordinary man, somewhat illiterate if not entirely so, the work of the new administrators was visualised as being very much what it had been under the old régime. At the same time the name of the new régime was quite clear to his intelligence: *kung ho min chu kuo* (united people lord country). That had its effect, the more so since the people were now styled citizens, and most of the old pomp and ceremony of official life was discarded. The elaborate official robes disappeared, and the old travelling chairs with their special bearers and the retinues of outrunners in uniform. The county head, or magistrate as he is commonly called in western books, might even be seen walking along the street like any ordinary person. If a man had to appear before an official, he no longer had to *kowtow* to him as representative of the Son of Heaven. There was an increasingly clear understanding that the new régime was not as the old, and that it gave the ordinary man more standing. The 'divinity that doth hedge a king' once gone soon became a tale of the past, the more unreal as years went on, so that attempts to revive the monarchy were received with indifference and even cynical amusement. For good or ill, the mould of ancient custom and ritual was broken; and when that happens a community cannot be preserved in the old pattern. Men's minds are forced to move on, and the way is open for social and political repercussions which are as incalculable as they are far-reaching.

The chief characteristic of the new habit of mind was the view of the state as a purely secular institution, and one of the main repercussions was the subservience of the civil official to the military. In the old days the military officer had neither the political power nor the social prestige of the civil. Now there came a mechanical drift in the other direction, and the new civil officials proved themselves helpless before the men who had behind them the power of the gun. This was the real revolution which took place after 1911. At first it came slowly, but by 1918 the provinces were being administered by generals in command of their own armies, and the chief function of the civil officers of the Republic was to extract from the people the money which the military demanded. All classes of men were caught in this utterly vicious system, and there seemed no way out except to let the country break up into separate states, as happened in Europe in the Middle Ages, each having its own master ruling by right of the sword. This was the failure of the first attempt at western republicanism. The experiment very nearly brought a complete social collapse.

There were other forces in the country which worked to save the situation. Education carried on rather inefficiently, but the new-pattern schools grew in number, and in them there were an increasing number of teachers who preached the doctrines of democracy and familiarised youth with the idea of parliament and votes. The political history of China was discounted, and the history of modern Europe exalted. Thus a new generation of educated men grew up who were to all intents and purposes the 'new people'. They believed that democratic institutions were possible: if the opportunity came they were there in every district in the country ready to be used. How that opportunity did come belongs to a later section of this chapter, and we must turn first to another type of political training and experience which was at work in the country.

As has already been noted, the principles laid down by Montesquieu and Bluntschli had made a deep impression on the minds of the reformers at the end of the nineteenth century. One outcome of this was that the law became a popular field of study for the students who went abroad, at first in great numbers to Japan, now more to America and Europe. These law students came back with a detailed knowledge of western legal systems, both constitutional and otherwise. They were convinced that their country must substitute government by the law for government by the individual. This was the type of mind which asserted itself in the councils of the Republic at its inception and which continued to have influence throughout the first decade of the new era. Once the decision had been made to establish a republican form of government, it is difficult to see how so unprecedented a situation could have been dealt with except through the making of a constitution. The machinery for this was already there in Peking. There was a department during the last years of the dynasty which had produced 'Constitutional Principles' and then, in 1911, at the outbreak of the Revolution, hurriedly issued its 'Nineteen Articles'. These were on the Japanese model, which was in its turn based on the German model. The republicans turned to America for the most part, and in the Provisional Constitution passed by the National Assembly of 1912 American elements predominated, though there were also some distinctively French features in it.

A parliament was thus brought into existence, and regulations for provincial assemblies such as figured in the constituent States of the American Republic were also put into force. At the time no one had any idea but that these bodies would function, inaugurate policies, pass budgets, and otherwise clarify the public will and see that it was carried out. In the Parliament, however, there was trouble from the very beginning. Dr. Sun and his party were obstinately convinced that parliament must be the ultimate authority in the state and must therefore be in a position to control the executive. The President, Yuan Shih-kai, and his followers were equally determined to keep the power in his hands. The outcome of this bitter controversy was a victory for the executive and the virtual death of parliamentary government. The Constitutional Compact promulgated in 1914 was one which made the President 'the President of the United States, the King of Great Britain and the Emperor of Germany all rolled into one'.[1] Some of the provincial assemblies worked for a time and they only faded out of existence when the war-lord régime had developed. They were then found by the men who gained control of the provinces to be both annoying and useless.

This might have been expected to be the end of constitution-making and even of any thought of democratic institutions. Actually the idea of coded law as a necessity persisted in the minds of educated people. The hope that a permanent and effective constitution could be agreed upon and made the basis of a new unity

[1] A criticism originating from Dr. C. T. Wang.

136

survived into the 'twenties. The law officers in Peking went on working, and in 1923 the Chairman of the Constitution Convention was able to pass a new proposal through the rump of a parliament still sitting at that time. It was this which made it possible in 1924 for negotiations to be opened between North and South, then at daggers-drawn, and which enabled Dr. Sun to go to Peking for discussion of terms of reunion.

Whatever may have been the nature of Chinese government in the past, however much it may have stressed personality in the administrators as more important than law, the trend for the last forty years has been in the other direction. Whether this is wholly due to western influence is another question, one which cannot be profitably considered until the historians have made a more critical study of Chinese law from antiquity downward.[1] The question is not merely one of constitutional law, but also of civil and criminal law, where the history of the Republic has been the same as in the more political field. Since 1904 there have been western-trained jurists at work and drafts of codes have been issued from time to time. In spite of unfavourable conditions the work has continued, and during the last few years been extended more widely than ever. There would seem to be some instinctive force in this which goes beyond any influence from the West, though that influence has been strong since 1912.

The general impression, then, which this period— 1912 to 1925—conveys at first sight is one of startling political contrasts: on the one hand, groups of intellectuals carried away by their enthusiasm for foreign institutions and having no practical knowledge as to

[1] Cp. Jean Escarra, *Le Droit chinois*, Peking, 1936; also Cyrus H. Peake in the *Political Science Quarterly*, New York, March 1937.

how to make them work; on the other hand, mercenary groups of adventurers building up spheres of military influence without the least concern for any principles, western or Chinese. It must be remembered, however, that the two groups were not out of contact with each other. Men passed from one to the other, and both were receiving education in practical and theoretical politics.

Meanwhile the country as a whole carried on, where it was not harried by civil war, through the momentum of its age-old system of village and clan life. At the same time people of all classes were coming to understand more the real nature of western life, both on its good side and its bad. For some ten years after the Revolution foreigners were almost universally popular, and were able to make friends with Chinese of all classes in a way which had been rarely achieved before. Whether they were diplomats, missionaries, business men, or teachers in Government universities, they enjoyed a remarkable prestige. All over the country there was a wave of interest in foreign customs and foreign articles of all descriptions. Wherever men congregated in their leisure moments, in tea-shop or wine-shop, in town or village, one of the main topics of conversation was the foreigner and his ways. And this was done not in the old spirit of curiosity which is exemplified in the old Chinese books on the barbarians and their astounding habits, but with a sober feeling that the nation was embarked on a new course and this outside world was part of their world. Newspapers from Shanghai were passed round. Schoolboys, primed with what they had learnt out of their text-books, were listened to with attention. Members of provincial assemblies back from the provincial capital were in demand that they might give inside information on the happenings there. Through all this the people of China began to lose their engrossment in family and local affairs. The new term '*ai kuo*' (love of country) began to take on meaning and a new kind of political-mindedness emerged to be taken into account alongside of their new sense of the secular in national and world affairs.

Whilst this development was taking place the Literary Renaissance surged into being in 1917. As a movement in literature and education it does not concern us here, but it had important political implications. It provided a new and more facile medium of expression for political ideas. Instead of having to subject itself to the rigorous requirements of certain long-recognised styles of 'fine writing', youth was now able to say what it liked in its own way. There was in fact a very real democratisation of literary expression. The reams and reams of print which were published were not only an index of intellectual ferment: they were also indicative of the extent to which western political ideas had penetrated. The terms which Liang Ch'i-ch'ao and his fellow writers had first popularised were now the common property of students, certainly in the secondary schools and even to some extent in the elementary schools. Chief among these were '*p'ing-teng*' (equality) and *tzu-yu* (liberty), but alongside them were *kung-ch'uan* (rights), *kung-fa* (public law), *kung-i* (public discussion), and *yü-lun* (public opinion). These terms sprang straight from the living deposit of traditional language. They might not have been in current use, but they were there, tucked away in one book and another, some of them with the very connotation they received in this new age. There was no need to coin new words from a Greek or Latin source, though, possibly because the sound of it tickled people's sense of humour, 'democracy' became '*ti-mo-chia-li-si*'. In the Chinese language learned terms could be adopted in simple self-explanatory forms. Thus self-government (*tzu-ch'ih*) and independence (*tzu-li*), seldom if ever used under the old régime, had an entirely natural ring; whilst '*tzu-wo*' (this I of me, this individual personality of mine), achieved an instant popularity.

The literary revolution came at a time when the world was ringing with such expressions as 'making the world safe for democracy' and 'it is the youth of the world on whom the future depends'. With this new power of self-expression at their command, the students of China felt that the mantle of the old examination scholars had fallen on their shoulders. It was for them to mobilise popular opinion against the war-lords and politicians, who could not be trusted to meet the challenge of Japan's Twenty-one Demands or the trickery of the Versailles Conference over Shantung. The completion of the telegraph system made it possible as never before to stir the whole country into action. Student societies were formed in every college and secondary school, and whenever a crisis emerged these were circularised with inflammatory letters. In this way the student headquarters in Peking could go into committee with over a thousand telegrams demanding the action which was believed necessary to save the country. This happened on six separate occasions between 1915 and 1928, and on five of these occasions the agitation was effective in influencing the Government's action.

The consequent loss of morale among the students, and increase of suspicion and ill-will in foreign governments whose interests might be affected by this kind of mass action, is another matter. The point to note is that these outbreaks, disturbing as they were, were regarded all over the country as both legitimate and necessary. From time immemorial the method of public agitation had been the accepted way in which the Chinese people kept a check on their rulers. In the Classic of History it is said, 'Heaven sees as my people see; Heaven hears as my people hear'. Although the students' minds were full of western ideas, their action was in conformity with ancient tradition. The same must be said of the committee work of the student and other societies which were formed in great numbers. They might appear to work according to rules adopted from American handbooks of committee procedure; but as a matter of fact the course of affairs was governed by the old ingrained habits of mind which for generations had worked in the discussion of family, clan, and village matters.

The truth would appear to be that the inrushing tide of western influence did not create an artificial appetite for democratic government but stirred up an appetite which was already in the Chinese people, one created by long ages of local self-government and fostered by hard experience in standing up for their rights. There was one man in the country who proved himself capable of interpreting these impulses and enthusiasms and directing them into practical channels. That man was Dr. Sun, and we must turn now to his later political development before going on to the Nationalist Revolution (1926–28) which he inspired.

In 1913 Dr. Sun and his followers were goaded into rebellion by Yuan Shih-kai's insistence on setting his authority above that of Parliament. They failed, and the 'Father of the Revolution' again became an exile. Dr.

Sharman in his critical biography [1] suggests that this failure caused a moral or rather a spiritual collapse. It is perhaps more correct to say that the visionary, whose dreams had come to him so much apart from his own people, now awoke and saw for the first time that he had been dreaming. It is the effect of this process on the mind and soul of Sun Yat-sen which we now have to examine, bearing in mind the earlier stage of westernisation through which he passed. He had been thinking to make a republic by the inherent force of a provisional constitution and an oath of allegiance. He had expected the good-will and support of sister democracies even against their own interests. In a book published in England in 1918 [2] he ascribed his failure to the idea rooted in the Chinese mind for two thousand years that 'action is difficult, but knowledge easy', a theory which he had himself believed but which he now saw to be the most fatal of mistakes. He set himself, therefore, when nearly fifty years of age, to a detached study of the economic conditions of his country and to a more realistic comparison of China and the West. Nothing could cure him of being a visionary, but he became at last a visionary striving to found his dreams on social and political facts. In one sense he succeeded, for he came to know his own people very much better, both in their weakness and their strength. His earlier admiration of the West, however, was seriously affected. The years of his retirement coincided with the years of the Great War, and when he emerged from that retirement with his changed outlook, he came back into a world which also was radically different.

[1] Lyon Sharman, *Sun Yat Sen: His Life and its Meaning*. New York, 1934.
[2] *Memoirs of a Chinese Revolutionary*, p. 8; also chaps. i and ii *passim*.

The effect which the War years had on Dr. Sun's view of the West is particularly significant because many of his countrymen were suffering from a like disillusionment. The shock which the War gave to Chinese minds was a staggering one. Coming at the time it did, when enthusiasm for western civilisation was like a flowing tide, it took time for the full seriousness of what was happening to get home, but in the end, thanks to sedulous propaganda, at first by the Germans and then by the British, all China came to know the horrors that were being enacted in these civilised Christian lands. The large-scale slaughter, not of professional soldiers but of ordinary men drafted off by the thousands, attacked the Chinese moral sense in a particularly sensitive spot. To them, with their ancestor-worshipping, filial-piety soul, the family was at stake, for youth was the repository of the sacred life handed down from the past. The moral prestige of Europe suffered very badly. Other events, notably the sacrifice of China's interests at the Treaty of Versailles, also conspired to make the Chinese cynical about the peoples whom they had been admiring.

This vein of cynicism was very noticeable in Dr. Sun after 1918. He did not expect the 'friendly Powers' to act except for their own interests, and it was on this ground alone that he appealed for help for China. Also he came to see that democracy after the western pattern was open to criticism in a number of ways. He never lost his faith in the democratic principle, but he felt that for his own country it would have to be abandoned for the time being in face of the need for national unification. Most striking of all was the change which he advocated in the policy of the Kuomintang (Nationalist Party) in 1921, when Adolf Joffe came offering the help and co-operation of Soviet Russia. Whereas in 1905 the oath of the Revolutionary Party (Tungminhui) contained the words 'the spirit and the binding principle of our various aims are Liberty, Equality, and Universal Love', in 1924 Dr. Sun urged that 'there is one thing of the greatest importance in a political party, that is, all members of the party must possess spiritual unity. In order that all members may be united spiritually, the first thing is to sacrifice freedom, the second is to offer his abilities. If the individual can sacrifice his freedom, then the whole party will have freedom. If the individual can offer his abilities, then the whole party will possess ability.' There was thus a swing back to the ingrained tradition of the Chinese family and state, that unity and harmony are the ultimate requisites for which, if necessary, the liberty of the individual must be sacrificed.

Dr Sun told Joffe candidly that he did not consider Communism suited, as a form of social order, to the mentality of the Chinese people, but since their common objective was to save the proletariat from their oppressors there was no reason why China and Russia should not work together. That his relegation of individual freedom to the second place should also be characteristic of Soviet politics was a bond of sympathy and mutual understanding. This was no capitulation to the Soviet idea: on the contrary it was the legacy of generations, and the Secret Societies of the last hundred years had enlisted it in the sacred cause of revolution.

Westerners have been inclined to think obstinately in terms of a 'changeless East', but this is to ignore a psychology of revolution which is common to every race in the world. It is only unimaginative people who fail to realise that, with a race as patient and long-suffering as the Chinese, there must be a corresponding consciousness that if things go beyond a certain point, then an explosion is natural and inevitable. This is part of the biological mechanism of freedom without which human beings wilt and die. It means that under those conditions the man or group who has been strained beyond the pitch of bearing any more breaks out into all the actions which under normal circumstances are to them morally wrong. This is recognised in China by many proverbial sayings, such as 'If you rule the people by fear of death, the time will come when they will not fear death.'

The violence which attended certain phases of the Nationalist Revolution was not therefore either an unheard-of contradiction to the Chinese horror of bloodshed, nor was it simply inspired by Bolshevik theories. The Russian experts lent the aid of their technique to men and women who felt that China under the war-lords' régime had reached the point of being 'no world at all', where the men in control did not respond to the moral implications (*tao li*) of any situation. With the normal human values thus in abeyance there was nothing for it but violent revolution. Further, in subjecting themselves to the Russian training, Chinese youth found, as youth in other lands has done, that the new group life gave them an amazing sense of personal release and fulfilment. The new technique and the new vocabulary which it produced seem at first sight redolent of Russia, yet the revolution was based in China itself. There is in the Chinese social organism a deep underlying sense of community in the soil, that soil which is the basis of life for them all, whether scholar, farmer, artisan, or merchant. This gives to Chinese civilisation its fundamentally rural and proletarian character. Agrarian movements command immediate sympathy. The Chinese language therefore took on with ease the Communist ideology; apt expressions were found for all the terms, expressions which the semi-illiterate could read and understand.

During the years 1924 to 1926 Michael Borodin and his assistants were at work in Canton, whilst picked young men were sent to Moscow for training. So the idea grew and spread that the great bourgeois self-governing countries of the West had not said the last word in political wisdom or political idealism. The Chinese nation, suffering from the twin curse of militarism and imperialism, must break those curses in their own way and by their own united initiative. Then they must go further than any other nation had done in the application of democratic principles to the renovation of the people, and set up political machinery directly subservient to the social and economic needs of the time.

Fifteen years after the anti-Manchu Revolution broke out, the Kuomintang moved its forces out of Canton on the first stage of its campaign to save the country from its enemies and oppressors, domestic and foreign. The outcome of that campaign has been the establishment of the present Nationalist Government in Nanking. The man who had led the first revolution was the leader of the second and more real one. Though he was dead and his body lying embalmed in a temple near Peking, his influence was even more potent than when he was alive, for the leaders of the party took immediate steps to canonise him as the patron saint and martyr of their cause. His Will and his writings became the Bible of the movement.

Among those writings the most famous, and the one

most concerned with political thought, is the *San Min Chu I*—the Three Principles of Democracy—which consists of speeches delivered to the party in 1924. The book is significant both positively and negatively. The three principles or guiding aims behind the revolution are race (or nationality), self-government (or democracy), and the livelihood of the people. There is good evidence to show that as leader Dr. Sun attached primary importance to the third principle. His mind ran to the social uplift of his people and the ordering of the country's economic resources. But he saw no hope for this apart from a knave-proof democratic form of government. This, as the means to the end, is placed second. But the immediate problem, at the time the speeches were delivered, was the creation of enthusiasm for his policy, not merely in his party but throughout the country. He therefore placed first the race principle, and set out to unify the country through a sense of grievance against foreign nations and their interests in China.

It is not surprising therefore that in the first section there should be a quantity of highly controversial material. Some positive mis-statements are made, and often the worst side is painted without mention of the existence of ameliorating conditions. Thus Dr. Sun informed his party that China was 'paying tribute' to foreign countries to the prodigious extent of 12,000 million dollars—a calculation based on an estimate of the profits on foreign business of all kinds, including real estate. He says nothing of any profits coming to Chinese through the operation of these interests. On the other hand, the book contains a large amount of incontrovertible material, especially in relation to the treaties concluded under the Manchu régime, and the embarrassment and loss to the country which some of these treaty privileges granted to foreigners have entailed. He is alarmist on the question of population, affirming that unless something be done quickly the growth of the white races will involve the absorption of China and the liquidation of her people. He divides the world into imperialist nations who are using equally economic penetration and political chauvinism to achieve wealth and power, and the oppressed nations who are suffering from this aggrandisement. The chief exponents of imperialism he regards as England, France, and Italy. He calls on China to fit herself to lead India, Siam, and the other downtrodden peoples to a new freedom and self-determination. It is at this point that the influence of the Third International is most marked.

In Part II, on self-government, the atmosphere changes to one of cooler appraisal. He is not as in earlier years looking at the political achievements of Europe and America through rose-coloured glasses. Emphasis is laid on the necessity for China discovering her own type of democracy through a due appreciation of her own political experience in the past. The following criticism of the West is typical: 'Revolution in Europe and America has been a fight for equality and freedom, and innumerable lives have been sacrificed over the struggle. But after the fight had been won many errors have come into existence. Through their experience in this way we must beware of treading in their footsteps. We must not concentrate on a fight for equality but on a fight for the authority of the people. With the growth of the authority of the people there will be true equality.' From this the argument goes on to an indictment of western democracy as having left the working class at the mercy of the capitalist, to which working men have replied with the weapon of non-co-operation. He maintains that, potent as this weapon is, its use is productive of very dangerous results, witness the fact that workmen in the West have developed the habit of not obeying their own leaders. Another criticism is that 'the people of Europe and America nowadays act in opposition to able administrators' and 'it is very easy there to remove them from office'. This arises from a terrible experience of tyrannical government in the past. The Chinese have not had so bad an experience, so they have no such rooted suspicions. They have on the contrary a great tradition of rulers of genius coming from the lowest ranks in society—a cook, a tailor, a carpenter—and the happy results which came from giving them free rein for using their ability for the good of all. Administrative authority must be given to the men who can really exercise it.

This brings Dr. Sun to what he regards as his great discovery, though he admits that the Swiss have something of the same idea in their new constitutional developments. He first of all makes a sharp distinction between *chen ch'uan* and *ch'ih ch'uan*, the authority of administrative rule and the authority of controlling rule. The latter belongs to the people, the former to the administrators. The people must have powers of election of administrators, of recalling them, of initiative in the matter of general principles, and of the referendum. The administrators if they are to do good work must have five sets of authority: legislative, juridical, executive, examinatory (for Government service), and that of the censorship. With regard to the relation of the central government and the provinces, Dr. Sun denounces the idea of a loose confederation. There must be certain powers granted to the provinces viewed both as people and as administrative groups, but outside these defined and guaranteed rights the country must be one under a central authority.

Part III of the *San Min Chu I* reveals the same revulsion against the idea of western superiority. There is recognition that China has much to gain by making use of the technical discoveries of the West, but there is also criticism. For example, the power which has come to be in the hands of a few controllers of capital is regarded as an evil thing and a direct menace to the necessary authority of the state. It is emphasised that when the industrialisation which China needs takes place there shall be special precautions taken against private capital getting the whip hand.

He discusses the land problem as follows: 'The land problem has not yet had any satisfactory solution in Europe and America. If we want to solve it we have to do it now. It would be too late if we should wait until our industry and commerce were developed. By that time the difference in wealth would be too great. . . . The best solution is the equalisation of land-ownership. This measure will naturally meet with the resistance of landowners; but, fortunately, as they are mostly small owners, the problem can be solved without great difficulty. The method to be adopted by the Nationalist Party is that the Government shall tax the land according to its value, or purchase it at its stated value. How should the value of a piece of land be determined? According to my opinion the value should be determined by the owner himself, and on the value he reports the Government should exact one per cent tax. . . . How can we prevent fraud over this? By the Government prescribing two regulations, one that the tax should be collected according to the stated value, the other that the Government has the right to buy at the stated value. Thus, if a landowner should report one hundred thousand dollars' worth of land at ten thousand dollars, the Government would have the right to buy it at that price, and the landowner would lose ninety thousand dollars. . . . After the value is fixed, any future increase in the value coming from improvements made by society and the progress of industry and commerce shall belong to society.' In this and in many other ways Dr. Sun reveals himself as very definitely a socialist, though not after the same pattern as most western socialists. He himself draws a sharp distinction between socialism in Europe and socialism in China, and there is, indeed, in his attitude an interesting combination of insistence on the authority of the state, the control of capital, and the continuance of private enterprise. This fits in with his position in Part II, where he advocates security of authority for able administrators. At the same time he appeals to ancient Chinese tradition. The welfare of the whole body of the citizens is to be the one object of administration, whether in the political or the economic field, and where the property rights of individuals are adverse to the interests of the community those rights cannot for a moment be allowed. On the other hand, there is throughout this Part III a recurrent discussion of Communism, with the unfailing conclusion that it is not the ultimate solution of the problem of livelihood. Private capital is not a pernicious thing if it be prevented from acting in pernicious ways. The Chinese have not suffered so grievously from an overweening capitalism that they must take violent measures to destroy its power. Let them take warning from the West and solve the problem in a more reasonable fashion.

Thus the *San Min Chu I*, which four years after its publication became the accepted policy for the whole country and the text-book taught in all schools, not to be altered in any essential particular since it had been given to the country by its sainted leader. His last charge was that the revolutionary struggle should be prosecuted with every effort until this policy could be put into force. Until that happened 'the revolution was not yet completed'.

The invasion of China by the West has now been examined from the angle of political thought and aspiration. The influence has plainly been profound, so much so that at one point men whose minds had largely capitulated to the West were looked to as the saviours of the country. Since that time (1911 to 1912) there have been a large number of people in influential positions, notably in education and in the law, whose minds were subservient to what they had learnt in the West. On the other hand, there have been striking revelations of a deep-rooted culture-consciousness in the Chinese people as a whole, so that it does not occasion surprise that there should be a revulsion against the tutelage of the West. The nature, however, of that revulsion is not one which can easily be understood. The attraction of the West to such men as K'ang Yiu-wei was, in the last resort, that its civilisation opened up a vision of a world civilisation. They were stirred to the marrow of their being, and, being Chinese, assumed that so impressive a civilisation must be correspondingly complete in its political organisation. In this they were of course deceived, as they learnt during the troublous years from 1912 to 1925, the years in which the western order has been subject to as drastic a test as the Chinese order. Out of the misery and anarchy of this testing period men's minds both in the East and the West have emerged in a state verging on confusion. The only principle which seems to have final validity is that of nationalism. The West accepts this as a matter of course. To the Chinese it has been a spiritual difficulty requiring a radical readjustment of their views of life and society. They have, however, made strenuous efforts, as the *San Min Chu I* shows so clearly, to make such readjustment, and this process has been going on for the eight years during which the Nationalist Government has functioned.

Dr. Hu Shih in some lectures delivered in America in 1933 made the following statement: 'A Chinese scholar once remarked: "It is easy for China to acquire the civilisation of the West, but it is very difficult to master its barbarism. Yet I suppose we must first master this barbarism before we can feel at home in this new civilisation." By barbarism he means the military side of the western culture, which does not consist of mere up-to-date equipment, nor mere efficient organisation, nor mere resourcefulness in man and money power, but which must presuppose the existence of what may be vaguely termed "the martial spirit," under which term we may include the love for adventure, the almost primitive delight in competitive combat, the instinctive love and worship of the warrior, the painstaking cultivation of bodily strength, the habits of obedience, and the readiness to fight and die for an impersonal cause.'[1] Dr. Hu puts it extremely well, and in the light of the facts behind such a statement the western political idealist finds himself on the horns of a dilemma. Either he is obliged to confess that the whole democratic advance in the West has been a mere by-product of national

[1] *The Chinese Renaissance* (Chicago), p. 14.

chauvinism, something which served that end under certain conditions and which under the new conditions to-day may very easily disappear. Or he is obliged to confess that the national chauvinism of the West is incompatible with the principles underlying true democracy, and so long as this chauvinism exists, self-determination and self-government cannot bear the fruits expected of them. The trouble about the British and the French and the Americans is that they will not recognise the dilemma. They would both eat their cake and have it. To the Chinese also it has been and is an excruciating problem. Being without the chauvinistic spirit, they welcomed the democratic idea at the valuation which late nineteenth-century Europe and America put on it, only to find that they had made a mistake. No democracy could live in the world of white imperialism without being able to defend itself. Without modern armies they were at the mercy of their foreign bondholders. With modern armies they were at the mercy of their war-lords. Their response to this situation has been to summon up their ancient revolutionary spirit and imbue it with a new nationalistic vehemence which they have learnt from the West. To many Chinese to-day this new spirit is in the nature of a capitulation, one into which they have been forced by a world in anarchy. From the political point of view it is the negation of everything they prize in their own tradition.

CHAPTER IV

THE DESTRUCTION OF THE OLD EDUCATION

IN modern controversies over education Chinese writers commonly refer to it as the *hsüeh mo*, the main arteries, that is the very life-blood of the nation. This is stated as a self-evident proposition; and it is true that nothing so stirs their sense of the ideal. If foreigners are to understand the significance of education in China, they must realise that there is a peculiar religious sacredness attaching to it.

From the early days of Confucius, their first great educator, all down the ages the conviction has grown that learning is the root and branch of civilisation. After every national upheaval the new rulers in the imperial palace commended their régime by endowing scholarship and encouraging education, and it is a moot question whether men did not regard the promotion of education as the prime function of the state. There has been no duty of the Emperor more exalted than that of governing the great examinations; and if corruption spread into this field the nation judged the dynasty and condemned it without mercy.

It is also characteristic of the Chinese people that they did not organise education in the way in which modern European states have organised it. The Chinese love of local initiative has been at work here. Hence there has been wide variation in different provinces and districts; where acute poverty has prevailed, there education and scholarship have suffered. But there could be no more fascinating journey through China than for a traveller to go from place to place and learn the history of its educational life: to see before the humble peasant homes the pillars commemorating some ancestor who had distinguished himself in the Examinations: to see the charming club-houses built by local scholars for their literary activities: to hear of the magistrates who had inspired a new fervour for education: to learn about the clan endowments, the yearly allocation of so much rice to the support of students and graduates: to wander round the old book-shops in the cities, turning over the mellow books, and penetrating to the storerooms where are kept the wood blocks for this book and the other, the work of local scholars. Twenty years ago any such traveller would have seen all these and many other evidences of a great system of education, one with a history of two thousand years and more. He could even have seen a few of the old Examination Halls, still left, though fast mouldering to decay.

There was no government organisation of the system except in so far as the nature of the State Examinations determined the studies of those ambitious for public office; nor was there any state endowment except that candidates for the highest examination went to the Capital at provincial public expense, and if they were successful became members of the Hanlin Academy with allowances commensurate with the high, though plain, dignity of scholarship. Schools were not organised on lines familiar to the West, with teachers taking graded classes of children. Neither the subject-matter of education nor the technique of pedagogy which had grown up generation after generation required such methods. Schools were very much one-man affairs. The boys went on each with his own task as allotted to him by the teacher, who, at the end of the day, checked over what had been done. For the most part the subject of study was the Canon of the Classics, but by no means exclusively so. There were all sorts of variation from district to district, or from one scholar family to another. In some schools history would be more studied, in others poetry, in others *belles-lettres*. But the Canon was the all-pervading and unifying influence, being both Bible and the main Greek and Latin Classics and the legends of the Saints and the rubrics of the Church all rolled into one.

From most points of view it was an extremely intellectualistic education, and, of course, in every way emphasised literary values. Mathematics was little taught, if taught at all. But the underlying principle of the whole was the making of a man, the development of personality and the training of moral character. The educated man took his stand before society as an expert in moral principles. In all the relationships of life, whether precedented or unprecedented, he was the man to point out the right word, the right act, the right ritual. Such was the theory. In practice, since the scholar made the aristocracy of the country and the only way to the dignity and wealth of public office was through scholarship, the worldly side bulked very large in the minds of most students. This was more than ever the case after the Manchus conquered China. K'ang Hsi and Ch'ien Lung with their shrewd, calculating minds saw that the way to preserve their inheritance was through generous treatment of the scholar class. Heterodox opinions were as much an object of suspicion as sedition, and although some notable movements in learned study took place, the relation of learning to

157

life and society and its needs was seriously affected. Too many of the nation's spiritual trustees became the slaves of imperial policy. The majority of the *literati* fell to the temptation of sycophancy, and when they became officials found safety for their minds in elegant literary trifling.

This roughly was the state of affairs at the beginning of the nineteenth century. The invasion from the West was destined to break up the traditional order of education as much as any other part of the nation's life. It began, however, very gradually and in a way which seemed quite remote, for the first foreign school for Chinese was that founded by Robert Morrison in Malacca in 1818. After his death a society was founded for promoting schools in China in which emphasis should be laid on the teaching of English as a means of imparting western knowledge as well as Christian teaching. This method was adopted in most of the mission schools which came to be founded as missionary activity extended, and it had far-reaching consequences. The primary object of these schools was the training of catechists and teachers and the building up of a Christian community which could read the Bible. They did not attempt to give the specialised training in the Classics which led to success in the official examinations, and were therefore considered negligible by the *literati*. But to the poorer classes they offered an opportunity of gaining that knowledge of English and western mathematics which might lead to remunerative employment in the new business world of the Treaty Ports.

Both Roman Catholics and Protestants emphasised the need that the women of the Christian communities should share in this education. Throughout China's history there have always been women of education who shared their brothers' lessons with a tutor or elder relative, and some are famous as poets and essayists. But it was a new idea that all girls should receive some education, still more strange that they do so in schools, which necessitated either a daily walk through the streets or the leaving of their homes to live in a boarding school. It was not until after 1900, and still more after 1911, that girls' education became part of the Chinese national system. But it was the mission schools, some of which were founded before 1860, which led the way, and trained many of the pioneers of the women's movement in China.

After 1860 the steady growth of the missionary movement gave opportunity not only for an increasing number of schools but for a raising of their standard. Boarding schools for both boys and girls provided a high-school course; some were called 'colleges', but there was not yet any work in western studies which reached university standard. This higher education was perhaps more emphasised by the American missionaries than by those of other nationalities. It was they who founded in Peking, Shanghai, Nanking, and Canton the first college institutions, which were incorporated in America and received American degrees. Only one Englishman of the time was far-sighted enough to press for university education. Timothy Richard in 1885 proposed to the Baptist Missionary Society a scheme for a strong union college in each provincial capital, but he failed to carry his fellow missionaries with him. A large number of people in fact, both in China and in Europe and America, looked unfavourably on this new development as something outside the missionary's proper task. But whether it had results in the field of religious conversions or not it had an effect on society which became more and more marked towards the end of the century. An increasing number of young men and women received a grounding in western knowledge and educational methods, and some of them went from these schools to complete their education in America and Europe.

While the official Chinese world was not interested in these educational experiments, there was one branch of western knowledge which they began to realise must be studied in the face of the growing menace of western barbarism, namely technical science. The building of ships and the manufacture of guns and ammunition was, however, a task for artisans, not for learned men, and the earliest Chinese schools of western learning were purely technical schools for the training of workmen. Tseng Kuo-fan established in 1867 a school in connection with his arsenal at Kiangnan, which is important for the translation work which was done there on engineering and allied subjects. In the same year another of the great viceroys of the time, Tso Tsung-tang, established schools in Foochow in connection with his shipbuilding plans. In 1879 the Telegraph College was founded in Tientsin, and in 1890 the Naval College at Nanking. Viceroy Chang Chih-tung prepared a more elaborate scheme for a 'Self-strengthening College' at Wuchang which was to provide courses in agriculture, foreign languages, mechanics, mining, and military science. For this college he engaged teachers from America, Belgium, England, Germany, and Russia. The Tung Wen Kuan (1862) was primarily an *ad hoc* institution for the training of interpreters and the like in the same way that the technical schools trained engineers. But the students were of a different type. They were very carefully chosen men of education, coming from good families with a tradition of learning behind them. It was soon found necessary to have two auxiliary schools in Shanghai and Canton. The next step was that the Tsung-li Yamen, in response to various forms of pressure, sanctioned the teaching of mathematics and physical science, western history and international law. The college also acquired a printing-press and published translations of all kinds of books, copies of which were sent to the governors of the different provinces.[1] In this way an entirely new idea of the scope and significance of western thought and education began to penetrate the minds of the scholar class.

There was as yet no recognition of western subjects and methods of teaching as needed in general education. That field was still dominated by the State Examinations, with their traditional form of the 'eight-legged' essay and the *Li* poem. There was therefore no inducement for candidates to apply themselves to anything but antiquarian erudition and elegant orthodoxy. Before any real change could take place there was a long battle to be fought. In 1869 the Governor of Fukien memorialized the Throne urging that a test in mathematics should be introduced into the Examinations. In 1875 Li Hungchang proposed that there should be a test in science as an alternative. In 1878 the Emperor gave permission for this, but no serious attempt was made to appoint

[1] The *Calendar* of the College for 1879 gives the following list: Wheaton's *Elements of International Law*, Martin's *Natural History*, Malguti's *Chemistry*, the Code Napoléon, the *Guide Diplomatique*, Woolsey's *International Law*, Keat's *English Grammar*, Fawcett's *Political Economy*, a *History of Russia*, Tytler's *Universal History*; books on Chemical Analysis, Mathematical Physics, and Human Anatomy.

examiners with the requisite knowledge, and, as on the one or two occasions when candidates offered the subjects they were promptly ploughed, there was but cold encouragement for those whose minds were attracted in this direction.

None the less it is clear that feeling was intensifying and in time must make itself felt. As an example of this feeling take the following quotation from Chang Chih-tung's book *An Exhortation to Learn*, published in 1898: 'From Ming times to the present day, this system has been going on for five hundred odd years. Preponderance is given to style and manner, and the matter deteriorates. Rules which are old give occasion for abuses, and the examiners follow their own convenience and so hide their stupidity, whilst the successful candidates are vulgarly proud of their good luck. Both in their exegesis and what they quote the scholars turn up their noses at anything except cram books from the shops. With regard to the original meaning of the classics and the thought of former decades they do not really know anything at all. During the last few decades style has become continually more trivial, and not only do they not understand the past but even the forms of modern style are entirely disregarded.'

Chang Chih-tung had still no thought of western learning as in any way affecting the soul of China. It was the reformers, K'ang Yiu-wei and his disciples, who first adopted western history and philosophy and science as part of their own heritage in the world. To them the old learning still held its place as of first importance, but it was now in relation to the other forms of learning which were sweeping into China. From now on it was no question of meeting barbarians on their own level but of learning from another civilisation those things which China might have discovered for herself but had not. K'ang Yiu-wei was the prophet of the Reform Party, releasing men's minds from old inhibitions, and in that sense setting them on the path of educational reform. But the man who was most successful in interpreting these things to that generation was Liang Ch'i-ch'ao, and it is to him that we must turn if we are to understand the revolution in thinking which took place.

Take the following two passages: 'There never has been a case of a man being ignorant of other countries' systems of learning and at the same time being able to master his own country's system; and likewise there has never been a case of a man being ignorant of his own country's learning and at the same time being able to master other countries' learning. . . . To-day in studying the western learning we must make political science the basis of learning and technical science the addendum. . . . The usefulness of political science is on a wider scale, of the technical sciences on a narrower. If you can give the country political ability and no technical skill, it does not matter, because the political administrators can promote technical advance.' That was written in 1897 while he was still in China. In 1902, an exile in Japan, he wrote the following on the need for education 'settling its objective': 'A country's education is in principle the same as an individual's. A father or elder brother in arranging their son's or younger brother's education determines his approach according to whether he is to be a scholar, farmer, artisan, or merchant. . . . If he is to make baskets, they will not teach him something else. . . . So with a country and its public education. The education is the means by which it nurtures its own kind of people, welding them together as a whole that they may be independent and struggle to survive in this world where victory goes to the fit and defeat to the unfit. To achieve this end is impossible with daubs of easternism and westernism, to-day learning some foreign language, to-morrow establishing some special study, in slipshod confused fashion hoping to reap the fruits. Those who have a mind to this great business of education must first recognise the two principles of education, the one the tool for manufacturing the people of the country, the other an indispensable means for understanding the world's experience, for examining the tendencies all over the world and the special characteristics of our own race with a view to arousing its whole strength.' Both passages show how far thought had moved, but there is a significant contrast between them. In the earlier one his attitude is identical with that of his master, K'ang Yiu-wei. In the later one he is moving away from K'ang's universalism, becoming both more nationalistic and at the same time more dazzled by the efficiency of the West.

The defeat of China in 1894, not by a Western Power but by Japan, proved a match to gunpowder. From 1895 there was for three years a continual succession of memorials pleading for modern studies and examination reform. One of the chief measures proposed in the 'Hundred Days of Reform' was the destruction of the examination system. That effort failed; yet seven years later the very forces which had killed it made a complete *volte-face*, and the great historic system was abolished, never to return. Centuries of Chinese idealism had gone to the making of it. The Ming Emperors had stereotyped it, the Manchus had prostituted it for their own ends, and now, with all its virtues and all its vices, it was abolished, not because it was good or bad, but because the Manchu imperial house saw that the alternative lay between its life and theirs. With its abolition went a whole hierarchy of vested interests, from the Hanlin Academy—its buildings already destroyed through the Boxer trouble—down to the humble village teacher in whose hands had lain the opening of the door to place and power. Most radical of all was the destruction of the *shu-yuan*, the centres of scholarly research, half colleges, half clubhouses. Their endowments went to the financing of the new education.

During those last forty years there was one quarter from which an influence on education might have been expected, namely, from the men who had studied in foreign countries. Actually their influence was very slight. Yung Wing, sent by missionaries from Hongkong, graduated from an American university as early as 1854. Consumed with the desire to serve his country, he urged upon Tseng Kuo-fan the advisability of sending a number of boys to America. One of the provisions of the treaty with America in 1868 was that Chinese should be welcomed in American schools; and on the strength of this Tseng memorialised the Throne. After his death the plan was supported by Li Hung-chang and finally received imperial sanction in 1871. Thirty boys between the ages of thirteen and fifteen were to be sent each year for four years with the expectation that they would stay fifteen years and return as fully matured and responsible members of society. These hopes were not realised. The boys were kept under Chinese supervision, were expected to retain their queues and Chinese dress, and had to spend some time studying the Classics under their Chinese tutors. None the less, being exposed to their foreign environment, they absorbed some of the ideas around them. Thus, when an official was sent to enquire into their progress, they refused to make the traditional *kowtow*. The report, therefore, went to Peking that they were learning bad foreign ways and, however clever they might become, could never be of real use to China. In spite of many protests the edict went forth, and they were recalled. One of the group, however, did not forget what he had learnt: Tang Shao-yi was to become one of the leaders of the Revolutionary Party.

No such systematic plan was made for sending men to Europe, but a few went, mainly through Li Hung-chang's influence, as the need arose for trained engineers and military and naval instructors. In 1875 a French engineer working in the Foochow shipbuilding yards took several apprentices with him to France. In 1876 a German officer, who had been engaged by Li Hung-chang as military instructor in his new army, took seven men with him to Germany. Of these, two were sent back as unsuitable, two remained in France, one because of illness, and the other three returned after three years as military instructors in Chihli province. In the same year, also by Li Hung-chang or through his influence, thirty or more men were sent to England and France to learn shipbuilding and navigation; another ten went in 1880. In 1890 five commissioners went to study conditions in Europe and each took with him two student attachés. In 1895 another sixteen men were sent to Russia, England, France, and Germany. These first adventurers into foreign lands were all more apprentices than students. Few, if any, had scholar standing, many of them were very young, and while they proved of some use in the army and navy, they had little or no influence otherwise. Among them, however, was one Yen Fu, who, although sent to study navigation, developed a taste for philosophy and gave himself to the translation of such authors as Huxley, Spencer, and John Stuart Mill. His translations were very widely read, and taught many Chinese *literati* for the first time that there was something of ethical and philosophical value behind western material civilisation.

After their defeat by Japan in 1894 the Chinese realised that if they wanted to learn the naval and military arts of the West they could do so much more quickly and cheaply through Japan. The first group of Government students were sent in 1896. They were welcomed by the Japanese authorities, and from that year onwards there was a steady and rapidly increasing stream of students, some sent by the imperial Government, some by provinces, many going at their own expense. After 1902, when the Government revolutionised the educational system, there was a great demand for teachers for the new schools. Thousands went to Japan with this in view, and when, after one or two years' study, they returned with a smattering of western knowledge, they were regarded as qualified for the new posts.

The new era in education began with the promulgation of a complete modern system of schools of every grade, beginning from the village and leading up to provincial and national universities, the whole to be under a Ministry of Education with Provincial Commissioners. It sounded very well, but to put it into actual practice was a very different matter, the chief difficulties being lack of properly trained teachers and of suitable buildings for class teaching. The returned students from

Japan met the need in entirely inadequate fashion. There were very few equipped for the vital task of training teachers in Normal schools. Text-books were prepared and elaborate time-tables drawn up, but the method of teaching was still very largely the old repetition method sacred to the classical tradition. The immensity of the problem is shown by the following figures given in a report by the Ministry of Education: in 1911 there were 52,650 modern schools with 1,625,534 scholars as against 4,222 schools with 102,767 scholars in 1905.

The new attitude on the part of the Government sent many pupils into the mission schools, which, instead of being despised as being no help in mounting the official ladder, were now recognised as providing, for the time being, a more efficient education than the new Government schools. The enrolment in Protestant mission schools in 1889 was 16,836; by 1911 it had risen to 102,533. A kind of higher-grade boarding school became specially popular. Most of these were American schools, but there were several founded by English missions, such as those at Swatow and Amoy, Foochow, Hankow, and Tientsin. It will be noted that these were all port cities. It was, however, university education which made the most striking progress. St. John's University in Shanghai raised its standard year by year and became very popular with the new business middle class which was beginning to emerge. The colleges in Canton and Nanking developed a special agricultural side; and there were other growing universities in Foochow, Soochow, far west in Chengtu, and in Tsinanfu and Peking. Although started originally by different missions, these institutions came more and more to be worked on a union basis, international as well as interdenominational.

The Young Men's and Young Women's Christian Associations also began work at this time along definitely educational lines, at first slowly and then, after the foundation of the Republic, with immense speed of expansion. They drew their foreign staffs almost entirely from America, and thus brought into the country a body of keen, alert young university graduates, all convinced of the need for healthy minds in healthy bodies and of the superlative value of democratic institutions. They were prepared to put the democratic principle to the test, so that they early adopted the practice of local responsibility and Chinese control. The influence of the Y.M.C.A. was exerted, not only in colleges and schools, but also through city associations which came to have great club buildings in which day schools and night schools were carried on. After 1912 its influence extended into Government colleges and schools. Since these young, energetic men and women came as helpers and not as competitors, they were very popular, and in the matter of physical training and games were instrumental in arousing the interest of students. The associations in the big cities became centres of citizen-training schemes. The buildings, it must be noted, were put up for the most part by Chinese money, subscribed locally, so that people had the feeling that this was their property. This fostered local initiative to a degree which was not found in missionary work generally. Young China used here what of the West appealed to him, and used it in his own way.

So far no attention has been given to education by Roman Catholics. The reason for this is that while some Protestant missionaries saw in the 'self-strengthening movement' an opportunity for propagating the Christian faith, there were few, if any, Catholic missionaries who looked at things in that light. What Catholic education there was had as its aim, first, the training of the children of Catholic families in the habit of intelligent worship; second, the training of catechists and priests. For the children the simplest of curricula was sufficient, and throughout the nineteenth century there was very little change in these schools, some of which had had quite a long history. The same applies to the seminaries where training was given for prospective catechists and priests. The missionaries on the whole preferred to have no non-Christians in their schools, and it was not till the beginning of the twentieth century, when the demand in Chinese scholarly circles arose for western learning, that Catholic educators began to think in terms of a secular side to Christian education. Even then the vast majority of the missionaries stuck to the old position that the sole concern of the Church with general education was to produce second and third generations which would be Catholic in the sense that no new-made convert could ever be. Whether viewed from the angle of non-Christian society or from that of the Christianising missionary, it must remain a question whether the Protestant educators or the Catholic were more effective in their attack on the spiritual life of the Chinese. By the beginning of the twentieth century Protestants were exercising a much wider and, in a secular sense, a much deeper influence on Chinese life and thought. The Catholic method went deeper in the narrowly religious sense, but it failed to attract those who were ready to break away from old spiritual affiliations.

In 1903 the Jesuits founded Aurora University in Shanghai, and arranged for faculties in law and science as well as in arts. Science included, significantly enough, civil engineering and medicine, instruction in the higher classes being given in French or English. By 1908 there were two hundred and three students. About the same time a few Catholic secondary schools were started, for the main part in the ports, whilst the curricula of the seminaries were widened to include a greater number of secular subjects. Finally came the plan for a great university in Peking, which was begun in 1925 under the auspices of the American Benedictines.

There have been widely divergent views as to the value to China of this foreign-controlled education. In his *History of Christian Missions in China*, Professor Latourette states more than once that mission schools were the best in the country and had an influence out of all proportion to their numbers. He points to many of the leaders of modern China who passed through these schools. T'ang Leang-li, the spokesman of the Kuomintang, on the other hand, has said:[1] 'The new schools were based on the missionary schools with their tradition of dogma and authority and with their antiquated methods. They were from the nature of the case incapable of becoming the centres of advanced scientific and cultural education.' That is to say, what Professor Latourette regards as a great benefaction to the Chinese people the Chinese writer regards as the reverse. He has also said that 'few or hardly any mission schools can provide teachers fit for the Government schools', and adds the indictment that 'Christian educated Chinese cannot read or write their own language properly, and lose their sense of national self-respect by being taught to look on their past as dark ages of heathenism.' Another writer, himself the product of missionary edu-

[1] *China in Revolt.*

171

cation, has said:[1] 'The mission schools vindicated, either consciously or unconsciously, the superiority of occidental civilisation, and inclined to neglect the beauty, the genius, and the dignity of Chinese culture. The result was the creation of a class of superficial beings who did not belong to the East or the West.'

The truth would seem to lie somewhere between these assertions. That these schools did 'vindicate the superiority of occidental civilisation' must be admitted, but it has to be recognised that up till ten years ago the students who went to mission schools were those who wanted all the westernism they could get. Since the larger the institution the more its dependence on non-Christian support, the indictment loses some of its force; and if a number of students lost 'their sense of national self-respect' it was part of a general lack of self-confidence which could be found in all ranks of society during these years. As for looking on 'their past as dark ages of heathenism', there were plenty of people outside the range of missionary influence who regarded the culture of the past as half superstition, half benighted autocracy. Those people would strenuously deny that it required religious propagandists to teach them that.

The truer estimate would appear to be that the revolution in education gave the missionary societies an opportunity to serve China at an hour of need, that they took the opportunity and worked with zeal and devotion, in many cases with expert educational knowledge; but in other cases they did not use trained foreign teachers, nor did they make but very inadequate arrangements for the training of Chinese teachers. The zeal and devotion were primarily directed to making converts, and in their efforts to achieve this end Protestant missionaries did not

[1] Theodore E. Hsiao, Ph.D., *History of Modern Education in China*, p. 131.

as a body grasp either the central importance of Chinese studies or the unsatisfactory nature of the uncorrelated aims and methods of their western education. They failed like most of their generation, and as the Government of India under the influence of Lord Macaulay's ideas of education failed, to understand that education must be rooted in the soil.

There was one educational experiment which in view of its inherent significance and the way it has been ignored by the controversialists needs special reference. The people of Shansi were more implicated in the murder of foreigners at the Boxer time than any other province. In their fear of retaliation they turned to Timothy Richard to intervene for them. The result was that a fine of half a million taels was imposed, but an agreement was reached by which the money was used for the foundation of a modern university with Richard as chancellor and with foreign control to continue for ten years. It was an amazing institution. The students were all old degree men knowing no English, the teachers nearly all foreigners who knew no Chinese. Instruction had to be given through interpreters, and many of the text-books had to be translated. After the transfer to Chinese control the institution fell on evil days. It was not wisely administered and now stands very low in the rank of Chinese universities. But the chief moral of the story lies in the fact that the graduates of its early years became men with great local influence and were very largely responsible for the state of affairs which has made Shansi known for years as the 'model province'. In other words, during its foreign-controlled period the university stood for mutual forgiveness and understanding, and the educational values were not trammeled by narrow religious propaganda.

173

The Republican revolution brought an immediate development of western education on lines adopted very largely from Japan, who in her turn had adopted them from Germany. For the time being the system inaugurated under the imperial régime was continued, though with two important differences. One was an increased emphasis on girls' education, equality of opportunity being a principle of the Republic. The other was the dropping from the curriculum of the study of the Confucian Classics. Instead of having put into his hands the actual texts which he was expected to memorize, the child was now given Readers of all sorts and descriptions, modelled chiefly on American patterns. There was the National Reader, which he used as an American child did, to gain a mastery of reading, and which contained stories from the Classics and moral teaching as well as much miscellaneous matter. There were also History, Geography, Sociology, and Ethics Readers.

The idea of the sanctity of education still held, but the content of education was anything but holy. It was taken for granted that a new people had to be made to meet the new world and that what Confucianism stood for had very little to do with this. The more conservative people, like K'ang Yiu-wei, who felt very dubious about sacrificing so much of the past, were pooh-poohed into silence. Education was secularised, as it has continued to be ever since. The mind of those in power is shown by the pronouncement passed by the interim meeting of the Educational Association in 1912, with T'sai Yuan-pei, the Minister of Education, presiding: 'The emphasis on moral education must be supported by practical learning and by military training, and the moral side must be completed by aesthetic training. If we compare this new ideal of republican education with the old

Manchu ideals, we shall realise where they differ and agree. "Loyalty to the emperor" and republican government are incompatible: "honouring Confucius" and religious liberty are not incompatible. "To exalt force" is the militarisation of the nation: "to esteem reality" is the principle of utility. "Respect for the common good" is what we call public spirit. There may be some difference in the width of application, but the fundamental idea is the same. A world view and aesthetic training are things which the past did not take into account.' Such sentiments, with their background of western secularism, could not of course make much of an impression on inland teachers, but they successfully enough muddled them into accepting a purely secular régime.

During the next ten years efforts were made to put the new system into force throughout the country, and new schools and colleges came into being everywhere. But those were years of increasing chaos. Not only was school work often interrupted by actual fighting, during which students were turned out of their school buildings in order that these might be used as barracks, but there was no strong government to implement the plans of the Ministry of Education which functioned at Peking. Very little progress was made with the training of teachers or the improvement of teaching methods. Ideas such as practical science teaching, handwork and physical training were adopted in theory, on instructions from headquarters. It became the ambition of every college and middle school to have a science laboratory, and much money was spent on buying expensive foreign apparatus, but too much of it suffered from carelessness and misuse. Few if any were the science teachers who ventured to perform an experiment, while it was out of the question to allow students to touch the apparatus: the most they could learn from it was to recognise the illustrations in their text-books. Athletics have won their way in China to-day, but twenty-five years ago it was an effort for a schoolboy to shed his long gown to take part in a game of football. Handwork was mainly represented by drawing.

Mr. Chou Yü-tung in his *History of Educational Thought* laments that during the last sixty years there have been no educationalists pure and simple in China. The men who controlled and influenced educational thought, such as Chang Chih-tung, Liang Ch'i-ch'ao and Ts'ai Yuan-pei, have been primarily either politicians or philosophers. The adoption of western methods has been largely opportunist; at first, as we have seen, purely a means to an end, the strengthening of the country to resist foreign aggression by naval and military preparation. Then with the growth of the realisation that a change of government was needed came the study of politics and economics. The abolition of the examination system and the organisation of modern schools was still the expression of the old idea that the object of education was to train officials: a new kind of government necessitates a new kind of official, that was all. While in places like Peking and Shanghai returned students might bandy catchwords and officials frame educational systems, in the schools and in the society from which the students came there was all the time tension between the surface modernisation and the subconscious pull of the deeply rooted past.

In contrast to this, the idea was slowly gaining ground that education is an end in itself, the necessary training which every boy and girl has a right to receive to fit them for life and not for any one special profession. That it did so was due to two influences which made themselves felt in the second decade of the twentieth century. The decision of the United States Government to use Boxer Indemnity Funds for education of Chinese in America had far reaching results. In the first eighteen years about 1300 men and women went to America from Tsing Hua College alone, and there were also those from other institutions who won scholarships in open competition, as well as many who went at their own expense. To all of them the United States was the Mecca of enlightened modernism. They did not go there as the earlier students did in order to master western crafts, but to get the 'new learning' in all its branches, and more particularly to study education in order to become teachers. For this reason a favourite place of study was Teachers' College, Columbia University. The full force of this influence became evident in the reforms which took place about 1922, but before considering these we must turn to the other influence, that of the *Pai Hua* or 'plain language' movement, which owed its inception to one of the Columbia graduates.

In 1917 Hu Shih, a student just completing his Ph.D. thesis and recently invited to become philosophy professor at the National University of Peking, wrote to Ch'en Tu-hsiu, the editor of the *New Youth* magazine, a new and radical weekly in Peking. The letter was meant for publication, and the editor, himself a professor in the National University, not only published it, but gave it his whole-hearted support. Part of it ran as follows: 'Looking at it generally, the cause of the decline in literary studies may be summed up in one sentence, "Matter is the slave of manner". This means form and no spirit, appearance at the expense of spirit.

To remedy this fault we must direct the emphasis to meaning in what we say, the matter behind the manner, the living kernel within the shell, as found in the old saying "with words unadorned and action undelayed". The quotation brings us to the question: If there is nothing in the words, what is the use of the adornment? In recent years I have thought over what has come to me, and to-day I want to declare a revolution in literary studies with eight objects to be achieved: give up the use of classical quotations and allusions, of conventions of courtesy, of parallelisms both in prose and poetry; do not avoid common everyday words and expressions; set ourselves to the construction of grammar; avoid unfelt exclamations; do not take the men of old as a pattern; in all expression there should be an individual "I" present, there should be something in everything we say.'

This movement, which has been rather inaccurately called a 'Renaissance', was not a revival of the great classics of China's past, but it was a 'New Tide' (*hsin shih ch'ao*) sweeping into men's minds, and was to a large extent the direct outcome of the western invasion of thought. There can be no doubt that the main driving force behind the movement was a growing dissatisfaction in the minds of the best kind of students abroad. They had been trained to express themselves in the elegant cadences of literary prose, but in their studies abroad they were compelled to apply their minds very strictly to the matter of the books they read. They reached the consciousness of language which any philosophically minded student is bound to have when he studies a foreign tongue and wakes up to unthought-of aptitudes for logical expression. There is a release of the mind: it is no longer slave to its conventional patterns; and that release leads on to a new power in the use of the native tongue.

Hu Shih and his friends, having had this experience, were brought up sharp against the situation in China, where expression had become over-stylised, over-dependent on ancient modes, unable to break its bonds and give free rein to every kind of thought. They denied entirely what some radicals were suggesting, that the Chinese written language was intrinsically unsuited for the expression of scientific or other modern concepts, but they maintained that there must be a complete break with the rigid conventionalism of the traditional styles. They turned to the colloquial literature of plays and novels, hitherto scorned by the scholars, and found there a medium through which the modern man could express his thoughts with lucidity and freedom. For three years the battle raged in all educational and literary circles, and in the end the reformers won a complete victory over the conservatives. The proof is to be seen in an order issued by the Ministry of Education in 1920: 'Starting in the autumn of the present year all elementary schools in their first and second years are to change to colloquial . . . all old-style text-books in elementary schools for the first and second year grades are to be discarded . . . third and fourth year books may be used until 1923 and then must stop.' It was estimated that by 1925 all Higher Primary as well as Primary schools would be using colloquial style text-books.

Let us turn now to the schools in which this revolution was made to take effect, more especially the elementary schools. The change came into an educational situation which was full of defects, not to speak of positive evils. Since 1905, and more especially since 1911, the elementary education of the country had been given in western-patterned schools; western-patterned in theory and in some cases in practice, with the division into classes and a teacher to each class. But in the majority of these schools there were not enough teachers to go round, and in many cases the teachers were still old-fashioned scholars steeped in the routine of the old-fashioned educational methods. The Readers which had taken the place of the Classics were in subject-matter more adapted to a child's intelligence, but in style they were still modelled on the classical tradition. Thus each lesson remained a task to be learnt by heart in the same fashion as the discarded Classics had been, and although the child's mind was to some extent stimulated by his understanding of what he was learning, this gain was offset by the loss to him of not having great prose to commit to memory and in having to keep step with his class. Nothing more boring could have been devised for a bright youngster than being faced with a lesson which he could master in a few minutes but which was supposed to keep his attention for the best part of an hour. The amount of valuable time wasted must have been colossal.

The introduction of the colloquial Readers into the school, good as it was in some ways, was yet bad in others. The pendulum swung too far in the direction of consideration for the child. The professed educationalists, trained for the most part in Japan and America, had now a golden opportunity to achieve 'reading without tears'. The new Readers were not merely childlike in thought and diction, they were even childish, and so served even less than the old ones to strengthen the sinews of the mind. The old vice of repetition still continued, and students became even more slipshod in their habits of study. None the less, there was some good accruing from this change. The young student was taught to write as he thought and spoke, and to make his writing a means of self-expression. Thus in the schools all over the country there was a great outburst of juvenile authorship in school magazines and the like; and from an educational point of view this must be regarded as proof of an excellent new vitality. Significant also is the fact that a whole new vocabulary came into vogue, fashions of speech which showed very clearly the influence of current western journalism. Take, for example, the constant harping on social and every other kind of phenomena as 'a problem', and the devising of a new 'ism' to solve it. As Dr. Hu Shih in an *Essay on Problems and Isms* pointed out in 1920, with a very fine barb of ridicule, everyone was thinking in these terms: 'Please discuss this problem at length with a view to solving it. Please do not trifle with this "ism", new and strange as it is; do not trifle with that "ism", profound and mysterious as it is. The number of problems which China must solve is simply colossal . . . every one of them with a firebrand tied to its tail.' That was the weakness as well as the strength of the New Tide in education. Everyone from twelve years up began to talk and write and what they put forth was a mass of the new *clichés* which were going the round.

At the other end of the educational scale there were immensely exciting results. The rebirth of learning in Europe was acclaimed as the revolutionary force which had made Europe 'the impressive, brilliant Europe we see to-day', as Ch'en Tu-hsiu said. It had brought revolution in every field of thought. So in China the New Tide must mean release from old dogmas about history and religion, must bring a new and realistic understanding of the past. To the university students in Peking, therefore, life was thrilling in the extreme. Those who were studying in the departments of National Studies were shown a vast area of tradition from which the accumulated debris of ages required to be removed in order that the real contours of their national history might emerge into the light of day. This was a great inspiration to youth and came at a singularly opportune moment. Ever since the founding of the Republic and the disestablishment of Confucianism the influence of the great past had been declining and there was nothing to take its place except unadulterated westernism. To many this was the solution of China's problem, and echoes of this viewpoint can be found in the school text-books of the period. But the main bulk of public feeling was against such a solution. In a revaluation of the past, conducted on the principles of critical research, the Chinese people might hope to find the clue to their salvation in the modern world. That was the appeal which came to students, especially in Peking; and the response, both then and in a continuous line of development since, has been one of great educational value to the country. The study of their national history and literature has been imbued with a new seriousness of temper and impartiality of approach. As a movement it attracts some of the best minds in the country, and in these days of warring slogans it gives quiet, responsible people a hope for the future in which old sanctities may attain a new reality.

In the midst of this excitement there arrived in China three distinguished educators from the West: Professor John Dewey of Columbia University in 1919, and in 1920 Mr. Bertrand Russell from Cambridge and Dr. Paul Monroe, also from Columbia.

They came at the invitation of the Ministry of Education, and those who were instrumental in getting them invited had very definite ideas as to what they might do. Professor Dewey was, for those who had studied under him, the great apostle of philosophic liberalism and experimental methodology, the advocate of complete freedom of thought, and the man who above all other teachers equated education to the practical problems of civic co-operation and useful living. Dr. Monroe, with his unique knowledge and experience of class-teaching and the organised technique of secondary education, was to examine into the state of the schools. Mr. Russell, on the other hand, came as the foremost exponent of a critical attitude to the old, a scientist who knew how to evolve from his science a philosophy of life and the universe.

The choice of these three distinguished men is highly significant, the more so as they proved from the point of view of popularity an enormous success. It was not merely that there were influential men in China who had studied under them, but that these men were able to convince others that what they reverenced in them was the very spirit and teaching which China needed. Everywhere in society there was spreading the feeling that this new education just did not educate as the old had done. As an indication of what a great many people felt, there were in Nanking about this time 500 private schools of the old traditional type, in Canton, the city which prided itself on being more go-ahead than any other in China, there were 1000 such schools with 20,000 pupils.

It was not enough that the New Tide should flow into the minds of students, not enough that the Ministry of Education should give its blessing to the popularisation of literary thought and expression. The movement had to be translated into terms of academic education, and for that to be done the aims of true education had to be redefined. Elasticity was needed in view of the widely varying economic levels and requirements of the provinces. Under these circumstances it was to foreigners that the educational leaders turned for advice and inspiration.

The effect of Mr. Russell's visit belongs more to another chapter. Dr. Monroe's survey resulted in two further invitations being issued to American experts. One was to Professor Twiss of Ohio State University, that he should make a thorough examination of the science teaching in schools. The other was to Dr. McCall of Teachers' College, Columbia, who came 'to construct scales and standardise mental and physical tests, specially in primary schools'. A psychological laboratory was started in Nanking under his direction. It is doubtful whether much was really achieved along these lines, except a better understanding of the vital importance of laboratory work in science teaching, and of the study of the child itself as a factor in education. This fitted in with Dr. Dewey's message, which was what really made a deep impression. His lectures in Peking and elsewhere in all the large Government centres were very carefully organised and fully reported and translated. The published form ran to ten editions within two years, and altogether we can see both in this and in the records of the educational conferences held in 1921 and 1922 that American influence was very powerful at this time. Thus, for example, a new and very vigorous institution came into being in the National Association for the Advancement of Education, a large number of the members of which were graduates of Teachers' College.

As a result of pressure from this and other quarters the Ministry of Education agreed to make radical revisions. In November 1922 the aims of education were set forth as follows: (1) to adapt itself to a new and changing society; (2) to promote the spirit of democracy; (3) to develop individuality; (4) to take into special consideration the economic status of the average citizen; (5) to adjust education to the needs of life; (6) to facilitate the spread of universal education; (7) to make itself flexible enough to allow for local variation.

Dr. Dewey was both America at its educational best and the West as the new Chinese scholar class was most able to understand it. There is need to emphasise this because, as we saw with the Reformers in 1896–98, it is only when the Chinese make their own response in their own way, when their intellectual and moral consciences are satisfied, that things begin to happen. What happened in 1922 was the release throughout the country of great unifying forces. There was no reason why the Ministry of Education should be able to function in all the independent satrapies into which the country was divided; but it did so function to a large extent because teachers everywhere willed to have it so.

In 1912 the Japanese pattern had been followed with the German aim of achieving power through education. Now it was American ideas, both aims and methods, which took hold. Three main emphases in American education were relevant: the emphasis on making a new people, that on making every department of learning clear and simple from the beginning, and that on making every child fitted to earn its living and contribute to the general life of the community. These features in American education had sprung from her particular conditions, especially the influx of a continually increasing number of immigrants with their widely divergent social and religious traditions. Thus American educators saw in a way which, for instance, British and French had no need to do that education is aimed primarily at effecting change.[1] Since this fitted precisely with what the liberals in China had in their minds, there was, from the first, acceptance of this principle, and the new education set out to make a new people. As, however, the subsequent years proved, this system was lacking in the efficiency which characterised the American system. The Chinese leaders in education made too many assumptions as to the intelligence of students. They indeed showed that they could memorise, but they also showed that they did not necessarily understand what they learnt. There was, therefore, a very great need for the American emphasis on clarity and simplicity. So also with making every child a contributor, both economically and otherwise. The new Chinese system had, as we have seen, been under the dominance of the old idea that education was primarily for state service and that an educated man as such was of moral value to the community. This by now was clearly seen to be a delusion. The bulk of the graduates of secondary schools, that is, those who had not the brains for a university training, were not fitted to take professional or business posts, not even to make reasonably good teachers. The self-strengthening which Japan had accomplished had not come in China. Hence the leaders turned to America and its 'education for life'. The ordinary boy and girl must be trained to be of use to their family and nation. In turning thus from an aristocratic to a democratic type of education China not only followed American aims but American methods. Six years were

[1] E. L. Thorndike, *The Principles of Teaching*, 1919, ch. i, pp. 1-3.

given to the elementary stage, six to secondary and three to the university. Half-way through their secondary course students were to be started on vocational curricula. Also, the credit system was followed, and with it came a further extension of the American method of introducing students to a wide variety of subjects and making examinations purely piecemeal affairs. Lastly, there was official approval for student self-governing societies, the idea being that through the life of these societies students would develop social initiative and public spirit.

A National Association of Vocational Education had been founded in 1917 under the leadership of Mr. Huang Yen-pei, a Chinese scholar of distinction and a leader of educational reform in his province. In 1921 he was appointed Minister of Education, but he declined office in order to concentrate on vocational problems. In six years the membership of the Association went up to the total of 4000. It made careful enquiries into all sorts of industrial and trade conditions. It united all the voluntary educational associations, and became in fact the spear-head of the growing agitation for reform. Owing to the high respect in which its leaders were held it was able to bring pressure to bear on educational authorities in the provinces. By 1925 there were 1548 vocational schools in existence, and it was becoming increasingly the practice in Shanghai and other industrial centres for large employers of labour to organise night schools in connection with their works. Universities and schools also did this in their neighbourhoods, the students giving voluntary teaching.

To this period also belongs the founding of a National Association for Mass Education. The peasant farmer, being the least literate class in the community as well as by far the largest, was felt to be the chief educational problem. Here again the man who showed himself leader was a private citizen, a young Y.M.C.A. secretary named James Yen, who organized educational work among the Chinese labourers in France during the Great War. On his return to China he continued with this work and produced a Thousand-character Lesson Course, based on calculations of the most commonly used characters in the written language. Having gained support for this work among illiterates, he went further and made careful studies of farming needs, both technical and social. After 1923 there were five experimental centres started, some by private enterprise, some by provincial authorities, and one, Dr. Yen's centre in Hopei Province, with strong financial support from the Central Government.

Further, all over the country there was quite a furore for 'proletarian schools' (*ping min hsüeh hsiao*), in the towns night schools, in the country seasonal schools for the farmer's off-seasons. These schools claimed to teach an adult to read in about three months by the use of the Thousand-character Course or other simplified textbooks. Vigorous efforts were made in some quarters to overcome the initial difficulty of Chinese script by the use of phonetic scripts, though the experiments on the whole have proved a failure. Experience goes to show that they could never be more than a half-way house to a knowledge of the real language. They are, however, of interest from the angle of our enquiry into western invasion. They show how very far some educators were prepared to go in the sacrifice of the literary tradition of the race. But they also prove that the invading force of westernism could reach a certain point and then could go no further, however useful in the narrow

188

utilitarian sense its methods might appear to be. The people who respond to simple education require literature in the high sense of the word, and they can only be satisfied by the real thing. That means the Chinese language of the Chinese people; only this lies next door to their heart. The daily life of the peasant or artisan contains all sorts of interests and relationships which are educative in every way, stimulating his intelligence and bringing home to him the richness of national traditions. This non-academic education can be reinforced by academic education, but only if it is in harmony with peasant and artisan life. A number of Chinese educators in recent years have visited Denmark with its systems of Folk schools. This invariably strikes them as an admirable illustration of what needs to be done.

The effect of the Nationalist Revolution (1926–28) in education is difficult to estimate, and that not merely because the results are continuing to emerge. On the one hand, its effect was slighter than might have been expected. The central and provincial authorities carried on with the new system which was already being put into practice. Dr. Sun's emphasis on the 'livelihood of the people' only served to stress the importance of vocational training. On the other hand, this great wave of national consciousness had a very marked effect both on the spirit in which education was given and on the position of mission and Church schools in the country. As the Second Convention of the Nationalist Party in January 1926 laid down, 'there must be emphasis on education, and it must be made revolutionary and proletarian, with special emphasis on the extension of mass-education, whilst the nationalist administrators must also make positive efforts to recover authority in education'. A few days later the Anti-Christian Alliance published its intention of attacking the Christian Church as the intimate ally of imperialism in China.

As the revolution swept the country, so everywhere schools came under the virtual control of the Nationalist Party. Whilst the main curriculum was not interfered with, new and thrilling lessons were introduced on the basis of the Three Principles of Democracy (*San Min Chu I*). Special teachers were added to the school staffs whose business it was to inculcate these principles; and although the scope of Dr. Sun's famous lectures was very much wider than an attack on western imperialism, yet the sections containing the attack were the spiciest in the book. These, therefore, attracted the bulk of attention, as also did the fiery speeches which characterised the weekly memorial services held in honour of the Dead Leader. From a dozen different angles, with all sorts of pithy illustrations, the lesson was driven home in class-teaching that the stronger races were making colossal fortunes out of their special trade privileges. As a method of teaching history, if somewhat garbled history, nothing could have been more calculated to make an impression on the nation's youth. History became alive and full of meaning, a very grim meaning when the modern expansion of the white races was shown to have involved the extermination of weaker races like the Red Indians.

For some four years there was a wave of anti-foreignism strong enough to induce in a whole generation of students an anti-imperialist complex. As part expression of these feelings, came the attack on missionary and church schools. The conflict raged round the question of registration, that is to say, whether schools of foreign foundation must recognise the authority of the Ministry of Education. The earlier attitude of the Republican Government had been to discourage registration. The authorities preferred to be free of treaty complications which might thereby arise. But as the danger of national disunity became more and more apparent, dislike and suspicion of mission schools and colleges had grown in various influential quarters.

Missionary educators on their side, in all good faith —and even it might be said in all goodwill—prized the freedom for educational experiment which was theirs under the Treaties. They found it difficult to realise that their increasingly prosperous institutions might warrantably be regarded as alien and divisive forces in the country. They did not think of themselves as invaders but as benefactors and philanthropists to whose efforts no one could reasonably object. At the same time, they claimed for themselves the right in equity to control the institutions which their money and expert work had created. And if such an institution was actually registered under the State Department of another country, and the property—valuable foreign buildings occupying a conspicuous site in the city—belonged to a body of foreign trustees, that, after all, was only a businesslike proceeding in view of the general insecurity prevailing in China. Yet all the time this attitude ignored the basic contention of a large and influential body of opinion among the Chinese that education is a main artery of the nation's life, and it is for the country's leaders and them alone to decide what kind of education should be given.

The bitterness of the issue lay for the missionaries in

the fact that since 1922 the leftist spirit of the Nationalist Party had made it a zealous supporter of the anti-Christian movement. Mission schools were accused of catching the young life of the nation at its most impressionable stage and inoculating it with other-worldly notions and ideas of universal love which, in the last resort, meant only 'submit yourselves to the imperialist and capitalist who are exploiting you'. On this ground compulsory attendance at religious services and classes in religious doctrine and history was denounced. In a few provinces the policy of the authorities was that they would have no religious teaching at all, not even optional, whilst everywhere the weekly service in honour of Dr. Sun was insisted on, and a special teacher of the revolutionary programme, a party member appointed by the local headquarters, had to be paid by the school.

From 1927 to 1929 the conflict raged. Some mission schools did not survive the local opposition, others were closed by order of their trustees. The main part, however, came to be registered under the Government. They then found that the situation was not so impossible as had been feared, and they have since carried on under Chinese principals with managing boards having a majority of Chinese. To-day they are recognised as a part of the legitimate educational organisation in the country. The better-run schools and colleges are perhaps more popular than they ever were.

The wave of anti-foreignism has subsided, as such waves have subsided in the past, but the effect remains in an attitude of cynicism towards the West, coupled with a new appreciation of the material significance of education. The avowed aim of all training to-day is to make citizens who can take part in the struggle for national salvation. The aggression of the Japanese naturally only tends to accentuate this, with the result that military training is now regarded as an indispensable part of school work, with training in first-aid and nursing for the girls. In other words, education is more than ever a material means to a material end; and if an old conservative scholar were asked how this has come about, there could be only one reply: this is the central principle of western education, and it has conquered the mind of China.

Here the Report of the League of Nations Commission on Education (1932) is highly suggestive. This Commission, composed of a German, a Pole, a Frenchman, and an Englishman, in the forefront of their report put themselves on record as follows: 'The chief danger lies in the purely formal imitation of the methods and substance of foreign civilizations. A notable characteristic of contemporary China is the cultivation by a group of the specific tendencies of some foreign culture, whether it come from America, Germany, France, or some other nation. . . . A considerable number of young Chinese intellectuals imitate the outward forms of American life without appearing to realize that Americanism springs from conditions which are peculiar to America, entirely different from those which prevail in China. . . . The old Chinese traditions are rightly considered out of date. Most of the springs of China's high civilization have run dry. At the same time one cannot but deprecate the tendency to misunderstand and underestimate their educational value. It is in its literature, whether it be philosophical, historical, or poetical, that the spirit of a nation is expressed. To replace these traditions by the products of a foreign civilization would be to disregard the spontaneous relation between the mentality of a people and its cultural manifestation.'

The warning of the Commissioners is unquestionably right, and if it had been given twenty years earlier it would have been all the more valuable. But what they failed to realise is that half the educational problem they were asked to investigate consisted in the relative failure of exactly that formal imitation which they deplored.

In spite of the 1922 reforms and the emphasis on western subjects and western methods, academic results have been predominantly poor. Responsible-minded educators have come to see that the lowered standard of Chinese cultural studies, with the loss of conviction as to their value, has created an impossible situation. Men of the calibre of Hu Shih, Chiang Mon-lin (President of the National University of Peking), the moving spirits in the Rural Teachers' Training College at Wusih, and some of the workers in James Yen's rural education movement, show behind their absorption in western technique a quick sensitiveness to the fundamental spiritual values involved in real education. This is specially marked in Liang Shou-min, ex-professor of philosophy in the National University of Peking and now head of rural citizen training in Shantung province. To him it is a matter of life and death that the soul of Chinese education should be saved from western materialism. This is in agreement with Dr. Sun himself, who laid down in the *San Min Chu I* the old nineteenth-century principle that Chinese culture must be for the essence of education and western learning for the technical application. The best minds concede all that the League Commission had to say about preserving the vital elements in their cultural tradition, but the question is: What are the vital elements which the modern mind, after scientific scholarship has sifted the evidence, can lay hold of and pass on to the new generation? The education of to-day has to solve the problem of what and how to teach during the transition period, while the historians, philosophers, and poets are occupied in the process of rediscovery.

CHAPTER V

WESTERN SCIENCE AND MEDICINE

IN *Science and Civilization* published in 1923, Professor Whitehead has a chapter on the 'First Physical Synthesis' by which more than by any other intellectual achievement western thinkers were able to establish the autonomy of natural science. Professor Whitehead draws attention to the year 1642, the year of Galileo's death and Newton's birth, as marking the change from the old to the new. He emphasises the happiness of the coincidence by which the one man followed the other, Galileo 'a supreme experimentalist and enough of a mathematician' and Newton 'a supreme mathematician and enough of an experimentalist'; and he then goes on to point out that if just at that time there had not been these two men with their special gifts, the history of the West might have been vastly different. The point of the Professor's remarks is enhanced by the fact that the Papacy in Galileo's day did its best to make him recant and it was not until the nineteenth century that the Roman Church recognised that the earth went round the sun; and that a study of Newton's life reveals that he had religious scruples over spending so much time on his calculations. Also we have to note that it was not until the seventeenth century that Bacon's plea for the experimental method in science was made, whilst Darwin and Wallace belong to the nineteenth century. Thus western civilisation went its way for nine-tenths of its history before the scientific mind began to come into its own and break away from the tutelage of theology and philosophy. For over 2000 years it worked under grave disabilities, and progress in knowledge of the universe was correspondingly slow. The same applies to Chinese civilisation with this difference, that the conditions from the seventeenth century on were singularly adverse to progress in science, but that, when by the end of the nineteenth century the western idea of natural science had penetrated the Chinese mind, there was amongst intellectuals a widespread and enthusiastic welcome of it, a welcome which has continued down to the present day. It is this cultural influence which we now have to estimate.

There are eminent Chinese who take up the position that science is alien to their characteristic modes of thought. Thus Dr. Lin Yu-tang in his *My Country and My People* (1936) devotes a chapter to 'The Chinese Mind' and in the third section of it deals with what he calls the 'lack of science'. So also Dr. Feng Yu-lan in an article in the *International Journal of Ethics* (1923) boldly asks, 'Why has China no science?' Both writers, one a philologist, the other a historian of philosophy, have very pertinent arguments to advance in support of their theory, but both fail to do justice to three facts. One is that so much of the semi-philosophical, semi-scientific thinking of the Greeks can be duplicated by the same kind of thinking in China of about the same time. Between the sixth and second centuries B.C. both civilisations were at work discovering the way to think rationally and to link events by the nexus of cause and effect. Those who have studied the works of Mo Ti and Hsün Ch'ing can have no doubt as to the definite advance that took place during this era. The great system which

was built up about the second century B.C. of five ele-
mental physical, or metaphysical, forces—Wood, Fire,
Metal, Water and Earth (soil)—is proof that the Chinese
as well as the Greeks made serious attempts to analyse
and then synthesise the universe on a rational basis.
Then in the first century A.D. there was Wang Ch'ung
with his famous series of essays, the Lun Heng, in which
he stoutly argues for physical events being due solely
to physical causes. This was the high-water mark of
Chinese science in those days, and it must be noted that
the Chinese did not advance in mathematics as did the
Greeks. There was no counterpart to Euclid, though
some unknown philosopher, about the third century
B.C., was occupied with considering the nature of space,
and considerable progress was made in the practical
mathematics of astronomy. The first real advance in
theoretical mathematics came with Liu Hui in the third
century A.D., with whom is associated the discovery of
the π relation between the circumference of the circle
and its diameter.

As in Europe after the Greek flowering period, so in
China there was a long period of relative stagnation.
Contact with the Arabs in the seventh century brought
about a new interest in mathematics apart from its use
for the calendar and astronomy generally. The Chinese
then learnt algebra for the first time. But the great
T'ang Dynasty with its poets and painters dazzled
men's minds with the glory of poetic and artistic intuition, and, as the centuries passed, this artistic side to
scholarly activity became more and more a sacred tradition. The sage Hsün Ch'ing had urged: 'It is better
to treat Nature as a thing and regulate it than to admire
its greatness and meditate on it'; but in each succeed-
ing age there were but few who were ready to do this.

In the sixteenth century, when the Jesuits decided to send a mission to China, they had a considerable respect for Chinese learning and reached the wise conclusion that the missionaries must be in a position to attract scholarly attention by their wisdom. Matteo Ricci, therefore, and his fellows were specially trained in mathematics and astronomy, and when they arrived in Peking, took every opportunity to call attention to what they had to give. The results were just what the makers of the policy had anticipated. Scholars became interested, and some of them at least realised that they had much to learn. From 1611, for the better part of a hundred years, there was a steady stream of books published dealing for the most part with European astronomy and mathematics, but a few expounding the nature of western science generally. In view of what happened in the nineteenth century, it is significant that these works were produced by the co-operation of Chinese scholars of high repute, chief among them being Hsü Kuang-chi, convert to Christianity and the donor of the land which has since become world-famous for the Sikawei Observatory built on it. But the most outstanding achievement of the Jesuits was the reform of the calendar. At the time when they arrived this was urgently needed, and the Emperor, after years of testing, finally decided to hand the work to Nicholas Longobardi and John Terence. This decision was taken after the western astronomers had given a convincing demonstration that their calculations were more accurate than those of the Chinese.

It is impossible to estimate what might have happened if the Ming Dynasty had continued in peace. As it was, the Manchu conquest of China took place, and for several decades there was little opportunity for recondite studies. The Jesuit scientific books, however, were carefully treasured in Peking, as also their scientific instruments, and later, as society settled down to the new régime, they were included in the collections of worth-while books which became so great a feature in the literary efforts of the eighteenth and nineteenth centuries. For example, John Adam Schaal's works were republished in the *Chao Tai Ts'ung Shu* in 1697, and a second edition appeared in 1833. Matteo Ricci's works appear in the *Shou Shan Ko Ts'ung Shu* of 1844, and his collaborator Li Chih-tsao fills a whole volume in this collection. In the Emperor Ch'ien Lung's famous collection, the *Ssu Ku Ch'üan Shu*, there are eleven Jesuit works in the Astronomical and Mathematical Section. The *Tsung Mu T'i Yao* describes with honest admiration the stimulus which the Jesuits had given to these studies. Most of the old colleges (*shu yüan*) had some of these ponderous collections in their libraries, though it does not follow that the scientific sections in them found any but a very small number of readers.

The earlier chapters have already demonstrated the kind of temper which came to characterise the relations between the Chinese Government and the oncoming Westerners about the beginning of the nineteenth century. Those being the conditions of intercourse, we can well understand that the Peking Court circle never thought for a moment of welcoming foreign learning. When in 1839 the trading difficulties culminated in the Opium War and Lin Tse-hsü was sent to Canton as Commissioner to deal with the situation, he went with the feeling that he had ruthless and barbarous enemies to punish. It was an immense shock to him to find how very superior these barbarians were in their ships and their armaments. The significant thing is that he did not quail under the shock but on the contrary attacked the problem with immense spirit and energy. As a result there was a mobilisation of what technical ability was available, in order that guns and warships might be constructed after the patterns used by the enemy. The barbarians could only be beaten with their own barbarous weapons. This, for the best part of twenty years, was the only idea that the Chinese had in relation to the technical science of the West; and this was to continue to be the main idea almost to the end of the century. Along this line, therefore, there was a yielding to *force majeure*, but there was in no sense a penetration of the Chinese mind.

Nevertheless even in those bad days there were one or two signs of what was to follow. Commissioner Lin himself took a very personal interest in the plans and experiments that were made. He also started a special office in which he collected every bit of material on which he could lay his hands about the foreigners and their ways. He had western newspapers translated; and in 1844 he published, with Wei Yüan as collaborator, the *Hai Kuo T'u Chih* (Illustrated Record of Maritime Nations) in twelve volumes. In addition to geographical and general information about the different countries from India westward and some interesting maps with the latitudinal and longitudinal lines marked, there are special chapters devoted to the construction of warships, including paddle-boats, the manufacture of guns and shells, the building of forts and the strategic placing of them, and so forth. The preface by Wei Yüan states that the aim of the book is 'to increase knowledge and to make preparation for practical purposes', but in a section on Singapore special attention is given to the literary studies at the Anglo-Chinese College there. The writer—either Wei Yüan or Lin Tse-hsü—bemoans the fact that the barbarians make such efforts to know about China, whilst in China nobody is interested in understanding foreign ways. The work shows every sign of being written with a view to catching the attention of the ordinary scholar. In this presumably it succeeded, as in 1849 a second and enlarged edition was published, whilst in 1852 a third edition came out, double the size of the original.

Another early pioneer was Ting Kung-ch'en, a native of Fukien, who in his youth travelled either to the Straits Settlements or the South Sea Islands. He was interested in mathematics and engineering and picked up all the information he could. He published a book of *Drawings on Gunnery*, which illustrated, among other new ideas, the foreign method of sighting, the movable gun-carriage, and construction of forts. It also contained a section on 'fire boats' and 'fire cars', of which he made working models. Soon after the Opium War Ting was made superintendent of a cannon foundry and gunpowder factory at Canton.

In 1855 another work was published in Shanghai which was destined to find its mark. This was a compendium of natural philosophy by Dr. Hobson of the London Missionary Society. There was at the time a group of scholars in Wusih.[1] According to a contemporary statement the people of this city were specially intelligent, and the scholars found the old round of 'classics and history and verse-making very tedious: their stomachs required the study of physics and the exploring of scientific problems'. It was into their hands that Hobson's book fell. They had already been reading

[1] A thriving port between Nanking and the mouth of the Yangtse.

the Jesuit works with their exposition of the science of two hundred years earlier. Now they saw 'new truth had emerged, and that only China did not know of it. . . . It was as if two hundred years had passed in a flash and they met the new truth face to face.' They set to work as best they could to make the apparatus required for the experiments in the book, compared the results, and made detailed records. Unfortunately these were lost when the Taipings captured Wusih, and their studies were hampered by the confusion of those years. But when Tseng Kuo-fan in 1864 called for men of scientific knowledge to come forward, they decided they must give their services. Two of them, Hsü Shou and his son, settled in Anking and built without foreign help a 25-ton steamer which was able to cover eighty miles in seven hours against the stream. Hua Heng-fang went on with mathematical studies and got in touch with another brilliant mathematician, Li Shan-lan, who afterwards taught in the Tung Wen Kuan in Peking. They all made visits to Shanghai, where Alexander Wylie, devoted missionary and ardent student of mathematics, was living. Works on Geometry, Trigonometry, and Differential and Integral Calculus were produced, whilst Edkins, another missionary, joined with the group in producing a translation of *Whewell's Mechanics*.

This group felt increasingly when they were put on to technical work that they had not sufficient grasp of the underlying principles. We have to note, therefore, at this point a forking of the ways. One set of men stuck to the job which the State required of them and went on with various kinds of technical work. Machine-shops were set up in Foochow and Kiangnan, and a large number of Chinese artisans were employed under the supervision of a few foreigners, mainly French and English. The idea behind this was entirely that which the Peking Government had set forth, namely, 'self-strengthening'. It was the idea behind the plan a few years later of sending picked students abroad for study. In a petition of Tseng's (1871) he said, 'We already know what are the essential things overseas, for example, geography, mathematics, astronomy, navigation, ship-building, and manufacturing—every one of these has a close relation to military operations'.[1] On the other hand, in men like Hsü Shou, Hua Heng-fang, and Li Shan-lan there was the pure love of knowledge for its own sake. Thus while some men may have been better patriots—in a good many instances feathering their own nests—these others were the better Chinese, more true to the highest traditions of the literary caste. In their approach to the study of natural science they showed more the spirit of the true scientist.

The spirit of the western scientist in those days is to be found in the Reports of the British Association for its first thirty years (1830–60). The urbane gentle-men who were its presidents expressed sentiments which remind us vividly of sentiments in the Confucian literature. They felt that in the last resort there was a great harmony of Nature, a vast system of order, which it was their high privilege to explore; and as they explored and came to understand, so they should apply the new knowledge to the welfare of mankind. In doing this they saw visions of 'many fraternities of fellow-labourers working for a common cause on a common plan with a perfect mutual understanding' (1839). It was because these Chinese scholars had much the same mind that they were attracted. They

[1] Gideon Chen, *Tseng Kuo-fan* (Peiping, 1935), p. 65.

would have agreed whole-heartedly with the statement that Priestley's analysis of water was 'important not merely because it banished water from among the elements, but that while it accounted for an infinite number of phenomena it introduced into chemistry distinctions of thought and accuracy of reasoning and led to the general prevalence of a sounder logic'. Here, they would have said, is where we Chinese have made our great mistake during the last 800 years. We came to the point where we saw that knowledge consisted in 'the examination of things' (*k'e wu*), but we construed things to be the things of the mind and the social order, and we have more and more descended to looking for the laws of the universe in old books. So we have fallen behind in the acquisition of real knowledge, and we must start by making up our deficiencies from the people who in the last 200 years have made such progress in these studies.

Hsü Shou and his friends appealed to Tseng Kuo-fan to found in connection with the Kiangnan Arsenal a translation bureau in which they should take an active part. It is doubtful whether Tseng ever quite saw the force of this plea for science. His diary reveals a man of pious temperament, conservative to a degree, and in his heart of hearts only interested in the building-up of moral power. But he saw the force of Hsü's arguments that if the only way to save the country was by examining western ways, then the examination must be thorough and must get down to basic principles. He granted the request therefore, and work began in 1868. In 1871 they began to publish, and by that time they had John Fryer and C. L. Kreyer working for them. Their first plan was to take the *Encyclopaedia Britannica* and translate it; but they finally decided it was not sufficiently up to date. Things were moving rapidly in the scientific world—Darwin had published his *Origin of Species* in 1859 and was working on his *Descent of Man*. The policy which they adopted was to issue works in the main fields of natural science. In 1880 Fryer published a report of the work accomplished: 98 works, running to 236 volumes. In Mathematics there were 22 works in 52 volumes; Astronomy, 9 works in 27 volumes; Geography, 8 works in 12 volumes; Engineering, 7 works in 17 volumes; Physics, 6 works in 14 volumes; Geology, 5 works in 20 volumes (including Mining); Chemistry, 5 works in 19 volumes. Also in deference to the 'self-strengthening movement' there were 15 works on Naval and Military Science in 41 volumes and 13 works on Arts and Manufactures in 15 volumes. The circulation is given as 31,111 copies; in all, 83,456 volumes. The report also goes into detail in describing the principles which the translators adopted in translating scientific terms. There were not wanting people who insisted that the Chinese language was an impossible medium for the expression of scientific processes and the creation of scientific terminology, but in the light of his experience Fryer states his conviction that it could be done—with care could be well done. But he states, however, in an article in *Nature* a year later that 'most of the treatises produced were far too elaborate and profound'. In this criticism he is undoubtedly right. His Chinese colleagues were exceptional men, and the ordinary purchasers of those 31,111 books did not necessarily make very much of them. Fryer was also instrumental in stirring up the missionary body to undertake the systematic production of simple text-books for school use. One of his remarks in *Nature* has particular interest: 'She [China] is therefore willing to be taught even by the "foreign Barbarians" such useful things as she feels she is ignorant of. But she must do this of her own accord and in her own way or not at all. It is a matter in which she is not to be dictated to, as in the case of treaties or missionary rights. She has freely availed herself of what she considers beneficial and has not been sparing in funds to enable knowledge to be disseminated throughout the Empire.'

During this same decade the Tung Wen Kuan in Peking was also producing a number of translations.[1] With its big staff of foreign professors—English, American, French and Russian—the majority of them being scientists of one kind or another, it is somewhat surprising that the scientific works were few in number, nothing like so many as came from the Kiangnan Bureau. W. A. P. Martin had his own conviction that Law was the prime necessity of the situation, and the College was concerned also to produce historical works, whilst its prime purpose was of course teaching, with emphasis on the acquisition of foreign languages. However, works on Chemistry, Mathematical Physics, and Anatomy were produced. For instance, Pilleguin translated Malagirti's work on Chemistry, making ten volumes of it of 110 pages each, with a wealth of illustrations and the use of western symbols. These works were well printed on the best paper—in this respect a contrast to the Kiangnan productions, which had a very mean appearance—and they were circulated among all the provincial *yamens*. This was done by imperial orders, but, we may doubt whether the Empress-Dowager or Prince Kung expected these works to have any particular effect. There

[1] *Vide* p. 161.

is a question whether the books were on public sale in Peking, for we know that when K'ang Yu-wei wanted such he went to Shanghai for them. As for the Tung Wen students, they were specially picked with a view to their not being a revolutionary influence. There is no evidence to show that they developed any alarming fervour for scientific studies.

The first half of the next period (1890–1911), was the time in which the Chinese people generally woke up to the fact that there was a real invasion of their life going on. It was the first period of nation-wide apprehension as to what the outcome was going to be. Under the circumstances we do not wonder if people's minds were largely occupied with the political issues and in the matter of western science were mainly concerned with the technical side. It was the period in Europe when technical science was making enormous strides, and the idea became prevalent there that China was an illimitable field for the building of railways and the opening of mines, in other words, for the use of western machinery.

The Chinese response to this was to make further schemes for catching up with the West. There was Yung Wing's plan for 120 students to go to America for a training of fifteen years; and there were similar schemes in relation to France and England. From the point of view of their promoters' hopes all these schemes proved very much of a failure. Not that a certain number of fairly competent technicians did not eventuate, but conditions in the high official *yamens* were unfavourable for them when they got to work. If we look for in-fluential figures among these returned students, we can only find one, Yen Fu, who was sent to England as a naval cadet. He returned with the rough draft of a translation of Darwin's *Origin of Species* in his pocket, and it was the publication of this which brought him fame and influence. Railways were built and mines opened, but in practically every case by foreign engineers, and the result, generally speaking, was an increase of fear of the foreigner. There was no real penetration of the minds of the Chinese, but a strengthening of the feeling of suspicion toward the whole range of foreign activities. Even a shrewd man like Chang Chih-tung totally failed to see that science could be anything more than machines cunningly put together on the basis of calculations made by a curious kind of scholar called a mathematician. To the day of his death it was to him a sort of knack which these foreigners had evolved, and it was inconceivable that it could contain a philosophy of life which might take the place of the Confucian philosophy.

On the other hand, there was during the 'nineties, as there had been during the 'fifties, a small group of scholars setting their minds to work on the question of the western attitude to the universe and to life. This was the group we have already spoken of in other connections, headed by K'ang Yiu-wei. K'ang was never a scientist in the true sense, but a humanist philosopher, a man who saw visions. Science was only the window, suddenly opened, through which he looked out on these visions which his impatient and somewhat arrogant temper felt must be brought to pass. His biographer says of him that through acquaintance with the microscope and the electric telegraph he awoke to the harmony of the relative in time and space. After he went north his mind turned entirely to politics, but while he was teaching in Canton he had much to say on the wonders of western science, and his influence spread far beyond the immediate circle of his pupils.

Liang Ch'i-ch'ao also was not a scientist, but in his writings during the years he was in exile (1898–1912) he constantly called on his fellow countrymen to accept science as the master teacher of the world. What science really meant to him is not always clear, but there can be no question of the way it appealed to him. One quotation from an article written in 1902 must suffice to illustrate this: 'The heaven and earth of the twentieth century has drawn its curtain now for more than a year. During this time not a few famous writers have offered to the world of knowledge wild-swan works and massive productions. Standing out among these as the words of a man pressing on into a lonely path is *Principles of Western Civilisation*, by the Englishman Benjamin Kidd, a book destined to influence all the races of the world, to be a great light to the future. Kidd is not merely a great transmitter of the evolutionary thesis; he is also a stout upholder of the revolution of evolution. Since Darwin produced his *Origin of Species* a new heaven and earth has been opened to the world of thought. Not only was natural science changed, but also history, political science, economics, sociology, theology, and ethics all have been deeply affected. Spencer arose and took everything together and threw it into the melting-pot. He took the most diverse and inexplicable phenomena and linked them together on one principle, building up a great system with its trunk and branches. . . . Science—in the narrow sense of what in Chinese is called *k'e chih*—has advanced, and religion cannot hold its dying breath. By evolution the roots of age-old tenets have been thrown away. Every intelligent man recognises that the success of evolution is of the order of the universe. Then Spencer with his shrewd mind has created a synthetic philosophy, borrowing, as he says, the principle of biology to establish the principles for the race of man. That is so, and yet no one can point out for certain what the evolution of man is going to be, what is the road it must follow, what the end at which it must arrive. This is the great question of the world. . . . Therefore Marx, the great light of the Socialist Party, says jeeringly that the learned people of to-day regard science as having exploded religion: they say that man has come by evolution from the lower animals: by their law of evolution man is the highest point: but suppose that some day there might be another turn of evolution and another class of man emerge: the learned men have no answer to make to this. Huxley also criticises Spencer. . . . His criticism, although it is expressed extravagantly, is right. None the less both Marx and Huxley can make difficulties for others; they are unable to solve the problems for men. Kidd stands out above all others and takes a step forward. . . . Kidd maintains that man is like the other animals: without struggle there can be no progress. Whether it be a struggle between individual and individual or race and race, the outcome is that the unfit is defeated and perishes while the superior who is equal to the situation flourishes. This is an unchanging law, and in this movement of evolution *there must be the sacrifice of the individual for society, of the present for the future. Therefore the man who grasps at his own immediate profit entirely misunderstands the theory of evolution. He is indeed a criminal to the evolutionist. . . . He is not a help but an injury to the cause of man's survival.*[1]

The whole article is of very great interest and import-

[1] The italics are Liang Ch'i-ch'ao's.

ance, but the reader is familiar with the particular run of thought which captured the minds of so many at the end of the nineteenth century. 'Adaptation to environment', 'natural selection', the real significance of death and sex in the life of man—Liang weaves them all in with all the clarity and persuasiveness of a master of language. And that of course is what he was; he never set himself forth as a scientist, but as an expounder of the great movements of thought in the world outside China and an interpreter of what China's response must be. The real significance of his position is to be seen in his whole-hearted acceptance of the evolutionary principle. One is reminded of Hu Shih some ten years later studying for his doctorate in Columbia University and discovering—rightly or wrongly is another matter —a logic and symbolism of change in Confucius's system of thought, so that 'he [Confucius] conceived of human history as a continuous process of gradual development from crude ways of living to complex forms of civilisation'.

Liang's was the kind of writing which caused the minds of those thousands of students in Japan to burn with a sense of a new gospel. This was what they smuggled over into China, and indeed this was what the newspapers in Shanghai were beginning to print in their supplements. It came at a time when every honest-thinking man in the country was wretched with the futility of the Boxer outbreak and the shame of its aftermath; the time when the imperial Government still went on pouring out its grandiloquent hypocrisies of fiat and edict, and so dragging in the dust the hallowed dogmas of the old orthodoxy. Accordingly it was at this time that men began to feel that lack of self-confidence which became so marked as the years went on. The die-hard official, the pettifogging conceited *literatus*, the dreamy idealistic teacher, these were still untouched, a score of them to be found in every country neighbourhood, a hundred of them in every town; but increasingly there were the others who felt that the old learning did not work in this modern world. The first question for them was whether all this talk of democracy was to be trusted, and when they felt unable to see it working out in practice, they turned to this new philosophy of science and considered that. First, it had brought these Westerners, who were obviously not barbarians in the old sense, to a height of practical efficiency with which China simply could not compare. She was beaten at every point, most of all in the comparative wealth and well-being of the community. And all this was based on an understanding of Nature and its laws, the very thing which China's sages had emphasised as indispensable for the good life. This, then, was the real challenge of the West. In some such terms it was that men began to doubt and hesitate, and then turn to western thought and be imbued with western points of view. As they were so influenced, they were exhilarated with the thought which Liang Ch'i-ch'ao was emphasising, namely, that in acclaiming science as their teacher they would be placing themselves in the van of human progress. What they did not realise was that the philosophical side, the theory of it, came easy to them, but that without the practical side, the dirty work in laboratory and machine-shop, their conversion would fail to achieve the results for which they hoped.

The fatal division between scholar and artisan still continued, and to this must be attributed in part at any rate the tendency to inefficiency in all the different technical enterprises which were undertaken. The abolition of the old examination system in 1905, epoch-making as it was, did nothing to remedy this situation. Science was regarded as a number of subjects which the student learnt in books, and if later he was appointed to some administrative post which involved technical processes, he found himself entirely at a loss. At the same time able artisans saw no prospect of rising to high positions, nor were there facilities for them to acquire the principles of their work. Instead of dealing with this weakness in the radical way it demanded, the tendency all through the last thirty years of the imperial régime was to use foreign engineers and even foreign foremen. Only so could the suppliers of the capital for any enterprise be sure that costly machinery would not be irreparably damaged. The whole system was a vicious circle, though here again we have to note that these same foreign engineers and foremen testified again and again that amongst a large number of bad workmen always there were some who were intelligent and reliable.

The last years of the Manchu Dynasty were such that they gave an incurable list to men's minds. Political issues absorbed everyone's interest. After the establishment of the Republic things were better. There was nothing to stop the advance of science in the country, and for a time at any rate there was a new feeling of hopefulness. An able and liberal-minded, if somewhat theory-beridden, Ministry of Education set to work. Simple lessons on natural phenomena began to appear in the elementary school reading lessons. Western mathematics was taught from the elementary school up as a required subject, whilst secondary schools were required to teach chemistry and physics.

The two great publishing houses in Shanghai, the Commercial Press and the Chung Hwa Book Company, published systematic text-books. The only trouble, and this was a desperate one, was that there were so few competent teachers. Efforts were made by headquarters and provincial educational authorities through the training colleges which were started in all the provinces, but the supply of science teachers from them was entirely inadequate. Thousands of students who had studied in Japan were back in the country, among them men who were theoretically qualified to teach one or two branches of elementary science. It is open to serious question whether they had had the necessary laboratory training —Japanese education was deficient in this at the time —and in any case provincial authorities were seldom awake to the vital need of such equipment. Thus for the first decade of the Republic the science teaching in schools was in the vast majority of cases very poor.

This criticism applies to a less degree, to those government universities which had returned students from America and Europe on the staff. Christian universities and those of the mission secondary schools which were more generously financed, were somewhat better. But wherever science teaching went on, the tendency in society was to be rather awestruck with what students had to report on their studies. There was a great temptation to the student to think he was a better man than his father and correspondingly be satisfied with the merest smattering. The old prejudice for keeping your hands clean still survived in very large measure, so that we can find as late as 1919 an incident like the following occurring in a university of good standing. The examiner of the graduating geological class found 'that they could hardly distinguish a piece of granite from basalt, or sandstone from slate. I was told that they had a great field expedition once a year. They went on donkeys wearing their long coats with great dignity.' The same scientist—a Chinese D.Sc. of an English university—recalls seeing a student of chemistry pour alcohol into a lighted lamp; whilst the writer remembers on one occasion being taken over the science department in a university—not one of the best—and finding in the balance-room on a half holiday two of the balances left on cock. This we have to realise could happen at a time when the greater part of the student world in universities was talking with tremendous unction about the age of science as having arrived. The truth of the matter was that freshmen came to the university stage with the very poorest preliminary training, and of those who had the idea of studying science comparatively few were able to sustain the discipline of the scientific method. On the other hand, the two great technical colleges the Peiyang and the Nanyang, together with the Peking Union Medical College, always maintained a high standard of practical work. The same applies to the Government Geological Survey with its headquarters in Peking. Started in 1912 by Ting Wen-chiang,[1] a scientist to his finger-tips, it retained through all the troublous years its consistent practice of systematic laboratory and office work, alternated with long expeditions in which, if the assistants did wear long gowns, they tucked them up and got down to work.

At this point we have to consider a controversy which sprang up in 1924 and was carried on in a series of articles in the more serious periodicals. Twenty-nine

[1] Dr. V. K. Ting, M.A. (Glasgow), B.Sc. (Cantab), D.Sc. (Freiburg).

of these were collected in a two-volume book which ran into a large number of editions. The subject was 'Science and its view of Man's Life', the debate being conducted by some nineteen people, some with a philosophical, some with a scientific training. One of the philosophers in an introduction says: 'During the last thirty years there is one term which has reached the seat of supreme majesty in the country. Whether men understand it or not, whether they belong to the conservative party or the reform party, they all dare not publicly reveal an attitude of contempt towards it. That term is "Science". Whether this almost universal worship is of value or not is another question. The least we can say is that since the change came in China no one who can be counted a forward-looking person dared decry "Science" until about 1921 Liang Ch'i-ch'ao did so in his *Diary of Reactions on My Trip to Europe*. Then for the first time in China formal notice was served on Science that it was bankrupt.'

The controversy is illuminating, not because it points to a disbelief in science as helping to make human happiness, but because it shows the nature of the reaction against the dictatorship of science in human affairs. There is the revolt of the humanist against the mechanisation of life; and even the Communist, Ch'en Tu-hsiu, is not prepared to accept the idea of science as controlling human life. He makes use of science as a stick with which to beat religion and its superstitions; so also do Ting Wen-chiang and Wu Chih-fi with their denunciations of what they call mysticism, *i.e.* a combination of theology and speculative metaphysics. They stand in opposition to man being the slave of science, as they also do to the romanticism of the new literary men. They have the Classicist's sense of form and tradition.

In a word, they are humanistic scientists, and perhaps none the worse scientists for being so.

In 1928 the Nationalist Government brought into existence two bodies which bid fair to put more advanced studies in natural science on quite a new level. One is the Academia Sinica with its headquarters in Nanking and a branch in Shanghai, the other the National Academy of Peiping. The Academia Sinica, with Ts'ai Yuan-pei as president, was organised with nine departments of research: astronomy, biology, chemistry, physics, engineering and technology, geology, meteorology, psychology, and history and philology. This last quickly began to distinguish itself in archaeological excavations conducted with severely scientific accuracy. The National Academy of Peiping, with the physicist Li Shih-tseng as its president, was organised with three departments: physics, chemistry, and biology. For both these institutions ample buildings have been supplied, and a serious attempt is made to give scope to the best research minds in the country. A good part of the work done is in the field of pure science, *e.g.* on the structure of the atom and quantum mechanics, but both institutions also pride themselves on responding to appeals for practical help. Thus a crisis in the cotton industry brought about the allocation of large funds for the study of the problems involved. There is a growing series of journals which deal with these researches, for example, *Transactions of the Science Society of China* and the *Chinese Journal of Physics*. The Academia Sinica publishes a series of monographs, and results are also published in the science journals of England and America.

There are three or four smaller institutions also engaged in research of the same character, and in 1930 and 1931 three universities, Tsing Hua in the north, the National-Central in Nanking, and Chung Shan University in the south, started giving laboratory facilities for post-graduate research. These so far have been mainly in the field of chemistry, though Professor Huang of Tsing Hua has done some important work in thermodynamics. In industrial chemistry Nankai University,[1] under the presidency of Dr. Chang Paolin, has made a very good start with work on the hydrogenation of oils. With regard to agricultural problems, the best work so far had been done in two missionary institutions: the University of Nanking and Lingnam University at Canton. Both these now have Chinese professors working successfully with foreigners, and for the time being this seems to produce the quicker results. The University of Nanking has, with the help of visiting professors from Oberlin University, carried out a prolonged series of experiments with cereal seed stocks, and has finally arrived at the point where it has a new wheat which is 40 per cent. more productive and at the same time smut-resisting. Lingnam has done some equally good work on sericulture and animal husbandry.

Enough has been done already in the several fields of natural science, in archaeology, and in critical history to show that fears about the decadence of Chinese mentality are without foundation. At the same time we are not yet in a position to estimate whether Chinese scientists will prove to have any distinctive gifts. When we come to the general public of educated men, we find, as the narrative has shown, that for years the admiration

---

[1] A private institution. Dr. Chang started his career in the navy, but his experiences in the Sino-Japanese War (1894) turned him to higher education as the vital need of the country.

for science was far too much a merely theoretical one, more an expression of the nation's disgust at its political and economic weakness than an appreciation of the true spirit of science. But in the last fifteen years in academic education and in industry and pure research, there has been immense progress. China's intellectuals at last realise that science means drudgery, endless patient attention to details, disciplined observation, and accurate recording. But, while they appreciate this spirit and submit themselves to its control, they still find a delight in exploring the semi-scientific, semi-philosophic theories of the universe which profess to be based on science. In this they are applying old aptitudes, just as in their final opinions they tend in most cases to a humanistic rather than a mechanistic view of life.

In the treatment of science and its influence the sphere of medicine has been purposely omitted. It is better dealt with separately, since the penetration of western medical knowledge has taken a different course from the rest of the applied sciences, being subject to special disabilities as well as proving specially attractive.

The Chinese art of 'physicking' was highly developed long before the nineteenth century. A really notable work, the *Pen Tsao*, on the *materia medica* had been produced in the third century A.D., and from this we can appraise the high standard of accurate observation which had by then been achieved. Surgery of a rough-and-ready kind was practised, but both the Chinese family sentiment and the attitude of the law made any but the most confident of doctors afraid of it. The result was almost a total failure to achieve any advance in that field. So also with the study of anatomy; reverence for the dead, which extended to the corpse, made it impossible for any would-be student to have material on which to base his studies. The practice was universal for learned doctors to keep their knowledge and skill to themselves as a private acquisition, and pass it on only to their sons. Medicine was, however, probably in some ways, as advanced in China as in Europe until the beginnings of modern scientific knowledge. For instance, inoculation from human vaccine for smallpox was known and practised, and is said to have been introduced to Europe via Arabia and Turkey by Lady Mary Wortley Montagu in 1717. There was a great interest in medicine, and a considerable body of literature came into existence. In the famous imperial collection of meritorious works [1] made in the eighteenth century there are 196 works in the medical section. These works, however, with the *cachet* of scholarship attached to them, tend to ignore one side of Chinese medicine which at once strikes the western observer, namely, the use of fantastic remedies, the supposed efficacy of which is based purely on cosmological or analogical grounds. For example, nervous complaints arising from fear may be cured by a powder made from tigers' claws, since the tiger is the emblem of courage. This kind of physic is still believed in to-day by the great majority of the illiterate section of the population.

Dr. Wu Lien-teh, Director of the National Quarantine Service, and one of China's most distinguished medical men, has made a plea in a recent article [2] for the use of the names 'scientific' or 'new' medicine rather than 'western', and 'old' medicine rather than 'Chinese'. He regrets that the use of 'western' for the new methods 'has enabled the die-hards of medicine to utilise the term as

---

[1] Ssu Ku Ch'uan Shu, containing 5000 volumes.
[2] *Chinese Recorder*, August 1936.

a cover for their ignorance and to prejudice scientific medicine in the eyes of the public'. This accounts in Dr. Wu's opinion for the fact that 'one of the hardest things to break down among the people of this otherwise rapidly changing country seems to be the popular belief in the efficacy of the old system of Chinese medicine'. Possibly this is not a specially Chinese characteristic but one to be found among peasant folk everywhere. How many old-wives' remedies are still in use in English villages? However that may be, it certainly has been a great hindrance to the acceptance of western medicine that it has been associated with the 'foreign devils'. The yellow-haired, blue-eyed foreigner was an awesome sight to the Chinese villager and presented the appearance of having walked straight out of the old legends of red-haired devils. When the villager, hearing of marvellous cures, screwed up his courage to put himself in the hands of the terrifying person, it did not relieve his fears to be told he must be cut open, having first had a drug administered to deprive him of consciousness. As we have seen, Chinese medicine does not include much surgery, and no doubt the widely believed stories that foreigners took out the eyes of their patients and compounded them with lead in order to obtain silver, had their origin in operations for eye diseases. These diseases were the first to be tackled by foreign doctors; the surgeons attached to the East India Company and the early missionaries in Macao and Canton found that they could do much to relieve the very prevalent eye troubles.

It was the acceptance which this met with among the Chinese which encouraged Dr. Parker of the American Board Mission to open the first hospital in Canton in 1835. A hundred years later the *Chinese Medical*

Journal of 1935 gives the following figures: 33 medical colleges, of which 13 are under mission and foreign management; the graduation of 632 medical students in one year, of whom 79 were women; 500 hospitals with a total of 20,799 beds. Of these hospitals 214 are mission institutions. The total number of modern-trained practitioners is not yet fully known. So far only 7000 have registered under the new Government regulations, but there are probably as many more who are more or less fully qualified.

The popularisation of western medicine in China was due, in the first instance, to Protestant missionaries. Medical work, progressed alongside evangelistic and educational work as the Treaty Ports, and then the interior, opened. In this way a great deal of suffering was relieved and knowledge of elementary hygiene and antisepsis widely spread. But in many, one might say most, of these mission stations the medical staff was very small, often a single-handed doctor with possibly one nurse. In addition to his other work this doctor would have to train Chinese assistants in order to cope with the increasing number of patients.

Before the Republican era a growing number of influential men had realised the value of the western doctor and his drugs and appliances. After 1911 there came quite a boom, and mission hospitals became popular, many of them being built on a large scale with the help of subscriptions from local people. Medical colleges also were organised both by union missionary effort and by the Government, so that a much more efficient training could be given. Today patients and their friends no longer recoil in horror from the idea of a major operation; and we may say generally that the new medicine is an accepted part of Chinese life.

The training, given in the first instance in mission hospitals, appealed to many boys educated in mission schools who wanted another vocation than that of teacher or preacher, as well as to others who saw here an opening to a lucrative profession not inconsistent with a scholar's dignity. In this way there has come to be a considerable body of men capable of opening medicine-shops, but not fully qualified, owing to the limitations of their training. A few of these remained as assistants in the hospitals and did devoted work for comparatively small salaries, but the greater number set up for themselves. To-day the position is peculiar. In the big cities the number of fully qualified doctors, trained either abroad or in the large hospitals, is more than enough to meet the demand; that is to say, there are more than can secure the paying practice for which they look. In the country districts there is need for a far larger number, especially as the Government registration regulations will gradually put the half-trained man out of business. This need will, it is hoped, be met in future by the Government Health Service, an institution still in its infancy. The Nationalist Government set up a Ministry of Health and has spent large sums on its work. The Minister, Dr. Heng Liu, has now a large central hospital in Nanking, with a school of nursing and midwifery attached, and a strong medical school in Shanghai. Preventive medicine is being vigorously pushed, and the Central Field Health Station is giving training not only to doctors and nurses but also to sanitary inspectors and sanitary engineers, and has special courses for school teachers.

The trend of medical development is shown particularly clearly in the history of the Peiping Union Medical College. The first hospital in Peking was founded in

1860 by Dr. Lockhart, a missionary of the London Missionary Society. In the reorganisation which followed the Boxer troubles a union medical college came into being through the co-operation of three American and two British societies. In 1915 the growing feeling that medical training must be of the very best found a response in John D. Rockefeller, and the college and hospital were rebuilt on a much larger scale by funds from the Rockefeller Foundation. It then came under the control of the China Medical Board, and a board of trustees was appointed, six of whom were to represent the original missionary societies. In 1928 this board was reorganised to meet the demands of the time for Chinese control, and to comply with the requirements of the Ministry of Education. It is now self-perpetuating and independent of the bodies which had previously appointed members, and has a two-thirds majority of Chinese. In this institution China now possesses one of the finest hospitals in the world, with medical and nursing training-schools and research departments efficiently staffed and equipped. Both here and in the Lester Research Institute in Shanghai scientific research of first-rate importance is being carried on with complete co-operation between Chinese and foreigners.

In the beginnings of modern medical treatment in China nursing was left to the friends of the patients. These were for the most part men, so that the second stage was to train male nurses, it being unthinkable that such work could be done by women. With the increase of women patients came the training of older women to care for them; and finally, with the emancipation of women under the Republic, the woman nurse came into her own in China as elsewhere. The Nurses'

Association of China, started by missionaries, conducts examinations the standard of which is approximating to that of other countries; and an increasing number of young educated Chinese women are making nursing their vocation. The same emancipation opened the door for women to train as doctors, and to-day they are working as colleagues with men in some of the large hospitals as well as in special women's hospitals and in private practice. It is interesting to notice that several women qualified abroad even before 1900, among the best known being Dr. Mary Stone and Dr. Ida Kahn, both of whom were taken by missionary friends to the United States and educated there.

The missionary body has also made a great contribution through the translation of medical books. Although to-day most of the advanced training insists on a thorough knowledge of English and the use of English text-books, there are still colleges where this is not so, for instance, at Cheeloo University. In many of the smaller hospitals doctors have been trained entirely through the use of translations. Dr. Benjamin Hobson, whose scientific work has already been referred to, reported to his society in 1852 that he was preparing a second edition of plates for his work on physiology, encouraged by the demand for the book. Copies of this were purchased by many officials, and it was said that the Viceroy had sent one to the Emperor. Certainly he ordered a reprint of the book in the next year. In this everything referring to religion was expunged and it was published in a popular collection of Chinese authors, the name of the author being given only in Chinese. Since Dr. Hobson's day many other doctors have found time in the midst of a very busy life to do some translation work, and latterly this has been standardised and co-ordinated by the China Missionary Medical Association.

Thus western medicine is in a very strong position in China to-day, destined, it would appear, to oust the old medicine entirely. As a matter of fact, in spite of the 'new' doctor's nettled amazement, the 'old' continues to survive. There are old-fashioned doctors everywhere, even in Shanghai, where an able and learned man like Ting Fu-pao has a great reputation. These doctors tend to introduce a modicum of western medicine into their own methods of diagnosis and traditional principles of dieting. Research, such as is being carried on in the Lester Institute, is likely to show that there is permanent value in some of the old drugs and the prescriptions which make use of herbs unknown in Europe.

Meanwhile there is an acute problem of professional honour. The old practitioner had his code of traditional morality, and the sanctions attached to it were enforced partly by the old law codes, partly by public opinion. In the case of the new, the law is still inadequate, whilst public opinion cannot act, bewildered as it is by wholly incomprehensible factors. There are the gravest dangers in the situation. For example, some fifteen years ago there was a phenomenal growth in the use of injections, patients being under the impression that freedom from pain and the temporary exhilaration were signs of cure. All a dishonest tradesman had to do was to assure a sick man that this was the latest and best western medicine and that it was very expensive. There is also a sinister exploitation of the public with patent medicines, mainly imported from the west but also those of local and Japanese manufacture. The leaders in the medical profession are fully aware of these dangers, and the

China Medical Association,[1] in close touch with the Government, is devising ways and means to cope with the situation. Hence the recent insistence on registration for all doctors. But in a country so vast as China, with its traditional attitude to the restrictions of the law, the problem is not one which can be solved merely by legislation. Unless the full power of professional and general public opinion can be brought to bear, the new medicine may be only a doubtful blessing. Fortunately there is the present emphasis on preventive medicine, and also efforts are being made to break down the old tradition of guarding discoveries as family secrets, and to substitute the true scientist's principle of publishing all new information. But the real solution to the problem lies in a new application of Chinese humanistic traditions, together with their long-developed power of semi-official initiative. Provided that the practice of medicine throughout the world is true to its best, indeed its Christian, principles of service, it may be expected that the doctors of China will not fall behind.

[1] In 1925 the China Medical Missionary Association, at its own request, became an integral part of the China Medical Association, which makes no distinction of race or creed.

CHAPTER VI

THE NEW LITERATURE

FROM the foregoing chapters the reader is already aware that one great outcome of the western invasion in China has been books of every description. But so far we have only been concerned with these as conveyers of information; there has not yet been an opportunity to deal with the effect of western influence on literature as literature, with the works of imagination, the novels and short stories, the poetry, literary studies and essays in criticism, and, last but not least, the newspapers and periodicals, which have appeared during the last half-century.

The idea is still frequently encountered that Chinese literature consists almost entirely of the Classics and adumbrations of the Classics. Needless to say this is nonsense. True, an incredible amount of time has been spent on producing a sea of books on classical subjects—some modern bibliographers have estimated that in 1850 there were more books in China than in the whole of Europe. But the very writers and compilers and commentators who spent laborious days on these tomes, had also their lighter moments. There is nothing truer about the Chinese *literati* than that they loved their playing in literature as much as they loved their working. With dining and drinking, poetry and painting, leisured intercourse with friends and appreciation of Nature, with great officials being honoured the more when they left their high office and retired to the country to write elegant pastoral lyrics, it is easy to understand how there grew up a large body of exquisite literature. Any Chinese library or bookshop has a prominent section devoted to rows and rows of such books, a section quite as large and certainly more popular than those devoted to classical, historical, and philosophical works. Included in this popular section will be found the novels and fairy stories, the accounts of prodigies by sea and land. Young people were instructed not to waste their time on such trivialities, but very few reached years of discretion without having read a large number and having been thrilled by their imaginative power.

It was not really till the twentieth century was starting that the Chinese woke up to the fact that the West also had its great poets and essayists and story-tellers. The missionaries had been much too soberly engaged in the serious matters of their vocation, and even people with wide sympathies like Young Allen and Timothy Richard who set themselves to give a more all-embracing idea of western culture, tended to leave out this side. During the nineteenth century a large quantity of literature was produced, but it consisted of works concerned exclusively with the giving of information or instruction. They achieved that end more or less, but none of them to the Chinese scholar ranked as good literature. There was perhaps one exception, namely, the Delegates' Version of the translation of the Bible. Immense efforts were put forth to make this a work of outstanding literary merit; the most successful parts were the poetical books of the Old Testament, the least successful the dogmatic parts of the Pauline epistles.

The weakness was in the method employed. As a rule a foreigner set out the meaning as best he could, with a

Chinese taking down from dictation. After the Chinese had worked over the grammar, the result was gone over again by the two together, and finally passed as representing with reasonable accuracy the meaning which the foreigner wished to convey. By this means production was speeded up, as may be seen from the reports of the Kiangnan translation bureau and the records of the Christian Literature Society. But the dangers and weaknesses of the method are obvious. However able a linguist and a sinologue the foreigner might be, he could hardly accomplish an unfailing mastery of style or the fine shades of meaning which are if anything more important in Chinese than in most languages. The longer the Chinese assistant worked with a foreigner, the more he would tend to grasp his meaning through terms and phrases which were not obvious to the ordinary reader.

If such a method failed where the full zeal of religious devotion was exercised by a number of collaborators prepared to spend years in the completion of their task, it was all the more likely to do so with the technical works produced by one, or at most two, foreigners with their very limited staffs. Although, therefore, there was a large production of such works, we may doubt seriously whether much of this literature had any influence upon the ordinary man, though doubtless it conveyed a certain amount of information to the earnest student. Chang Chih-tung speaks with grave disgust in his *Ch'üan Hsüeh Pien* (1898) of the low standard of intellectual honesty to be found among the people who put themselves forward as learned in western languages. But most pungent of all are the criticisms made by Liang Ch'i-ch'ao in an article written in the same year as the *Ch'üan Hsüeh Pien*. He speaks of over 300 works having

231

been translated and six to seven out of every ten done vilely and inaccurately. To him the curse of the business was that both translators and readers 'knew and yet did not know; where they did not know, they thought they did'. Further, he makes great outcry against the principle which has dictated the kind of work to be translated. This was the principle of learning from the foreigners the secrets of their military and naval strength. Because of this more than half of the works translated were connected with war, engineering, and the like. To Liang this meant a fatal ignorance of the real spiritual and intellectual sources of the foreigners' strength.

In this attitude of his Liang was the forerunner of the new age which was so soon to arrive. By his example and the example of his leader, K'ang Yiu-wei, the door was opened to an entirely new kind of translation. These young reformers not only gave themselves passionately to the study of the culture of the West. They also developed a new style of writing, the *shih wu ti*, the style which was only concerned with setting forth the subject with entire clarity. That of course was what the older translators had been trying to do, but partly through defects of scholarship, partly through lack of sufficient zeal or conviction, had failed to accomplish. From this time on men were to be found whose literary gifts were of the highest and whose mental processes had exploded into new life under the influence of the West. They were men also who could not be satisfied with technical knowledge. They wanted to know the history and philosophy and, even more, the literature of the West. This new spirit was not confined to K'ang Yiu-wei and his disciples. There was that extraordinary personality, Lin Shu, who without any working knowledge of western languages was yet profoundly attracted by the western novel. He would sit and have a passage translated by an assistant who knew the 'foreign words'; and then he would take his brush and put it into faultless Chinese. He never tired of this, and the result was almost a hundred and fifty volumes,[1] not accurate in all respects but all of them immensely readable. To him the Chinese owe their first knowledge of Scott and Dickens, Robert Louis Stevenson, Conan Doyle, Victor Hugo and the Dumas, Balzac, Cervantes, Tolstoi and others. It is interesting to find that Rider Haggard appealed to him with great force. The point to notice is that he did not work under a sense of compulsion, neither as an official translator bound to show results commensurate with his stipend, nor with a solemn feeling that China must be saved by imitating the West. He wrote because he enjoyed what he wrote about. And there can be no doubt that this is the secret, not only of his felicity of style, but also of his popularity with his fellow countrymen. He opened an entirely new field of western life to them, one brimming with interest and so affording immense satisfaction. Since he made money out of this work, it was only a short time before there were others attempting to do the same, among them some of the students returned from Europe and America. This, then, was the way in which the Chinese began to be in touch with the literature of the West, the writings of poets and essayists and dramatists as well as novelists.

Throughout the first decade of the twentieth century

[1] Altogether Lin Shu translated 93 English works, 25 French, 19 American, 6 Russian.

the tide swung more every year in the direction not only of political Westernism but also of Westernism in literature. After the Boxer *débâcle* Peking lost much of its prestige—this in spite of the university founded there in 1897—and Tientsin and Shanghai, especially the latter, became the centres of attraction for those who were convinced that China must move with the times. It was in Shanghai that the newspapers and new publishing houses had the freedom they loved, for with the powers which the Foreign Settlements exercised, the Manchu Government found it very difficult to lay hands on the men it considered dangerous. These Settlements, therefore, were breeding-grounds of new thought, and it was impossible for Government officials or spies to keep pace with the endless books and articles which were being produced. The same thing was happening with the exiles and students in Japan. The Japanese language was easily learnt, and the western translations into Japanese were far more numerous and included a large selection of works of imagination. So started the new industry of making Chinese versions from the Japanese versions: not a particularly satisfactory way, but allowing of quick production and representing the new tastes of the translators. People translated what appealed to them and what they thought would appeal to their fellow Chinese. An idea of the wide range of influence exerted can be seen in the fact that between 1903 and 1907 seven different magazines were published in Tokyo by different bands of students hailing respectively from Chekiang, Hupeh, Kiangsu, Yunnan, Szechwan, Honan, and Shansi provinces. Some of these magazines ran to eighty-odd pages and they all contained, in addition to political articles, a number of translations of short stories and literary articles from western periodicals. Hu Shih has described the way in which the Shanghai students smuggled the new periodicals and books out of Shanghai into the interior.

The influence of Japanese stylisms began to be felt, and, generally speaking, after the abandonment of the traditional form of the Imperial Examinations with their elaborately artificial verse and essay-making, the mind of youth began to experiment with the language as it had not done before. Neologisms began to appear, many of them coming directly from the vocabularies of western languages. These were welcomed, and a corresponding feeling of impatience grew with the artificial parallelisms and rhetorical questions which characterised the old styles in writing.[1] It began to get home to people that the current literature in western languages was all written in current styles, that a man expressed himself on paper as he thought and spoke. This was construed by those whose minds were awake to such considerations as part of the freedom of political thought and institution which they associated with the West. So after the downfall of the Manchu Court in 1911, with a sense of a new-won freedom running like wine in men's veins, the situation was ripe for revolutionary developments. By 1914 a group of university students in the United States began to experiment in verse and prose styles, and their experiments were much more radical than their elders at home imagined. Three years later there was launched a campaign, known in China as the *pai hwa yun tung* (the plain-language movement), or *hsin shih ch'ao* (new tide), known to the West as the Renaissance.

There have been the most curious and inaccurate ideas about this movement and its leaders, so that it

[1] *Vide* p. 177.

were as well to get the situation clear. It was not, as so many Westerners have thought, a movement started and run by men who had sold themselves body and soul to Westernism and so had lost all their Chinese traditional sense of taste and literary discretion. Neither was it, as some others have more recently come to suppose, nothing but the rediscovery of certain despised elements in their own literature. There can be no question but that the origin of the movement lay in the discovery of the West by K'ang Yiu-wei nearly thirty years before when western history as well as western science became a living, palpitating reality to him and his disciples. As we have seen, they adopted the experience of the West as part of their own relevant human experience. From that it was but a step to adopt western imaginative literature as part of their own literary heritage. Having done that, they could not but realise the essentially vernacular spirit of current western literature. They quickly learnt, for example, that over 30,000 books a year were filed as new publications in the British Museum and that a huge section of this output was in language which could be understood by the common people. A fact of this nature was enormously significant to such a literary-minded race as the Chinese.

On the other hand, when we come to enquire into the early records of the Renaissance Movement there is also the clearest evidence that these literary reformers were by no means acting solely under western influences. They did discover the worth of certain despised elements in their past literature, and thus when they came to advocate the release of all writing from the shackles of the *wen t'i* literary styles, they had before them models from which they could adapt their writing. They could dig down into their own history and see how certain verse forms which in the twentieth century were antiquarian survivals had been in their youth new discoveries of living power. They could point to work done by Buddhist translators, who found the literary language of their time inadequate to convey their meaning and so used the expressions of current speech. Most of all they could exalt the vivid power of the Yuan, Ming, and Ch'ing novels and dramatic works. They set out to prove that it was these last which embodied 'the main line of development' in Chinese literature and not the strained artificialities of the examination candidates.

The movement started in Peking and more particularly in the National University. Ts'ai Yuan-pei, to-day the president of the Academia Sinica, had been made chancellor of the University in 1914 and proceeded to develop it with admirable energy. In choosing his staff he was not concerned with conventional reputations so long as he had professors with real learning and live minds. Amongst them were Ch'en Tu-hsiu, already known as an ardent radical and later to suffer imprisonment as a Communist agitator, and Hu Shih, still in America, studying philosophy under Professor Dewey and writing his famous Ph.D. thesis on the 'Development of the Logical Method in Ancient China'. Tu-hsiu organised a magazine, *Ch'ing Nien* (Youth), and there the question of 'literary reforms' was raised in 1916. Hu Shih threw down the gauntlet in a letter to *Ch'ing Nien* in October of that year, and when the storm of criticism broke, defended his position in the following January.[1] The charm and force of his reply lay in the brilliance with which he distinguished the illegitimate from the legitimate use of traditional imagery

[1] *Vide* p. 177.

and gave chapter and verse for the faults he denounced. The significance for us lies in its emphasis on every age having its own literature, different from that of every other age. This, he says, 'is not my individual opinion but the law of evolution in civilization'. So, too, in dealing with the ejaculations which are so marked a feature of Chinese fine writing, he cannot bear the modern essayists who take China's woes as their text and go back to old effeminate writers with their endless groans and tears. He would have his contemporaries write on the evils of the day as Fichte and Mazzini wrote.

We find the same underlying consciousness of western literary history in Ch'en Tu-hsiu, who supported Hu Shih with all the force of his revolutionary temper. In an article of the same date he starts with the question, 'Where does the strength and brilliance of Europe to-day come from? It comes from the grace of revolution. The meaning of "revolution" in the languages of Europe is quite different from the dynastic changes which are known in China as revolutions. Revolution means the stripping away of the old and the change to the new. Thus after the Literary Renaissance [in Europe] there was revolution in government, revolution in religion, revolution also in morals, whilst the revolution in literature was indeed an overturning of the old with a great advance to the new, indeed an evolution. The history of modern European civilisation may well be called a revolutionary history, and that is why I say that Europe's strength and glory come by the grace of revolution.'[1] Having made his point he turns to the history of Chinese literature, going right back to the poetry of the third century B.C. and giving a critical survey of developments since.

[1] Hu Shih, *Wen Ts'un*, 7th edition, vol. i, p. 24.

There is, therefore, the double background, the western and the Chinese, to both Hu Shih's approach and to Ch'en Tu-hsiu's; and the same applies to a strong supporter, a professor of Chinese Studies in the Normal University, Peking, Ch'ien Hsüan-tung, who put his views into print early in 1918. These were the three leaders, and each of them—it cannot be too strongly emphasised—was a scholar of repute. They knew what they were talking about when they embarked on long arguments connected with the different periods and phases of Chinese literature. They had practised themselves in the traditional forms of versifying: for example, Hu Shih tells in his Autobiography how, as a student in Shanghai, he had spent his spare time for months in doing the examinational style of poetry, arriving in the end at the conclusion that proficiency required only a mechanical kind of ability. It was this kind of revulsion against conceit and fantasy in current literary effort which drove them to look for something more direct, more honest, more naturally emotional, and more seriously thoughtful. And they found what they looked for, at any rate as far as prose was concerned. It was there in the novels which everybody read, but which were so despised by the high-and-dry traditionalists that the author of a novel hardly dared put his name to it. For verse the situation was more difficult. Forms which had been living in the past were now tainted with the stain of archaism, and the idea grew that the only way forward was through the medium of *vers libre*. For this there was a precedent. In an article on the 'Historical View of Literature' it was maintained that 'the seeds of plain-language writing are to be found lying in some of the T'ang poetry' (seventh to tenth centuries).

There was a good deal of moral courage required of

these reformers; not necessarily because Hu Shih and his friends were influenced by the West, for by that time few but a dwindling band of old die-hards were standing for China as a culture *contra mundum*. But the great bulk of educated people who agreed that China must learn from the West were not prepared to abandon their cultivated power of writing. Imagine three young classical dons in Oxford in the years just before the Great War, insisting that the Cockney tongue was the most virile medium of literary expression, as could be proved by the works of Barry Paine and Albert Chevalier. The instinctive sense of disgust which their fellow dons would have felt was much what the conservatives felt in China. The reformers stood in serious danger of losing their posts and finding no others open. Strong pressure was brought to bear on the chancellor of their university that he should call for their resignations. Fortunately Ts'ai Yuan-pei was equal to the occasion and refused with calm dignity to take any action.

If Chancellor Ts'ai had given way, there would have been a storm from another quarter, for the students, whatever their seniors thought, were almost to a man in support of the movement. Their enthusiasm knew no bounds, and almost every month some new magazine came into existence, dedicated to the sacred task of showing the possibilities of the vulgar tongue. Those who were in China at the time have the vividest recollections of how the fire leapt up in the capital and spread throughout the provinces into the remotest towns and villages. For one thing, the new cult brought a new art of letter-writing. Whereas the old stilted forms of correspondence had to be painfully learnt and the utmost care taken to give the right titles and express

240

the appropriate elegancies of sentiment—a letter was a test of scholarship—now the writer conveyed his thoughts directly and with complete spontaneity. The more extempore the sentiment and the more he spread himself freely over the paper, the truer he was to the new spirit. Every letter was full to the brim of the ardent young thing's *consciousness* of this and that, his *impression* of the one and the other. The result was floods of student letters to their home friends, together with copies of the magazines in which their articles were published. As Dr. Hu Shih has said, 'Everybody seemed to be rushing to express himself in this language which he could understand and in which he could make himself understood'.

A vast deal of this was, of course, very poor stuff, crude, verbose, and in a very short space of time falling into all the pits of introspective writing. On the other hand, unsympathetic sneering criticism is singularly misplaced in dealing with these ebullitions. We may have to look closely to find any 'bones and sinews' to what is said at such length, but even in the worst of these productions there is an entirely new power of expression. What is important for our purpose is that the initial impulse came from the West, and the West supplied them with some new terms, above all with the concept of social evolution. At the same time we must realise that the driving power was born of their Chinese tradition and Chinese needs. Their leaders might spend a deal of time in demonstrating the living value of certain trends in Chinese literature, but the students' response was to take all that for granted, and then to use the new medium for their own ends in their own way. Those ends almost immediately were political ends and not literary; and for just this very reason, because so much of their writing was done without attention to form, it is significant of the natural force of the literary revolution.

The situation reminds one of the fourteenth century in Italy when Dante and Petrarch began to use the vernacular instead of the polite Latin. The similarities are obvious, but the differences are equally important. There was in Europe at that time no such sense of evolution—the evolution of society and the evolution of literature—as there was in China in the twentieth century. Dante had an apocalyptic mind and also stood for a divinely appointed political order, the Holy Roman Empire. The use of the vernacular for literature came in France and Italy a hundred years and more before the release of the intellectual forces which made the Renaissance. In China the new intellectual forces came first.

The Literary Revolution was triumphantly successful. By 1920 the plain style was coming into use all over the country, with the possible exception of Kwantung Province. Not that Cantonese scholars were in principle opposed to the revolution, but there were special conditions there. Of all the southern dialects Cantonese was the furthest removed from this northern one, whilst the Cantonese people had their own vernacular literature. This was not easily to be read by northerners, but it had the same value for Canton as the old imaginative writers, now receiving attention, had for the north. It was the northern speech known as *kuan hwa* (mandarin's speech)[1] which became officially recognised by the Board of Education as the national language; and the new art of writing reproduced this both in syntax and idiom, add-

[1] Compare the expression 'King's English'.

ing on the neologisms to which reference has been made, and adopting western punctuation.

To the older writers, the men who had made their reputation in the *wen-t'i* (literary styles), the change-over to the new proved, almost without exception, too radical to be possible. It was therefore to the younger authors that the challenge came to prove whether they could 'deliver the goods' by writing works of real literary significance and power. Hu Shih himself was acutely aware of this challenge, and he immediately set to work to write an *Outline of the History of Chinese Philosophy*. He thus took up the gage on one of the most crucial issues, setting out to demonstrate the new style suitable for learned exposition. The experiment was a complete success; the writing was both beautifully clear and far more succinct than might have been feared. To the discriminating reader, however, it was also obvious that the audacious author could not have done it so admirably if he had not been a master of *wen-t'i* as well as of the new prose.

Hu Shih's book was the most outstanding literary achievement of the first years of the Renaissance. Other historians and philosophers followed this lead, but for the main part in articles rather than in lengthy treatises. Details of their work will come later, since their main importance lies in the field of critical research. We must first turn to the effect of the movement on newspaper-writing, and to the new schools of imaginative writers who began to receive public acclamation.

Newspapers for popular reading were an introduction from the West. In old China there was only the *Imperial Gazette*, which was sent to all officials, and which contained notices of appointments and other

Court news. The first periodical for general reading was the *Chinese Monthly Magazine*, published in Malacca in 1815 by the three missionaries, Morrison, Milne, and Medhurst, with the help of their convert, the first Chinese editor, Liang A-fah. In 1858 and the following years a number of Chinese daily papers were started in the Ports by foreign proprietors; it was not until the 'seventies that papers under Chinese management came into being. There was no great demand for them until the Japanese War, when public opinion began to be stirred. Then there was greater interest in news and in discussions of policy. All through the first decade of this century the demand for newspapers grew and was met, as we have already seen, by radicals in Shanghai and Tokyo. The coming of the Republic brought a further change. Journalism became respectable, as it could not be under the old régime. Sober dailies like the *Shen Pao* appealed to sober people, and their influence grew accordingly. With the coming of the 'new tide', dailies began to use the plain language style, and in other ways to cater for a less well-educated public. Circulations went up by leaps and bounds. The school-teacher was already a newspaper reader; now the merchant and farmer began to cultivate an appetite for news. The Postal Service, by now extending all over the country and working with astounding regularity in the midst of civil wars, enabled even subscribers in the far interior to get their weekly or daily paper. The standard of reliability in news was not very high, and there were other shortcomings; but for good or ill, from this time on, that part of the nation which could read at all became keen newspaper readers. The newspaper offices and companies were organised on western lines; and newspaper men in the Ports gave the impression of being more westernised, or perhaps Americanised, than any other section of the community.

Among the new imaginative writers were men who took the art of writing with great seriousness and worked hard at perfecting their individual styles. Also they read omnivorously, ranging from the by-ways of their own literature to the famous works of all nations. Literary criticism was a passion with many of them, and it is possible that in this they had an inherited facility which was a liability to them rather than an asset: it was easy for them to become *précieux*. Yet it would be a mistake to think of them as in any sense reverting to the finicking criticism which characterises some sections of traditional literary criticism. The contact that their minds had with the vigorous open-air world of common speech did not allow of literary pedantry of that nature. In addition, there was the contact of their minds with the western canons of literary criticism, many of these entirely new to them and proving highly provocative.

There are many names which should be mentioned. Among some of the most outstanding are the following: Lu Hsün[1] and his younger brother Chou Tso-jen, Ko Me-jo, Yiu Ta-fu, Chang Chih-ping, Hsü Chih-mao, Ping Hsin,[2] Pa Chin, Hsü Ti-shan, Mao Tun, T'ien Han, Hsiung Fu-hsi, Tseng P'o and Tseng Hsü-pai (father and son), Wang Tu-ch'ing.[3] Taken as a body, romanticism is their most striking characteristic, as one would expect, since theirs was a revolt against an excessive classicism. Every man did that which was right in his own eyes. He followed the impulse which

---

[1] A pen-name; his real name was Chou Shu-jen.
[2] The pen-name of a woman writer.
[3] Details of their lives are given in Appendix I.

came to him from the study of some poetic mind, Shelley, Goethe, Musset or Gorky, whoever it might be who gave him the experience of illumination. Through the insight coming from his own appreciation he translated his experience into the most living prose he could accomplish. There was nothing passive about these writers and the contacts they made with world literature. Their approach was active with all the vigour of an individualist seeking for means to extend his individuality. This individualism was perhaps their weakness rather than their strength.

With regard to the nature of their works, there is a very wide variety: novels; verse in the form of lyrics and elegies; essays of all kinds from contemplations of Nature to explorations of eroticism; appraisals of authors and literary periods; and, above all, short stories. In the writings of past ages there had been no stories of the modern realistic type, only fairy stories, but since the Renaissance came this has been the most popular form of writing. Demand has undoubtedly affected supply, but the power which men like Lu Hsün, Ko Me-jo and Hsü Ti-shan show, goes far beyond any such explanation. There is a new delight in the portrayal of man as man, the ordinary person in an ordinary situation, which, as the story unfolds, turns out to contain so much meaning. Every kind of social stratum affords material for observation. Lu Hsün, for example, excels in his stories about simple illiterate men and women, for whom life is too difficult and who find themselves in all sorts of trouble. Yiu Ta-fu, on the contrary, has a gift for portraying students and young teachers, bothered with the maladjustments of their lives in the new times, while Sheng Hsi-cheng writes stories born of his experience in the civil wars. Love troubles are the theme of many stories, for this generation of students has been vastly concerned with the right of the individual, whether man or woman, to fall in love and choose his own mate without any sort of dictation from the family.

The number of long novels produced was relatively small, and on the whole they do not display as much native individual force as the short stories. It may be that they were written less from a real creative impulse than from an enthusiastic appreciation of the modern western novel, with its craftsmanship of well-knit plot and subtle psychology of character development. On the other hand, it is more likely that the unsettled state of the country and the restlessness of men's minds was the main factor. Even scholars of the book-worm type could not easily concentrate over long periods when violent events were taking place outside their very doors; much less could high-strung writers whose sympathies were actively engaged on one side or the other.

The same conditions account in a measure for the hurried, unconvincing nature of the new poetry. But there is a deeper cause than that for the comparative unsuccessfulness of the modern experiments. The art of poetry in China has for so long gone hand in hand with the art of painting, and the two together have produced such deep-running habits of aesthetic appreciation, that the modern cannot achieve in words alone the freedom of mind which he requires. The question of verse-forms has been a continuous problem, and even Hsü Chih-mao, the most successful and most confident of plain-style poets, passed through stages of acute dissatisfaction. One is reminded of Petrarch and his divided mind, his preference for 'the "Africa", a dull epic written in Latin, to the charming Italian sonnets which

247

are his chief claim to immortality'.[1] If Piers Plowman is any guide, we may expect the authentically new poetry to come from some proletarian singer rather than from the ranks of the new intelligentsia.

Essay-writing, on the other hand, has been much more successful. Most of it is distinguished by a candour which can be as delightful as it is sometimes devastating. The authors plainly did not need much urging from Hu Shih to 'set up their individual I'; it was already effervescing within them. A writer seeks to make his effect by the personal impression, but sometimes a particularly recondite foreign illusion strikes the eye, which makes one wonder whether he has not purposely gone out of his way to make an impression of learning. The English reader must, however, be cautious in criticism, for among the writers there are men and women who are as versed in the literature of France or Germany or Russia as they are in that of England and America. There is more of a cosmopolitan atmosphere about the literary discussions in Peking and Shanghai than can be found in any one of the countries mentioned. Due weight must be given to the zest which comes with the exploration of hitherto unknown territory, and if the explorer should be found on examination to have unearthed a bauble rather than a treasure, there is ground for the hope that he will discover his mistake in time. There are no more ruthless critics in the world than the present generation of Chinese literary men.

In the exercise of their candour the new writers were in danger of falling into an excess of introspection. They have revolted against the static virtuosity of stained-glass moral attitudes and they revel in the intricacies of self-revelation. This cannot be said of Lu

[1] H. A. L. Fisher in *A History of Europe*, 1 vol. ed., p. 432.

Hsün, who shows his genius in objective observation. For this reason he is to some readers too cold, inhuman, cursed with the sardonic spirit. But the test in such a case is whether the writer betrays contempt for the human being he is describing. Lu Hsün survives such a test, for although he is contemptuous of professional writing men, his descriptions of ignorance and stupidity show his deep sense of brotherhood. The same spirit appears in Ko Me-jo, although his candour is at times so ruthless that he appears to be a pure cynic. Actually he has in him a deep well of pity for all those who suffer oppression, as his conversion to Communism proved. But many of the other writers, Yiu Ta-fu for example, go too far in their pity for students and their difficulties in life, particularly their problems of love and marriage. Their stories can become mawkish, and the effect then given is one of a literature of escape with an emasculating influence on the reader. It may be that this was an inevitable stage of revulsion after the repression of the Manchu era. It was only a stage, for ten years later there came a fresh revulsion; both writers and readers have become wearied of this individualism, and a sterner, more puritanical spirit expresses itself in new ways.

In order to understand that revulsion, some account of developments between 1922 and 1930 is necessary. Although the Ministry of Education under the reactionary Government of the Anfu Party, had come over on to the reformers' side and what Lin Shu, the veteran translator, called 'the vulgar talk of rickshaw coolies' became officially the 'national language', not everyone wrote in the 'plain language'. In Peking itself some of the younger and more critical scholars, men such as Dr. Feng Yu-lan and Mr. Ch'ien Mu, whose lectures on philosophy and history have attracted enthusiastic classes, have continued to write in the old style, though, of course, with a stern simplicity and attention to plain meaning. In Nanking also there was a centre of opposition which has continued right down to the present. But nothing could withstand the onrush of plain-style publishing which developed in Shanghai. By 1930 there were as many as eighty new publishing-houses, part publishing-house, part book-shop, nearly all of them in the Foochow Road of the International Settlement. Their names tell a story: the Present Generation Book Co., the New World Book Co., the China Light Book Co., the Crescent Moon Book Co., Rejoice in the Masses Book Shop.

The interesting fact about these companies is that many of them were established by little groups of writers. Partly the old-established houses like the Commercial Press and the Chung Hwa Book Co. could not afford to take the risks involved in some of the publications, partly a group wanted to make its own experiments under its own direction. Also it was thought that money could be made, an expectation which for the most part has not been fulfilled. Foochow Road became for some half-mile two solid lines of book-shops, after the good old fashion of Chinese cities in which each trade keeps itself to one district. These new book companies were organised on a semi-foreign, semi-Chinese basis, and all of them had a perpetually new supply of books and magazines printed on foreign-style paper and, as time went on, bound in covers containing designs and symbols of the most impressionistic description. Some publishers have even taken to adopting the western method of printing the lines of script, namely, horizontally from left to right, not in the traditional perpendicular fashion beginning at the right-hand of the page.

The history of some of these groups or coteries is instructive. From the early days of reform kindred spirits joined in organising literary societies, as had been the practice in China for ages past. The most influential of these was the Society for the Study of Literature organised in Peking in 1921. It had a large membership and published, with the help of the Commercial Press, a flourishing monthly devoted to short stories. For a time it had nearly every writer of note as a member. They were ambitious in their purpose to put out serious studies of world literature, and they embarked on a big programme of translation. But a year later Ko Me-jo, Yiu Ta-fu, and other students at the Tokyo Imperial University were back home. Their views were in a number of ways different from those of the leaders in the Society for the Study of Literature. They therefore organised the Creative Society and made it a publishing house. With the two rival organisations existing face to face it was not long before the sense of division grew increasingly strong. The Creative Group claimed that original work was their strong point, a claim which men like Lu Hsün found it hard to endure. Actually, the real point of distinction lay in the purpose of literature. Both were convinced that literature was a high art, but the one party averred that this art was for the sake of life, the other that art was for art's sake and art's sake alone—one seems to have heard something of this sort in western literary circles.

Other groups were also in existence for longer and shorter periods: thus the Young Students' Popular Association sprang out of the 1922 agitation and for a time had a great following among the students in France and Germany. But after three years most of its active members drifted into one or the other of the two stronger organisations. The impression one gets is that the spirit of the Young Students was exaggeratedly foreign, and therefore the bond of association was not real or permanent. The one exception to this was where the influence came from Russia. Owing to the Great War and the Versailles Peace Conference there was, as has already been shown, a general debunking of European idealism. The Russians were regarded as the only people who had had the courage and intelligence to break away from the ingrained sins of the old feudal régime with its latter-day capitalistic oppression. Russia too had proclaimed herself China's friend in a way in which no other country had, whilst the exaltation of science above religion and its dedication to the welfare of the common people had its own special attraction for Chinese youth. So in 1925, when the Kuomintang took full advantage of Dr. Sun's death and the May 30 incident in Shanghai stirred all China, the more radical writers achieved an enormous popularity. From that time on the feeling between the liberal sections—such as those led by Hu Shih and Lu Hsün—and the out-and-out revolutionaries became more and more marked. Under the political stimulus of the times the Creative group in 1927 prepared its great anti-bourgeois slogan of 'the revolution *in* literature now leading on to the literature *of* revolution': in other words, now was the time to discard all the pretty-pretty writing of the intelligentsia with their middle-class appreciation of art and *belles-lettres*; now was the time for real men to derive their entire literary inspiration from the wrongs of the under-dog.

So began the movement for proletarian literature

which has continued above ground and below ever since. The members of the Society for the Study of Literature were, on the whole, in opposition, with the result that a fierce controversy, known as the 'Battle of the Books', broke out and raged for over a year. Lu Hsün started it by an article in his widely read magazine, *Yü Ssu*. The title of his article was 'The Obscurity in Drunken Vision'—a provocative enough title in all conscience—and its author displayed not only his consummate power of sarcasm, but also, only too openly, his contempt. The challenge was promptly taken up by one Li Ch'u-li, whose reply was labelled, 'Pray look at our Chinese Don Quixote and his Wild Capers'. So they and their friends went at it hammer-and-tongs, and very soon a dozen journals were devoting much of their space to the controversy. Over a hundred articles were published before the fire died down.

It is impossible not to regret that such a quantity of energy was spent in such a fashion at the time when unity in the country was so desperately needed; impossible not to regret also that the controversy took so personal and bitter a form. But it must be remembered how much these writers were living in a high state of nervous tension, due to the ever-mounting misery of the years in which the Republic had proved to be no way of national salvation, but the very reverse. They were all desperately concerned to find 'the way out' for their country, and over and above the mutual jealousies of literary coteries there was the great political issue at stake. Should China copy the Russian way with all it involved of violence and outrage of human ties, or follow a way, possibly more tardy in results, but more in accordance with China's social tradition?

From the point of view of numbers and dialectical

ability, Lu Hsün and his friends may be regarded as having won in the controversy. From the point of view of public interest the Proletarians in the end proved that they had hold of the right end of the stick. Reading people, with many students among them, had begun to grow a little tired of romantic bohemian writing unless it was of a really significant quality. For instance, one recent development in literature had been a violent interest in sex problems. Sex literature of all kinds, from translations of passionate western romances to translations of the less technical parts of works on sex pathology, had had a great sale. But at this juncture the bottom dropped out of that market. There was a complete swing-over to interest in economic problems. Journals became full of statistics and policies for the economic redemption of the country. For a few months this new literature was very patently communistic; articles on Marx and Engels, Lenin and the Five-Year movement, figured in the magazines, and a translation of *Das Kapital* was published. In 1930, however, the Nationalist Government, in pursuance of their anti-Communist policy, banned this literature. Publishing houses in Shanghai were shut down with the help of the Settlement authorities, and a number of left-wing writers were imprisoned. But the public interest continued, not so much in Communism as in the economic aspects of the nation's affairs and of world affairs generally. This interest is reflected in the style as well as the substance of much recent writing.

Chinese drama was not affected at all until the Renaissance Movement began to have results. Indeed it was the Nationalist Revolution which first showed what possibilities of popular change there might be in this sphere. Students in university and school, both men and women, discovered a surprising quantity of histrionic talent among themselves, and the practice quickly grew of acting semi-written, semi-improvised plays centring round topics of immediate national interest. This was a striking development in two ways: the old Chinese actor was not a very reputable person in society, whilst women actors were as unknown as they were to the Elizabethan stage. Western influence was clearly marked in the manner of these productions and also in the more formal works of professional dramatists like T'ien Han and his friends. The tendency quite clearly is in the direction of western realism as against the idealism of the old Chinese theatre, and of all the western dramatic influences the modern Russian is notably the strongest. But the developments as they come are highly unpredictable, since the old classical drama has, through the influence of the Renaissance, become yet more esteemed, and is being studied to-day with a zeal which is as appreciative as it is critical. Also, there are some very brilliant actors, chief among them the world-famous Mei Lang-fan, who take their profession very seriously and work together with learned scholars in their study of the old drama. Some of the exponents of the old drama are experimenting with modern stage effects and have studied western technique, especially in Moscow and Paris.

Then there is another school which is interested in film work. For nearly twenty years efforts have been made in this direction, and there are now about ten studios at work. They tend to concentrate on modern films, and they show proportionately the influence of Moscow and Hollywood. But they also prepare films in which the old panoramic dramas appear with the actors in the traditional robes and masks. Some foreigners take a keen interest in this work. A wealthy German lady in Shanghai has considerable influence in dramatic circles there. But the general influence of Chinese films is small compared to that of the western ones. Almost every city of any size now has its cinema, and the big urban centres have many. Shanghai with its international population has more than one hundred. The majority show American films more than any others. The great middle class in these centres is very definitely being educated for good or ill by these shows, with their sex appeal, crook interest, and all that is associated with Hollywood. In drama as *in literature generally the proletarian idea is gaining ground in a new way, and finds inspiration in the imaginative writing coming from Soviet Russia. There is something in the Russian combination of mysticism and the brutal candour of realism which appeals to the Chinese. That power of intuition which is found in their own literary history and in their art is driving them on in this new world to find something—they know not what. Many of them believe that Russia is more able to help them to find it than any other country.

In this account of the Literary Revolution reference has been made at one or two points to historical works. The number of such works has grown rapidly. As we might expect from writers interested in their art and finding literary inspiration in works which had never been counted as good literature, the movement brought with it a whole series of histories of literature written from these new angles of approach. Lu Hsün has published a history of Chinese literature and a number of other literary studies, while his brother, Chou Tso-jen,

has written a history of European literature. He is one
of the few Chinese writers who read Greek and Latin.
Cheng Cheng-to also is a lover of Greece, given to expounding Greek and Roman legends. Ch'en Tu-hsiu,
the ardent Communist, has written most illuminatingly
on the T'ang poets. Some of these works incline to
iconoclasm; although this is not true of all of them, the
tendency is naturally in the direction of critical research.

Apart from the history of literature there has been a
most striking development in historical study generally.
Here, as in so many other fields of their intellectual life,
the modern scholars owe a great deal to stimulus that
has come from the West. Nevertheless in accepting
modern critical methods they have found in them the
same spirit which was at work in some of their own
students during the last three centuries. The story of
critical studies begins with Ku Ting-lin, the famous
geographer of the seventeenth century, before the Ming
emperors lost the throne. Some would say that he was
inspired by the writings of the Jesuit Fathers, but so
far this remains very much a matter of conjecture.
Whether it be true or not, the men who carried on his
tradition in the eighteenth century worked entirely
apart from western influence, and made considerable
strides in their powers of sifting historical evidence.
There came to be a Han Learning School, as it was
called, men such as Tsui Tung-pi, who worked all his
life painfully adding one volume to another and seeing
no chance whatever of publishing them. Since these
critics discounted the Sung interpretation of the Classics
and called for a return to the primary authorities of the
Han era, their work was frowned on by the Manchu
authorities as heretical in tendency, and so actually
seditious in intention. But the movement could not be

altogether stopped. Thus Yüan Yüan, Viceroy of Canton in the early days of the foreign Factories, encouraged textual emendation of the non-canonical books. The western merchants found him reactionary and unreasonable, but in his study he showed that he had a liberal mind. By the nineteenth century the great controversy of the Manchu era over Han scholarship had developed. Students of the canonical writings were divided into two camps, the *ching wen* and the *ku wen* schools, with the root of the controversy the question whether in the Classic of History certain component parts were infallible in the same sense as the rest of the book. This was the thin end of the wedge, the first subtle attack on the mind of faith.

The movement synchronises with the one in Protestant Europe, where the spirit of scientific enquiry claimed the field of sacred as well as secular history. It is the studies in the former which are specially comparable with the Chinese studies, because in both cases there was the inhibition of faith in an infallible book to be overcome. In Germany and England the second half of the nineteenth century saw immense strides made in destructive criticism; and at the same time not only scientifically minded students such as Wellhausen and Robertson Smith, but devout theologians also came to feel that behind the traditional patterns of sacred history lay facts which contradicted what the Church had hitherto accepted. In China the same process was at work, and was now reinforced by contact with western learning. Before K'ang Yiu-wei took to studying western history and science he was already making his teachers anxious by his radical theories about Confucius and the real gospel he had for the Chinese people. K'ang brought immense reinforcement to the *ching wen* school, and after his conversion to a world-view of history he went on with added daring in his criticism of traditional views. That a man of his learning should boldly label parts of the canon as forgeries had an effect on many minds. He was not the only one of his generation to get a new general perspective of the classical period. Hsia Tseng-yiu, without K'ang's daring but with a better endowment of the true historian's impartiality, produced a history of Ancient China which along its own sober lines was just as significant as K'ang's works were.

With the removal of the Manchu suppression of free enquiry, the study of history, and more particularly the early formative period, entered on a new phase. The same mind which was calling for a new people began to work on the making of a new history. K'ang Yiu-wei published his works, and they were reprinted again and again. Liang Ch'i-ch'ao settled in Peking and began to lecture on historical problems in the National University. He had a gift for setting young aspirants for historical study to work on the original sources, and the opening of the Imperial Palace library to students brought a great store of old editions into public use. Then came the Literary Revolution and with it a quickened sense of the need for studying and re-writing the history of the past. Hu Shih, Ch'en Tu-hsiu and Ch'üan Hsuan-tung, the three leaders in the Revolution, gave vivid expression to their new enthusiasm: Hu Shih in the field of the history of philosophy, Ch'en Tu-hsiu in that of the history of literature, Ch'üan Hsuan-tung in that of the history of classical times. The last-named nailed his colours to the mast by changing his name to I-ku (doubt antiquity). All three professors published works the matter of which was as radical as the style in which they were written, and which were read avidly. Hu Shih's *History of Chinese Philosophy* was reprinted eight times between 1920 and 1926, whilst his work on the history and text of famous Chinese novels had an equal success.

Liang Ch'i-ch'ao threw himself with ardour into this side of the Renaissance Movement. He described the work to be done as 'a whole continent waiting to be discovered', and he published in quick succession his *Method for the Study of Chinese History* and *The Political Thought of Pre-Chi'n Times.*[1] His lecture-room was crowded to the doors, as indeed were those of all the men who presented this new approach to history. The emphasis which they laid on the chronological realignment of source materials and absolute impartiality between canonical and non-canonical works had its penetrating influence on the students who listened to them. Amongst these were men who dedicated their lives to the study of history. Some of them passed on to American and European universities and there disciplined themselves in the technique of historical method. Others stayed in China and plunged into the sea of documents contained in the libraries.

Thus there came what may be described as the Peking school of historical study, centring in the research professors and students of the four universities, the National, Tsing Hua, the Normal, and Yen-ching, the last being a missionary institution. Until some years later when history began to be written by scholars belonging to the Communist Party, the work produced by these men was the most radically critical to be found in the country. It is difficult to estimate its real influence in scholar circles. In Nanking, for instance, recognition

[1] An English version of this was published by Kegan Paul, *History of Chinese Political Thought*, 1930.

260

is given to the need for higher critical studies, but the application of the historical method is much more cautiously made. The Peking historians are charged with being actuated by the lust of iconoclasm; and it must be admitted that the way in which they have elected to publish their results gives an edge to this accusation. Nevertheless, in spite of the appeal which is made to preserve the 'sacred treasures of the nation', the influence of the radical group has grown steadily stronger throughout the country. The tide in the direction of historical reconstruction flows too strongly to be denied its course, just as has happened in Europe and America.

Ku Chieh-kang, a pupil of Hu Shih's, has become the protagonist of the radical historians. In 1926 he published as editor a book, *Ku Shih Pien*,[1] which proved a landmark in this field of rediscovery. This volume contained reprints of recent learned articles with the criticism which they provoked. It was an attempt to introduce the element of public discussion into historical enquiry. The historians are disclosed in their laboratory, as it were, at work on this experiment and that, expounding the paths of enquiry which they follow and the clues which they think they have discovered. They do not claim to have achieved finality in any sense; they only ask that every theory should be judged on the evidence. The result is immensely illuminating at certain points, confusing at others; but there can be no doubt that the right questions are being asked and a new and better understanding of the past is being achieved. It is a slow process, and the men who have given themselves to the task estimate that it will

[1] *Discussions in Ancient History*, Peking.

be half a century before the historical material is really classified into good chronological order. The 1926 *Ku Shih Pien* has been the first volume in a series of four others, each longer than the last, and totalling altogether 3000 pages. The discussions are classified according to their subjects, and the original proposer of some theory may reappear three or four times to reply to his critics. Dr. Hummel, of the Congress Library of Washington, has described the work as follows:[1] 'The vitality of the present renaissance is no better attested than in this new doubting approach to the past, and the abandon with which younger scholars now break into print with new hypotheses'. He also says: 'An important phase of the new thought movement in China to-day is an insistent demand for a scientific re-evaluation of the nation's cultural heritage. A concerted effort is deemed necessary to preserve the continuity between the present and the past and to forestall a too-violent break between the old order and the new; thus confirming the truth of Ruskin's words that "the power of every great people, as of every great living tree, depends on its not effacing, but confirming and concluding, the labours of its ancestors".' That is true. No one can be in the company of these men for long without realising their earnestness. If they have dealt iconoclastically with the Golden Age of the Holy Emperors, their aim has been to find the real roots of their racial culture, to trace the real struggle out of primitive barbarism into relative civilisation. They are profoundly convinced that at this critical juncture in the long existence of their nation it is only the truth about their past experience which can serve their need. In seeking for the truth they are the children of their age, strongly inclined to believe

[1] In the *American Historical Review*, July 1929.

that religion is superstition belonging to a pre-scientific age and entirely explicable in terms of sociology. They have shown also a tendency towards the Marxist philosophy of history. But here the dogmatism of Communist historians is beginning to create a revulsion towards a more liberal appreciation of the spiritual side of their culture. There is a growing interest in their religious history. Hu Shih himself lectures on Chinese Buddhism; Hsü Ti-shan, now Head of the Chinese Department at Hongkong University, is a profound student of Buddhism; and they are not the only ones. The study of anthropology, a recent one and so far very much under western tutelage, also tends to make religion a study of central interest. Through it all the Chinese historian, critic and rationalist as he is, remains a humanist and a Nature philosopher, alive to the mystery of Nature and the dignity of man.

CHAPTER VII

CHINA TO-DAY

THE foregoing chapters have dealt with the western influences at work down to about 1930. That is now seven years ago, seven years in which there have been a number of major events, such as the Japanese invasion and occupation of Manchuria and Jehol, followed by the extension of Japanese influence in inner Mongolia and north China. In 1931 there were devastating floods in the Yangtse basin, and again in 1932, 1933, and 1935 on the Yangtse and the Yellow and Han rivers, whilst a severe drought in 1934 brought calamity to other parts in the North. An acute economic depression swept the country in 1933, but the inauguration of a radically new silver policy, at the time when Sir Frederick Leith-Ross of the British Treasury was studying the situation on the spot, brought about a remarkable recovery. The Communist Government in Kiangsi and Fukien provinces was eradicated. In 1935 the dissentient provinces of Kwantung and Kwangsi came into line with the Central Government. All these are events in which the national temper has been revealed. They also throw light on the attitude of the nation to western influences, clearing away some of the anti-foreign dust which was raised by the Nationalist Revolution. The three years 1926–1929 were, from the point of view of the past, a highly instructive time. From the point of view of the future

264

and the permanent attitude of the Nationalist Party and people generally, those years were, as we can see now, definitely misleading. The Chinese—it may be stated positively—have no intention of ruling out the West and all it stands for in their national life. Even Christian missions, so recently denounced as part, and intellectually speaking a disreputable part, of western imperialism, are now showing signs of revival. The Protestant churches have recovered from their attitude of defence, and the Roman Catholic Church in its latest report can point to over 100,000 adult baptisms in the year 1935–36.

These seven years present also a record of accomplishment in many directions. Most striking, perhaps, is the improvement in communications. There are the road systems which have been built in the maritime provinces, with a greatly increased use of public and private motor-cars; the regular air services now operating between Peiping and Canton, Shanghai, Nanking and Szechwan, and extending far into the north-west: the beginnings of a national telephone service: the completion of the long-planned Canton–Hankow railway, and the reconditioning and extension of the Lung-hai railway so that there is a clear run from Sianfu (Shensi) in the far west to a new port on the coast. It is noteworthy that in all these developments the greater part of the work has been done by Chinese technicians.

At the same time co-operation with the League of Nations has shown the Nationalist Government's willingness to receive help from the West in all kinds of ways. Distinguished experts from many of the western nations have visited China in the last seven years and rendered valued services.[1] Most of these experts have

[1] See Appendix II for a detailed list.

worked in connection with the National Economic Council which was set up in 1931 to co-ordinate various schemes of national reconstruction, and to undertake the execution of certain urgent schemes such as making a study of the conditions of land tenure and land taxation.

All this points to something more than readiness to use western appliances. It shows a determination to achieve western standards of economic prosperity, and a readiness, in the course of achieving this, to see the old organisation of society changed in quite radical fashion. The question, then, is to what extent such changes are already on the way. The main matters for consideration are the regrouping of social classes and the realignment of social, political, and economic power in the community; the structure of the family, with the relationships between men and women and the status of women generally; the growth of industrial towns; ways of living, eating and drinking, clothing and housing, recreation and athletics. The answers to the questions which arise in these connections may best be considered in relation to the new middle class, the new labour movement, and the new village life.

Old China may be said to have had no middle class. The traditional structure of society by occupation, scholars, farmers, artisans, and merchants, tended to give merchants an inferiority complex. Apart from a few exceptions, such as the famous Shansi Bankers' Guild, there was no such arrogation of merchant social prestige and merchant refinement of living as was found in the great trading cities of Europe. Big fortunes were almost exclusively made by Government officials, and they, for the most part, put their money into land and houses and the products of luxury art. Thus there was an aristocracy, but, since the imperial examination system was the only way to lucrative employment, and that was open to the son of a poor farmer as much as to the son of a wealthy official, it was not a permanent one. In China, as in Lancashire, three generations might see the rise and fall of a family's fortunes. The clan system tended to keep all four classes of society in touch with each other, since of four brothers one might be found in each class.

To-day the situation is different. An ever-increasing amount of wealth is coming into the hands of business men, mill-owners, bankers, contractors and dealers in urban house property, ship-owners, opium agents on a large scale, wholesale dealers, and also into the hands of lawyers, doctors, engineers, and soldiers. The requirements of modern business have made it necessary for all, except perhaps the opium agents, to have a modern education up to a high standard. Further, these men are all to be found in the big cities, and they invest their capital in commercial enterprises, so that they are able to put their sons into well-paid posts after giving them an expensive education abroad. It is these families, many of them now in the third generation, which make up the new middle class.

Communist agitators regard this class as having reached the position of a full-fledged plutocracy and exercising all the baleful powers of such. This is an exaggeration of the facts. For one thing the class is too new, and too many of its members are of the salaried or professional kind. But one section of it does lend some colour to the Communist's feeling. This is the banking section. During the last twenty years there has been a rapid development of modern banking, and during the last ten years a quite phenomenal development. The men who control the policy of these modern banks have a power with the Government and in the community which has not been seen before in China. The Nationalist Government could never have weathered the storms of these last years unless the bankers in Shanghai had supported it. And their support has been a voluntary one, not due to the kind of force which the war-lords of the previous decades would like to have exercised. On the whole, the bankers have proved themselves to be both public-minded citizens and men with a shrewd grasp of their business. They cannot be treated as a milch cow, and this they frankly tell the Government representatives when they get round a table together.

Shanghai, Tientsin, Canton, Hankow, in other words the Treaty Ports, have been the forcing houses of western culture. There these middle class families are at home, and to an increasing degree cut off from their 'ancestral village'. Some of them are members of the Christian Church, and for that reason barred in their minds from some at any rate of the traditional appeals. The great majority of them have through education come to a modern rationalist position, and see the ideals of old China as a lost cause. They have cultivated a taste for western-style houses, with two or more stories, modern plumbing, spring mattresses, and easy-chairs. Their reception-rooms have none of the old formality, and with the passing of that rigid arrangement of furniture has gone much of the formal pattern of the old manners with its elaborate courtesy and fine distinctions of age and sex. Young married couples have their separate homes, entertain their friends at restaurants, and spend their evenings at cinemas and dance-halls, or at tennis and swimming clubs. Most striking of all, in view of the old strict division between the sexes and the iron law that a man and a woman should not touch each other or even sit on the same bench, is the popularity of western dancing. Cigarette smoking for men and women has replaced the water pipe. So also with athletic sports: in old China seldom could a scholar be found who would take violent exercise, and the women were, of course, debarred by their bound feet. To-day Shanghai, for example, has its tennis tournaments, its football and basket-ball leagues, its golf and race clubs.

Clothes make an interesting study. After 1911 the younger men in the big centres were attracted to western clothes. They found the traditional long gown a nuisance, and in any case a well-cut foreign suit was a sign that its wearer was one of the 'new people'. Then came the Nationalist Revolution, and the regulation wear for members of the party was a simple kind of uniform buttoning up to the neck. But the smart young men soon came back to more elegant western fashions, while the older men reverted to the long gown with the *ma-kua* or short upper coat of ceremony. These last are still common in high social circles, and are *de rigueur* for weddings unless full western dress is worn. This fact is significant; it means that the wearers are not only more comfortable so, but also wishful to perpetuate something of the old order.[1]

With regard to the ladies, the revolution in clothes has followed a different line. They have not gone to the same length as the men in taking over western styles; even when living abroad they tend to keep to their own fashions. But during the last twenty-five years there have been some very marked changes. Schoolgirls

[1] The old round scholar's cap has, however, been replaced by the 'Homburg'.

generally have discarded the traditional trousers in favour of short skirts and plain coats of the uniform colour adopted by the school, but otherwise the usual style is a long coat fitting closely to the figure and fastening at the side in the traditional way. This fashion first appeared about 1925 when ladies in the West were wearing skirts well above their knees, and for a time this was followed by the more modern young women. Although to-day the coat reaches almost to the ground, it is slit up at the side and frequently gives glimpses of lower limbs which would have been as shocking to the Chinese of the last century as to the ladies of Victorian England. Even more radical is the adoption of short sleeves, which still finds many critics, but curiously enough there has been no movement in favour of *décolleté* for either day or evening wear. Bound feet have entirely gone for the young, and with them the old embroidered silk shoes. Instead, shoes of western pattern are worn with heels as high as any western woman delights in, though the variety of designs and materials is perhaps greater. Another most noticeable change is in hairdressing. The era of woman's emancipation in China coincided with the post-war fashion for short hair in the West, and during 1926 and 1927 there was as great a rush on the part of the modern young woman to cut her hair as there had been on the part of the men to discard their queues in 1911. Since then there has been the 'Eton crop' and nowadays the 'perm' following suggestions of fashion coming from the West. Cosmetics have always played a part in the toilette of the fashionable Chinese lady, but the western article has largely taken the place of the old, and 'Miss Shanghai' carries and uses her vanity-bag just like her western sister.

Under these conditions it is obvious that women have a status and live a life which is very different from that of their grandmothers. To all outward seeming the girl of a middle-class family in Shanghai has the same kind of education, the same chance of entering a profession, the same recreations, and the same freedom of intercourse with men, with the same opportunities of a marriage of choice, as the girl in the West. There is no question but that the new view of marriage has come from England and America and been fostered by western literature and the rapidly increasing number of cinemas showing sex films: Christian missionaries, too, undoubtedly had a hand in it at the beginning, some of them living to fear the forces thus let loose. For young China took to sex romance with an appetite as ardent as it was inexperienced. Marked developments came when the Literary Renaissance began to exercise its explosive force. Students abroad had already been struggling with the problem arising from falling in love with their fellow students while they were bound by family engagements made in childhood. Now the same problem arose in colleges and high schools in China, and the cry came for marriage freedom and the 'small family'. To-day it is safe to say that wherever a young man has a post which gives him enough money of his own, he will carry through a marriage of romance to suit his own tastes. Where he has not got enough money, he has to consult the family and may be guided by their choice, though not in the old blind way, since parents recognise the new situation.

Where the young couple marry without family consultation and set up their own establishment at a distance from the old home, the whole texture of the relationship is changed. The wife is not part of the 'large family', as she was under the old system, and is therefore much more at the mercy of her husband, although she is relieved from the domination of her mother-in-law. If, however, the wife is able to earn her own living, the husband has much less hold on her. The new marriage, therefore, may lead to the most poignant quarrels, and in the last resort entails a new kind of divorce. This the law of the country now recognises, as it recognises the new type of marriage. The contract is made between the two parties, and therefore can be dissolved without reference to their families.

All this means an urban-minded class in society engaged in building up a scheme of social life which is freer and more luxurious than anything China's rural civilisation countenanced, and which involves a technique as elaborate in its way as the older ceremonial. This technique takes time to learn and requires considerable aptitude and energy of will on the part of the young man or woman from the country. Thus the new middle class would appear to contain all the ingredients of a new plutocracy and to be well on the way to establishing itself after the pattern of New York or any other western metropolis. It would appear to be completely inoculated with the spirit of those places, and thus Young China may be thought to have 'capitulated to the West' socially, as it appeared at one time to have done politically. But, just as the experience of life under the Republic led to the Nationalist Revolution with its reassertion of a distinctive Chinese spirit, so this new class tends as time goes on to show itself Chinese as well as western. The ladies, as we have seen, have their own ways of preserving the distinctive charm of Chinese beauty. In athletics American basket-ball is adopted, but English cricket makes no appeal. Mah-jong is more popular than bridge. Foreign food restaurants have built up a considerable clientele, and no young man about town would respect himself if he could not deal with a western meal with a competent use of knife and fork. But it is still the Chinese restaurants which make money, and there is no sign of the use of chopsticks or the general style of serving the meal being altered either in public or in private. While foreign wines and spirits and a certain number of new articles of food may be introduced, on the whole the Chinese connoisseur and housewife wisely keep to their own menus.

In the field of architecture the same eclectic spirit can now be seen coming into play. In the first instance the growth of cities like Shanghai and the other ports involved the use of western architecture for factories, offices, banks, hotels, and so on. Buildings such as these, originally built by foreigners, have been copied by Chinese firms, until to-day the main streets in any port differ very little at first sight from those in any foreign town, except for the Chinese signs which still hang in the old way outside the modern shops. There is, however, a tendency on the part of the Chinese builder to take the old patterns and express them in plaster ornamentations. These may appear somewhat rococo to the western eye, but there is in them something of the old Chinese artistry trying to express itself in the new medium. Experiments in combining the colourful Chinese roofs and eaves with modern-style two- and three-storey buildings of reinforced concrete have been made by the Peiping Union Medical College and Yenching University, and are now being used in the construction of the Government buildings in Nanking.

Looking at the situation all round, there has been

widespread experimentation by this new class, and now its members have reached the point where they know what they like and what they do not. They hold the West in fee, rejecting some of its features, welcoming others, and where they welcome, not hesitating to transform to suit their own taste. In other words, a distinctive Chinese mind is at work, a distinctive Chinese sense of taste, a distinctive judgment of moral and aesthetic values. The real question is not whether this new class will remain predominantly western, but whether its excessively urban character will continue to make a sharp division between town and country, between capitalist and industrial worker. There are signs to-day in Government circles, in educational circles, and among responsible-minded people generally, of a strong revulsion against this urbanisation. Dr. Sun Yat-sen warned his countrymen against the dangers of breeding millionaires, and precautionary measures are part of the Nationalist policy which is committed to state socialism.

We turn now to industry and the new industrial class. In 1933 a Government survey of factories which would come under the factory laws, *i.e.* those employing 30 or more workers, showed 2435 factories in the whole country, of which half were in Shanghai. There are probably as many again which employ 10 to 30 workers. The industries include, as well as cotton and silk, the manufacture of woollen fabrics and garments, matches, cement, paper, cigarettes, machinery, glassware, sugar, stockings, soap, leather and rubber goods. It is extremely difficult to get any really reliable statistics of the growth of industrialisation, and even were it possible to do so, such statistics would not necessarily present the right picture, since they must be taken in comparison with the whole country. Factories are still mainly in Shanghai, Tientsin, Wuhan (Hankow, Hanyang, and Wuchang) and in a few places along the Yangtse. On the other hand the workers are drawn from the country districts over a much wider area, and the produced goods are spreading over the whole country. In this way the movement is affecting the minds and habits of a very much larger number of people than those actually employed in the factories.

Under the old conditions money was invested in land and the local industries. Now the handling of the outside product is more profitable, and investors hear of big dividends being paid on financial ventures in the cities. Thus money has drained away from the country, whilst employment in the city has become more attractive: a development which has already brought many country districts to the verge of bankruptcy. On the other side there is the growth of slum areas in the new factory districts and the evils attending unregulated cheap labour. All these are coming upon China, and they are accentuated by the extreme poverty of the villages, which have suffered for a century from the decay of government, from war, famine, and flood. Owing to poverty people are willing not only to seek work in the towns but also to accept it under conditions which are an inherent menace to society. In the village the family lived together, and the members cared for each other in poverty, sickness, or old age—in the International Settlement of Shanghai in 1935, 471 persons died without any responsible person to bury them. The farm-worker was in the fresh air at least during his working hours, and his food, if scanty and coarse, was nourishing and his vegetables fresh. The factory-worker lives either in a one-roomed tenement or a mud hut, or in a dormitory where the beds are occupied for twenty-four hours on the Box and Cox principle. He eats machine-milled rice and vegetables which have been exposed in the dusty market, or cheap tinned food. These conditions lower the standard not only of health but of morality. Disease, prostitution, and crime are more prevalent among the town labourers than among the villagers.

Among the factories there are a certain number which have been built for the purpose and provide reasonable conditions of space, light, and air. But the greater number have been erected with more thought of economy than of care for the workers, and very many small industries using rented electric power are carried on in ordinary dwelling-houses or outbuildings. The machinery imported into China has often lacked the safety-guards insisted on by modern western legislation, and so the locally manufactured machines, copied from imported models, are also without them. Little or no restriction has been enforced in the use of dangerous processes or materials. For instance, children are employed in match factories for putting the chemical material on the outside of the boxes. Most factories work twenty-four hours a day and seven days in the week, since there is no legal Sunday holiday. Even at New Year and the other festivals some workers are willing to continue working for extra pay. The working hours per day vary with different industries, some having only $7\frac{1}{2}$–8 hours; but others have 12 hours for women and children as well as men. Daily wages vary from $1.65 (about 1s. 6d.) to 47 cents for men, 89 cents to 24 cents for women, and 42 cents to 20 cents for children. Female and child labour, being cheaper, is more in demand. Many of these women and children are brought in from the villages on contracts by which they are housed in dormitories run by the companies, and their board is deducted from their wages. The conditions are little better than slavery.

From the West, then, has come a factory system which reproduces all the evils which characterised the early days of industrialisation in Europe and America. There have, however, also been some attempts to remedy these evils. By her membership of the League of Nations, China is pledged to adopt the standards of the International Labour Office, and a beginning is being made with factory legislation.

In 1921 attention was first drawn to the conditions under which women and children were working in Shanghai. A joint committee for the study of industrial conditions was formed by the American, British, and Chinese Women's Clubs of that city. The secretary was a young Chinese lady just returned from college in America, Soong Mei-ling, now the wife of General Chiang Kai-shek. The next year the National Christian Council was formed and put social study into its programme. Through the influence of these two bodies, together with the Young Women's Christian Association, the Municipal Council of the International Settlement appointed in 1923 a Child Labour Commission, consisting of three British merchants and one Chinese and one Japanese merchant, with four women, two of whom were Chinese. Dame Adelaide Anderson, the pioneer of English factory inspection, was invited to come and study the situation. Since then some progress has been made, but in its report for 1935 the Municipal Council can only say: 'Achievement of any better standard of safety or of hygiene will, in any case, be a long process, and must be preceded by the dissemination of information as to accepted practice. In the meantime the Council will find ample scope in the cultivation of an understanding with owners and managers of factories and in a process of education based upon these relations.'

A few firms have introduced better conditions into their works, such as the Ta Seng cotton-mill at Nantung and the Commercial Press in Shanghai. The first of these was opened in 1899 by Chang Chien, one of the pioneers of the cotton industry. Before his death in 1926 his undertaking had grown to include the growing of cotton on reclaimed land and factories for every process connected with it. Among the buildings on the estate are workshops of all kinds, schools, and hospitals for the workers, and also gardens and a theatre. Chang Chien realised that a great industrial undertaking should not be run purely as a money-making concern, but should be related to the development of the country in other ways, such as the reclamation of land and the building of roads, and also to the education and welfare of the workers. The same kind of spirit animated the founders of the great printing-works, the Commercial Press, but in their case it had a definitely Christian origin, and their plans arranged for a Sunday day of rest as well as for schools, hospitals, and welfare work for their employees.

Industrial workers in China are still for the most part illiterate, though the importance now attached to mass education has increased the numbers attending evening and half-day classes. It is, therefore, hardly possible yet to speak of a working class which can compare with the working class which runs trade unionism in England. There is a Labour Movement which, from the beginning, has had a strong political twist to it. It owed its inception not to demands on the part of the workers but to socialistic theories in the minds of a few teachers and students in the universities. These enthusiasts organised a National Labour Party as early as 1913, but there was little outward demonstration of its vitality until 1919. On May 4 of that year the students organized an anti-Japanese boycott in which many of the workers joined. At that time there were some fifty labour unions in Shanghai. By 1922 the Seamen's Union was strong enough to carry through a fifty-days strike which paralysed the trade of Hongkong. It ended in a victory which made the Chinese coolie realise for the first time that the employer, particularly the foreign employer, was not omnipotent. The next year saw the first National Labour Conference on May 1 attended by fifty delegates. This was followed by a second conference in 1925 attended by delegates representing the Seamen's Union, Railway Workers' Union, Miners' Union of Hunan and Kiangsi, and Cantonese workers. The importance of this conference was the decision to unite with Moscow. The more moderate trade unions of Europe did not realise any more than did their governments the real nature of the crisis through which China was passing. Since Russia alone responded to Sun Yat-sen's call for help, it was inevitable that the workers' leaders should turn to the Third International.

The Labour Congress of 1926 having resolved to co-operate with the Northern Expedition of the Nationalist Party, their propaganda agents followed with the advancing army and everywhere organised farmers' unions, workers' unions, and women's emancipation societies. Again the emphasis was largely political; not to join a union was tantamount to being anti-revolutionary. When the short-lived Communist Government was set up in Hankow in 1927 it was reckoned that there were 3,000,000 members in these unions. These might have gained a stranglehold on the Government, but the conservative business element in Shanghai associated itself with the right wing of the Nationalist Party, and the Hankow Government fell. This was followed by strong anti-union legislation. Federations of labour unions were prohibited, and since then there have been only individual labour unions. Their energies have been largely absorbed in organising anti-Japanese activities.

There remains the question how far the western influences which have affected the new middle class and the new industrial class have also touched the villages. Can there be said to be a new village life? One thing may be said at the outset: there is no more hard-worked phrase in China to-day than 'rural reconstruction'. Whether it be governmental planning, educational experiment, or the Christian expression of the 'social gospel', all are concerned with the villages. And the reason of their concern, expressed in one way or another, is at bottom that the salvation of China is bound up with her village life. Although industrial workers and the new professional and business men find their occupation in the towns, the tie of the land still holds them. However much money he has in the bank, however good his job, the Chinese likes best of all to know that he has some *land*. If he has even one acre, he feels that his future is safe: his life is bound up with what has always figured in Chinese thought as the 'root' of society. One of the leaders of new China, Liang

Shou-min, has discussed this in a book which he calls, *The Final Awakening of the Movement for National Salvation*. In his opinion, neither European Democracy nor Russian Communism is to be taken as a model for China, but she should seek her future in her own past. In the work which he is now doing among the villages of Shantung, Liang Shou-min is showing that this means a rebuilding of village community life on the old foundations of local self-government. The same idea is behind Government training of young men from the villages as salaried village elders who shall carry on the traditional ways of dealing with the affairs of the community, a practice which has been endangered by the unsettlement of the last thirty years. The various agencies which are working on the village problem are seeking to encourage the farmer by co-operative societies and farmers' banks, and by experiments with new and improved seeds and methods: also to improve the conditions of village life by mass education, for adults as well as children, by public health services and sanitation and by the encouragement of home industries. All these things are still in the experimental stage, but the forces behind them make it certain that, given continued peace and reviving prosperity, village life will be greatly improved and standards of living, of literacy, and of agricultural production brought nearer to those of the West.

Although the new village life will be based on the old, it will owe much to the West. The inspiration for health services comes from the adoption of modern medicine. Many of the ideas for co-operative societies, village schools and community centres come particularly from Denmark. America has contributed to the study of agricultural problems, the new cotton and wheat being acclimatised from American seed. Social and family life is gradually moving, as in the towns, towards greater freedom of intercourse between men and women, and more personal choice in marriage, although conditions of village life tend to keep the 'large family' together. Such things as bicycles, thermos flasks, and electric torches are found in many villages, together with soap, matches, cigarettes and some tinned foods.

There is one other feature in the social life in China to-day which is directly the outcome of western influence. It is the growth of a new military class and, just recently, the introduction of military training and discipline in schools and in villages. Soldiers as such had no place in the fourfold order of old Chinese society. The proverb says, 'You cannot make nails out of bad iron or good men out of soldiers'. But a change of attitude began to come with the beginnings of a modern army at the end of the nineteenth century. In 1898 and 1911 it was Yuan Shih-kai, the commander of the new army, who was able to tip the scales one way or the other as he pleased. He was the first of the 'war-lords', the military leaders who have exercised so dominant an influence during the last twenty-five years. Some of them rose from the ranks, few of them were men of education: their power was not in moral character (*tao tê*) but in their guns. And the power of the generals was also the power of the lower ranks. Firearms, except antiquated fowling-pieces, were a new thing in Chinese villages. Half a dozen soldiers armed with modern rifles could terrorise a whole village. During the worst years of civil war it was no uncommon thing to see a village deserted, men, women, and children with their cattle and as much household treasure as possible, taking

282

refuge in the hills, rather than wait the arrival of an army merely passing through.

Under Generalissimo Chiang's régime, however, notable improvements have been made in the training of educated officers,[1] with a slow but steady improvement of the discipline and general morale of the rank and file. A new spirit of self-respect is observable with the growth of the military virtues so much prized in the West. In the military centres the new military social class, like the middle class, is cut off from its ancestral village and is making its own social and moral standards.

With civil war a million or more common soldiers had some sort of a living, whilst their buccaneer leaders had an avenue to wealth and power, but they were loathed by the rest of the nation. Now has come military training for all. The hated soldier and officer are becoming the country's gallant defenders. The mind of the nation is becoming militarized. Every boy, whether in elementary school, high school, or college, is given military drill, and the elder ones have to spend three months of the summer in camp. Every girl has to learn first-aid and nursing. The farmers have to drill and learn to dig trenches for protection from air attacks. All this is entirely without precedent in Chinese history. China has had her warlike periods, but never has the organisation for defence or the inculcation of the military spirit been attempted on such a scale. Under the old educational system there was a section devoted to training for Government service in the army. In this section martial exercises had their place, though not a very conspicuous one. But, for the aspirant for civil honours or the student who aimed at scholarship,

[1] The military college at Nanking employs a number of German experts.

regarded as he was as on a higher social and moral plane altogether than the military man, any idea of military drill would have been entirely repugnant.

In so far as this militarization consists in preparation to resist an aggressive neighbour, it cannot be put down directly to western influence. Yet the imperialist policy of that neighbour is confessedly one which she has learnt from the West, notably from the principles and methods prevalent in the great days of colonial expansion. Moreover, all the weapons and technique employed are taken directly from the West. To what extent this influence will destroy a priceless temper of reasonableness and pacificism which the Chinese have possessed is a question which the world should consider.

The year 1939 will mark the centenary of the Opium War, that is to say, of the first formal clash between a Western Power and China. Looking back over this hundred years from the vantage-point of to-day, the first impression may be one of a continued series of lamentable mistakes, of strains and stresses which were as unnecessary as they were costly in human happiness; neither China nor any of the Western nations concerned doing justice to their best traditions. Such an impression, inevitable as it is, is not one with which the historian's mind can rest content; and it is for this reason that the study of the contacts from a purely cultural standpoint is so necessary. It enables us to avoid two untenable positions, both of them so easy to slip into and so calculated to bemuse our judgments. The one is that our forefathers were devoid of wisdom and common sense, not to speak of moral discernment, and that this generation is the only one which can see things as they really are. The other is that Chinese and Westerners being what they were, there could not but be mutual misunderstanding and suspicion and injury followed by the oppression of the weak by the strong.

The story told in these chapters goes to show that the second of these points of view is not true. Even at the worst of times there were men and women who represented their own national traditions and interests and yet were able to break through to some sort of understanding and appreciation of the people and the traditions on the other side. Lord Elgin, Sir Robert Hart, Anson Burlinghame, W. A. P. Martin, Timothy Richard, are highly significant, because on the Chinese side there were men of like stature and understanding: Tseng Kuo-fan, K'ang Yiu-wei, Liang Ch'i-ch'ao, and in these latter days Dr. V. K. Ting and Dr. Hu Shih. And besides these there has been a whole host of others —consuls, business men, missionaries, and teachers— whose names may be entirely unknown to history but who each in his own way went on making relationships on a basis of sincerity and friendliness, and found men of like spirit on the other side—officials, scholars, merchants, and even simple peasants and coolies. It is these men on both sides who saw quite clearly that it did not pay the West to thrust trade and culture at China with the violence and arrogance which was so often employed, just as it did not pay the Chinese to repel the invasion with their own type of arrogance and violence. This enables the historian to state dogmatically that, just because the Chinese and the Western peoples were what they were, they could have come together in a way which would have made the story of their relationships a happier one.

History, however, is not made up of exceptional

individuals, and the history having been such as we have seen it, we can now try to sum up the cultural relations which have actually emerged from the strain and stress of these hundred years. The discussions in the foregoing chapters have given the story of the growth each from its own angle. Is there anything which can be said of the growth as a whole? This may appear if we review the various stages from the Chinese side.

First, at the beginning of the seventeenth century came the urbane welcome of the Jesuit Fathers by the Emperor. Second, at the end of the eighteenth and the beginning of the nineteenth century, there arose a different sentiment, an acute mistrust and contempt for the rough traders 'from the Southern Ocean', followed by a recognition on the part of a few responsible people that the military arts of these traders must be learnt. Third, after the middle of the century came the discovery by a few scholars that the peoples of the West had something more than superiority in arms, something of culture and learning which China must take into account. Fourth, in the twentieth century came the sudden conversion of educated youth to the idea that their own culture was effete, unfitted for the modern world in which China had to join in the biological struggle for existence. Fifth, came the suspicion that the West was neither as friendly nor as moral as the reformers had been thinking, and that it was time that China worked out her own salvation in her own way. Finally, there is the sixth stage, the post-Nationalist Revolution stage through which China is now passing. Here we find a new attitude emerging with increasing clarity and force. It is marked in men of all classes by a new confidence in themselves and their ability to adjust their half-traditional, half-newborn national conditions so as to produce unity, efficiency, and the well-being of the whole community. Along with this confidence has come a new feeling to the outside world, a belief that there are friends there as well as exploiters.

Thus we may say that the pendulum having swung far to the West after 1911, swung back to the East after 1925 and is now coming to rest between the two. Through these distressful years a process has been going on in which the mind of youth has become less volatile, less impressionable to every new wind of doctrine, whilst middle age, itself born in a period of change, has become satisfied that the passing of the old order is not necessarily the prelude to a new order which will be wildly inhuman.

Under these conditions the attitude to western culture has changed. There is not the same heat of approval or disapproval. As far as the material implements of western civilisation are concerned, even the great mass of the peasants is now familiar with them and accepts them as a matter of course. If they are useful they are adopted; if they are not useful they are ignored. Their western origin has lost its glamour. In the matter of beds, for example, the new middle class may rejoice in a spring mattress, but the general feeling goes against them, and that not only on account of expense. Easy-chairs would appear to be more attractive, but even here the Chinese sense of tidiness and formality for a reception-room asserts itself. Indeed, the nation as a whole has a predilection for simplicity. The western bourgeois ideals of down-lined comfort give Chinese a feeling of moral discomfort, just as the waste of cooked rice at the table gives them the feeling that they are sinning against the farmer who has sweated to produce it. The pattern of Chinese civilisation has always been essentially rural, whilst the aristocracy of the nation has been a scholar class of which the greater part has lived in the country. Wherever he lived, the scholar found in his sacred Confucian literature, as also in traditions of poetry and painting, an extolling of the charm in simplicity which country life embodied and which was essential to the good life.

It is this sense for the country and its basic importance to the life of a civilised community which must be taken as our guide in estimating the trend of the times to-day. In the realm of politics, the wise way, if China is to be democratically governed, is for the sources of political authority, the power to determine policy, to centre in the country at least as much as in the towns. In their emphasis on rural reconstruction Government leaders as well as leaders of thought very much have this in mind. It is a realisation on the one hand that the Communist success in certain areas was due in large measure to agrarian discontent, and on the other that a peasantry which is intelligent as well as prosperous, and able to express its will in national affairs is essential to social stability in these days of international and interclass upheaval. The situation is viewed as one which requires the best results of modern science. Thus a constant stream of university graduates come over to America and Europe to take specialised rural courses, and to research on particular problems which have emerged in China: problems of soils and manures, of seed selection and crop-variation, of economic marketing, and so forth. Western experts are invited to spend a year or more studying some particular aspect on the spot. When they get to China, these experts find trained assistants waiting to work under them with a view to taking responsibility after their departure.

No one is worrying much about the form of the political authority which is to be exercised by the revived farming communities. The Nationalist Revolution brought a new consciousness of past mistakes, of which the chief one is felt to be too much attention to democratic forms and failure to work for the democratic spirit. Hence the preparedness to scrap the forms of democracy and to have a one-party government. Now the aim is to foster a spirit, and let forms be discovered later. There is, therefore, a decline in iconoclastic fervour directed against the old clan and family system; and there is no proposal to organise the voice of the people on a unitary basis of one consumer one vote. If one may judge from the past and the present, that idea which is characteristic of urban-centred democracies will have but little appeal. It is the producer who is the centre of interest, and since there existed in the old days the organisation of farmers' and craftsmen's guilds, the future units of power for determining local policy will almost certainly be developed along those lines. As to the questions of provincial and national policies, these are much more difficult to visualise. The solutions may, from the point of view of machinery, be anything. Yet here again the old political wisdom asserts itself. The idea of administration by the *shan jen* (the expert) is too deeply rooted to be torn up and thrown away in favour of any new-coined *vox populi vox dei* theory.

The modern version of the *shan jen* is, however, a serious problem. In the traditional philosophy of the State he was pre-eminently the expert in moral values. He spoke out of the clarity and profundity of his knowledge of what was indispensable for the good life of the community. He did not necessarily claim any wisdom on technical matters of industry or agriculture. In fact he tended to despise these mundane intricacies and to leave them to the farmers and merchants themselves. To-day education under western influence has produced an entirely different kind of expert. He is preeminently the scientific expert, whether his knowledge be in applied science or in social science. The danger is, therefore, that the technical experts may wield too much power, a danger which is all the greater for two reasons. One is that in the sacred realm of education the destruction of the old education in favour of a new and untried system necessarily involved bureaucratisation. Even in the worst years of the period of disintegration (1912–27) the Ministry of Education in Peking exercised some control over the provinces generally. It was the one department of State which did this, and the mantle of that Ministry has descended on the shoulders of the Nationalist Ministry in Nanking. The other reason is that the nation is now being regimented for national defence against aggression, and that means a determination to achieve quick results— efficiency rather than personality. There can be little question, however, but that the bureaucratised State has come to stay. If foreign advisers are to be trusted, this is the chief need of the Chinese people to-day. The old *laissez-faire* principle with its easy-going concessions to local self-government, or non-government as the case might be, with its concessions to inter-provincial jealousies and provincial semi-independence, cannot work under modern conditions. If the Central Government should follow the course of central governments in the past, namely doing nothing very much and doing it very well, then there is bound to be a collapse. None the less, the final answer is that bureaucratisation is a danger as well as a necessity. There are not wanting government officials and leaders of thought who realise this, and it is significant that the recent pronouncements by Wang Ching-wei, the most whole-hearted and influential of Kuomintang leaders to-day, are a passionate denial that his party and the Nationalist Government are anything but inveterate democrats. There have been serious doubts raised in the press on this issue, but it would appear that public opinion is inclined to believe Wang Ching-wei and to endorse the principle which he enunciates. Fascism after the Italian and German pattern has no following except among a few intellectuals of no particular influence.

The 'New Life' Movement sheds an interesting light on these two concurrent trends towards expert administration and the building-up of the people's power to govern themselves. The Movement was inaugurated by General Chiang in 1934 and grew out of the reconstruction of Kiangsi province after the expulsion of the communists. The idea behind it was that a new national consciousness should be built up on the old social virtues, and that this should be done by giving the people something definite to do as expressions of these virtues. It is concerned, therefore, with the personal habits of the people and in its detailed orders and exhortations is a perfect example of the bureaucratic mind. So also is the way in which those orders are carried out, not only in Kiangsi but in many other parts of the country. Such details as cigarette-smoking in the public streets, walking on the left of the pavement, queuing at railway ticket offices, and young women refraining from *outré* fashions in dress, are dealt with by the police. To all appearances the movement is not only curiously occupied with trivialities but also very near to being an intolerable infringement on personal liberty. Yet to the Chinese people generally it is something which is both useful and, if one may put it in that way, an excellent joke. Naturally some susceptibilities have been wounded and tempers lost, but taken as a whole the New Life propagandists enjoy a good-humoured popularity, and some of their main ends are on the way to successful accomplishment.

The somewhat heavy moralistic line taken by the exponents of the New Life Movement, together with the good humour with which the man in the street responds, tends to conceal the fact that in the eyes of a number of people this movement is an attempt to introduce a religious note into the reform movement. In fact there is now in place of the outcry against religion a feeling to be found in all sorts of circles that the integrating power of religion is a requisite for the life of the community, and that somehow the old spiritual values which have suffered in these last thirty years must be resuscitated. To some this arises from a deep instinctive faith in the *ju-chiao* (traditional Confucianism). There are others, and they more probably the larger number, whose attitude is very much that of the Durkheim school of anthropologists in France and elsewhere, which holds that the only reality in religion is the power which it has of inducing social cohesion: it is man's special instrument devised for this purpose. So far, however, the New Life Movement has shown little sign of substantiating such hopes. The historic *Li-chiao* (Confucian *cultus* religion) had its mystic sacramental approach to man and Nature on the one hand, and an austere sense of art on the other. It is difficult to see how the New Life Movement proposes to achieve this numinous majesty which characterised the old culture, without which it cannot become a really religious force.

There is a religious problem to-day in a sense in which there has not been heretofore. Not only have traditional forms been discarded by the large number of the educated; the superstitions of the illiterate section of society have also been vigorously assailed and belief in them shaken. The Government, which has ever since 1912 taken up the official position that religious liberty is the law of the land, tends to convey the impression that secular interests are of greater importance to the country. Buddhism and Christianity are the two distinctively religious forces at work in China. Of the two Buddhism is of course by far the larger institution, by far the more intimately welded into the fabric of Chinese life. Moreover its leaders are awake to the movement of the times and active in schemes for retaining their influence on the people. There are Buddhist modernists, notably T'ai Hsü Fa Ssu, who can converse learnedly on the Hegelian element in Buddhism and similar topics. This, however, does not prove that Buddhism has within it the power of serving present needs. Christianity is another matter, if only for the reason that by far the largest body of westerners in China is the missionary group, and its members are scattered all over the country. They maintain that China is dying for lack of the Christian gospel and can never reintegrate her national life without widespread acceptance of it. Their opponents maintain that the Chinese are temperamentally irresponsive to religion in general and will never in large numbers become Christian in the sense in which the Western peoples are.

Here is a question which goes deeper than any question as to rightness or wrongness in the methods used by the earlier missionaries. It is also a question the answer to which will very much affect the cultural relations between China and the West. Of the second point of view it can only be said that whilst Confucianism may be religion in rather different ways from the Christian ways, yet it is shot through and through with the appearance and content of religion, whilst the religious influence of Buddhism and Taoism in the past is unquestionable. There would therefore seem to be only a very doubtful validity to the claim that the Chinese are temperamentally irresponsive to religion.

With regard to the claim of Christian missionaries, it would appear to be only imperfectly substantiated by the existence of the Protestant and Catholic Churches as they are to-day. The undoubted tendency in the past has been to hail modern science as the gospel of salvation, whilst the broad lesson of the revolution in education points in the same direction. Culturally the deepest influence which the West has exercised in China is to be found here and not in the specifically religious influence. But this has been the case in the period in which a good deal of breaking-down was felt by the Chinese reformers to be necessary. Now that the country is entering on a period of building-up, is it possible that the way is open for Christianity to exercise a much bigger influence? To this question only an answer dealing with factors can be given. First of all, in a class by itself comes the factor of Christianity's power in the world generally. If it should prove in the future to be as nationalistic as it has been in modern Europe, unable to mediate the spirit of peace on earth and goodwill amongst men as it claims to do, this failure will be a factor of major importance in China, where the common sense of the people expects a religion to be one of accomplishment triumphing over the forces of evil and disorder. One of China's representatives abroad made the statement recently in a speech: 'If the Churches are unable to give the lead required in producing a will for international peace, we must turn to the universities.' The second factor is the Chinese Churches, Catholic and Protestant. If they should become marked out as more able than any other bodies to foster intelligence and initiative in the village communities, and to give an interior peace and happiness which glorifies all labour for the common good, that would be a factor on the other side. A third factor is the possibility that that section of the Church will become most prominent which preaches Christianity as a religion of escape from the unredeemable world. But in this respect it is likely that Buddhism will prove more widely attractive than Christianity. The final factor is in relation to the Chinese attempt in the field of historical research to find out the abiding elements in their traditional culture. If the Churches were able to produce scholars with a plainly surer insight into the lessons of the past, or if they produced a distinctive school of historical appraisal and commanded the respectful attention of the learned world, that again would be a factor making for the acceptance of Christianity. So far some slight attempts have been made in one or two Christian universities, but nothing yet has been achieved of any conspicuous note, just as the study of Christianity has only produced one or two Chinese thinkers of originality and power.

The main point here, and one which applies to the whole of our investigation, is that the Chinese are to-day not in a position of isolation, and show no signs of wishing to go back to that position. For good or for evil, China is now part of the family of nations. Her problem is the problem which presents itself equally to every other nation: how best to use all that the modern world has to offer for the upbuilding of her national life on the basis of her peculiar tradition, while at the same time, through her outstanding men and women, to be part of the world fellowship of religion, philosophy, science, and art. As that fellowship transcends the bounds of nationality, so in it disappears the temper which assigned a special position to East or to West. All have contributions to make, and all share in the life of the whole.

APPENDIX I

BIOGRAPHICAL NOTES ON SOME OF THE MODERN CHINESE WRITERS[1]

LU HSÜN (Chou Shu-jen) was born in 1881 of semi-educated farming stock in Chekiang province. At eighteen he entered the Naval School at Nanking, as it was the only school which would take him without fees. Six months later he changed to a mining school, and after graduating there he scraped together money for study in Japan. There he entered a medical school. He was anxious to get to Europe, but was called back to China by home claims and took a post as science master. After 1911 he got a post in the Ministry of Education and settled in Peking. There his real genius began to blaze, and by 1918 he was publishing short stories and satirical studies in quick succession.

Ko Me-jo was born in 1895 in Szechwan province. When he was nineteen he went to Japan to study medicine; returning to China in 1921, he refused a medical post and settled in Shanghai, with his Japanese wife, to make a living by writing. One way and another he was drawn into political writing and developed communist sympathies. The Marxist interpretation of history captured him, and he began to study the social history of China from that angle. But perhaps the biggest influence on him came from the May 30 incident in Shanghai (1925). It gave him a horror of imperialism. Allied to this is his sensitive revolt against the oppression of women. When the Nationalist Revolution started he threw himself into its activities, but before long the break with communism turned him against the success-

[1] Taken partly from *A History of Chinese Modern Literature*, by Wang Chieh-Fu (Peking, 1933).

297

ful Right Wing, and he had to retire to Japan. There he has devoted himself to studying the Bronze Age in China and has produced some half-dozen brilliantly suggestive and beautifully produced books. They are primarily inspired by the archaeological discoveries of the last thirty years, but his researches have carried him deep into the records of the past.

YIU TA-FU was born in 1897 of an old-fashioned scholarly family in Chekiang Province. When he was fourteen he went to Japan, where he was for eleven years, first in High School and then in the Imperial University. He studied economics, but became more and more engrossed in the study of western literature. After taking his degree he returned to China and devoted himself to writing short stories. Many of these show his revolt against the old family traditions.

CHOU TSO-JEN is Lu Hsün's brother, younger by four years. He too studied in the Naval School at Nanking and finished the course. He also studied in Japan, at first in the Law School of the Imperial University. He was drawn to the study of Greek. On his return he taught for some years, in 1917 getting a post in Peking.

PING HSIN (pen name) is a native of Foochow, daughter of an official in the Navy. Her later education was under Christian influences in Peking, both in High School and University. She owes a great deal to an uncle, who taught her to read the best Chinese novels as well as the Confucian Classics. She started trying to write when quite young and then in 1919 turned to the new style. She went to America, and on her return taught in her old university until her marriage. The western writers who have most influenced her have been Tagore and Tolstoy.

CHANG CHIH-PING, a Cantonese, was born in 1893, and studied geology in the Imperial University in Tokyo. On his return in 1922 he taught geology for about ten years. The pull of literature became steadily stronger, and finally he devoted his time entirely to writing and the organising of publishing houses.

MAO TUN (pen-name) was born in a country town in Chekiang in 1896. He came to the fore in 1919 and was soon well known as a vigorous exponent of naturalism in writing. From the beginning he has been strongly revolutionary and the National Revolution saw him on the communist side, working in the propaganda department. Since the collapse of the Communist Government he has confined himself more to imaginative work, but is still somewhat suspect with the Nationalist Government.

HsÜ CHIH-MAO, born in 1895, was another Chekiang man, brought up in Shanghai. He started his university course in a Christian university there, but migrated from there to the National University of Peking. From there he went to England, where he studied Political Science at Cambridge. He returned in 1922 and took teaching posts in the Peking universities. He became a friend of Liang Ch'i-ch'ao's and later spent a great deal of time with Tagore on his visit to China. He translated Tagore's verse and went with him on his visit to Italy, where they studied Roman culture together.

HsÜ TI-SHAN was born in 1893 and brought up in South Fukien in a family in which Buddhism was deeply studied. Coming under Christian influence he studied in Yenching, the Christian university in Peking. He had four years abroad, two in Columbia University, New York, and two in Oxford. For some years he taught in Peking universities, and then he went to India for two years to study Indian philosophy. He is now head of the Department of Chinese in Hongkong University.

T'IEN HAN was born in 1899, a native of Hunan province. His university education was at the Imperial University, Tokyo, and when he returned to China he joined Ko Me-jo and his group in writing for the magazines they started. But he left that group and concentrated on writing plays. He is the most popular playwright of modern times, and he and his wife are the centre of the younger dramatic group.

APPENDIX II

EXPERTS SENT TO CHINA THROUGH
THE LEAGUE OF NATIONS

DR. RAJCHMAN, Director of the Health section of the
League Secretariat: three visits, the last being a special
appointment as technical agent acting as liaison officer
between the League and the National Economic Council.

M. ALBERT THOMAS, Director of the International Labour
Office, to enquire into labour conditions and problems.

M. AVENOL, then Deputy-Secretary General, to establish relations with the Nationalist Government.

MR. (now SIR ARTHUR) SALTER, then Director of the Financial
and Economic Section with M. HAAS, Director of the
Transit and Communications Sections.

DR. BORCIC, PROFESSOR FABER, of Copenhagen University, and
DR. STAMPAR, to survey medical education and advise the
Central Field Health Station at Nanking on Public Health
Administration.

PROFESSOR BECKER of Berlin, M. LANGEVIN of Paris, PRO-
FESSOR TAWNEY of London and M. FALSKI of Poland, to
survey the educational system.

DR. PAREJAS, Professor of Geology in the University of Geneva,
and MR. DAVY, Reader in English Literature in the University of Nottingham, and DR. WISEMAN, Professor of
Geography in the University of Berlin, to teach for two
years in the National Central University.

M. MAURETTE, Assistant Director of the International
Labour Office, to advise on relations between China and
the Institute of Intellectual Co-operation.

M. OKENCKI, formerly of the Polish Ministry of Public

Works, and a Dutch engineer, M. Boudrez, to advise on road-building.

Professor Carlo Dragoni of the University of Rome, to advise the National Economic Council.

Signor Benito Mari, Chairman of the Italian Association of Seri-culture, to conduct an investigation into the state of the silk industry.

Mr. Coode, London Institute of Civil Engineers, and M. Perrier, Inspector of Roads and Bridges in Paris, to advise on Hydraulic works.

Sir John Hope-Simpson, to assist the International Flood Relief Commission.

SELECTED LIST OF BOOKS
TO AID FURTHER STUDY

ANDERSON, DAME ADELAIDE. *Humanity and Labour in China.* London, 1928.

Anti-foreign Riots in China in 1891. Shanghai, 1892.

BALME, HAROLD. *China and Modern Medicine.* London, 1921.

BARBER, W. T. A. *David Hill, Missionary and Saint.* London 1921.

BERESFORD, LORD CHARLES. *The Break-up of China.* London, 1899.

BLAND, J. O. P. *Li Hung-chang.* London, 1917.

BREDON, JULIET. *Sir Robert Hart.* London, 1909.

BRINE, LINDESAY. *The Taeping Rebellion in China.* A Narrative of its Rise and Progress Based upon Original Documents and Information Obtained in China. London, 1862.

BROOMHALL, MARSHALL. *Robert Morrison.* London, 1924.

'Bulletins on Chinese Education', issued by the Chinese National Association for the Advancement of Education. Peking, 1923.

CALLERY AND YVAN. *History of the Insurrection in China.* Translated from the French by John Oxenford. London, 1853.

CARTER, T. F. *The Invention of Printing in China.* Revised Edition. New York, 1931.

CHANG, P. C. *China at the Cross Roads.* London, 1936.

CHEN, GIDEON. *Lin Tse-hsu.* Peking, 1934.
Tseng Kuo-fan. Peking, 1935.

CHEN, L. T. *History of Chinese Political Thought during the Early Tsin Period.* Adapted from the Chinese of Liang Ch'i-ch'ao. London, 1934.

China To-day through Chinese Eyes. London: First Series, 1922; Second Series, 1926.

Chinese Social and Political Science Review. Peking, 1917 *et seq.*

The Chinese Repository. Canton, 1832–51.

CORDIER, HENRI. *Histoire des relations de la Chine avec les puissances occidentales.* 3 vols. Paris, 1901, 1902.

COSTIN, W. C. *Great Britain and China, 1833–1860.* London, 1937.

CURTIS, LIONEL. *The Capital Question of China.* London, 1932.

ELGIN, JAMES, EIGHTH EARL OF. *Letters and Journals.* Second Edition. London, 1873.

D'ELIA, PASCAL M. *Catholic Native Episcopacy in China.* Being an Outline of the Formation and Growth of the Chinese Catholic Clergy. Shanghai, 1927.

Educational Association of China. Reports of Triennial Meetings. Shanghai, 1896 *et seq.*

FITZGERALD, C. P. *China, a Short Cultural History.* London, 1935.

GAMBLE, SYDNEY D. *Peking, a Social Survey.* New York, 1921.

HART, SIR ROBERT. *These from the Land of Sinim.* Second Impression. London, 1903.

HODGKIN, H. T. *China in the Family of Nations.* London, 1923.

HUBBARD, G. E. *Eastern Industrialization and Its Effect on the West.* London, 1935.

HUDSON, G. F. *Europe and China.* London, 1931.

The Far East in World Politics. Oxford, 1937.

HUC, ABBE. *Christianity in China, Tartary and Thibet.* 3 vols. London, 1857.

A Journey through the Chinese Empire. 2 vols. London, 1855.

HUMMEL, A. W. (translator). *Autobiography of a Chinese Historian.* Leyden, 1931.

HUNG, WILLIAM, AND OTHERS. *As It Looks to Young China.* London, 1932.

HU SHIH. *The Chinese Renaissance.* Chicago, 1933.

HSIA, C. L. *The Civil Code of the Republic of China.* Translated into English. Shanghai, 1930.

Institute of Pacific Relations, Reports of Conferences. 1928, 1930, 1932, 1934.

JENKINS, R. C. *The Jesuits in China and the Legation of Cardinal de Tournon*. An Examination of Conflicting Evidence and an Attempt at an Impartial Judgement. London, 1894.

JOSEPH, P. *Foreign Diplomacy in China*, 1894–1900. London, 1928.

KUO, P. W. *The Chinese System of Public Education*. Shanghai, 1915.

LANE POOLE, STANLEY. *Life of Sir Harry Parkes, K.C.B., G.C.M.G.* London, 1894.

LATOURETTE, K. S. *The Chinese, Their History and Culture*. London, 1934.

A History of Christian Missions in China. London, 1929.

LEGGE, H. E. *James Legge, Missionary and Scholar*. London, 1905.

LIEU, D. K. *The Growth and Industrialization of Shanghai*. Shanghai, 1936.

LIN SHAO YANG. *A Chinese Appeal to Christendom Concerning Christian Missions*. London, 1911.

LIN YU-TANG. *My Country and My People*. London, 1936.

LINDLEY, A. F. (Lin-le). *History of the Taiping Rebellion*. 2 vols. London, 1866.

LOCKHART, WILLIAM. *The Medical Missionary in China*. London, 1861.

LOCKMAN, JOHN. *Travels of the Jesuits into Various Parts of the World*. 2 vols. London, 1743.

LYNCH, GEORGE. *The War of the Civilizations*. Being the Record of a Foreign Devil's Experience with the Allies in China. London, 1901.

MARTIN, W. A. P. *A Cycle of Cathay*. Edinburgh and New York, 1896.

The Siege in Peking. Edinburgh and New York, 1900.

MAYERS, W. F. *Treaties between the Empire of China and Foreign Powers*. Fifth Edition, Shanghai, 1906.

Maryknoll Mission Letters from China. Extracts from the Letters and Diaries of the Pioneer Missioners of the Catholic Foreign Mission Society of America. New York : vol. i., 1923; vol. ii., 1927.

MEADOWS, THOMAS TAYLOR. *The Chinese and their Rebellions Viewed with their National Philosophy, Ethics, Legislation and Administration, to which is added an Essay on Civilization and its Present State in the East and West.* London, 1856.

MEDHURST, W. H. *Critical Review of the Books of the Insurgents.* Shanghai, 1853.

MICHIE, ALEXANDER. *Missionaries in China.* London, 1891.
The Englishman in China during the Victorian Era. Illustrated by the Career of Sir Rutherford Alcock, K.C.B. 2 vols. London, 1900.

MOORE, E. CALDWELL. *West and East.* Dale Lectures, 1913. New York, 1920

MORRISON, MRS. E. A. *Memoirs of the Life and Labours of Robert Morrison, with Critical Notices of his Chinese Works by Samuel Kidd.* 2 vols. London, 1839.

MORSE, HOSEA BALLOU. *The Trade and Administration of China.* London, 1913.
The Chronicles of the East India Company trading to China, 1635–1834. 4 vols. Oxford, 1926.
The International Relations of the Chinese Empire. 3 vols. London, 1910–18.

MOULE, A. C. *Christians in China before 1550.* London, 1920.

National Christian Council of China. Annual Reports. Shanghai, 1922 *et seq.*

PURCELL, VICTOR. *Problems of Chinese Education.* London, 1936.

RASMUSSEN, O. D. *The Reconquest of Asia.* London, 1934.

REINSCH, P. S. *Intellectual and Political Currents in the Far East.* Boston, 1911.

REICHWEIN, ADOLF. *China and Europe, Intellectual and Artistic Contacts in the XVIIIth Century.* Translated by J. C. Powell. New York, 1925.

REMER, C. F. *The Foreign Trade of China.* Shanghai, 1926.

Reorganization of Education in China. League of Nations Institute of Intellectual Co-operation, 1932.

RICHARD, TIMOTHY. *Forty-five Years in China.* London, 1916.

ROBBINS, HELEN H. *Our First Ambassador to China.* An Account of the *Life of George, Earl of Macartney, with extracts from his Letters and the Narrative of His Experiences in China*. London, 1908.

ROCKHILL, W. W. *The Journey of William of Rubruck*. Hakluyt Society. 1900.

RUSSELL, BERTRAND. *The Problem of China*. London, 1922.

SHARMAN, LYON. *Sun Yat-sen. His Life and Its Meaning*. New York, 1934.

SOOTHILL, W. E. *China and the West*. London, 1925.

STAUFFER, M. T. (ed.). *The Christian Occupation of China*. Shanghai, 1922.

STAUNTON, SIR GEORGE. *An Authentic Account of an Embassy from the King of Great Britain to the Emperor of China*. London, 1798.

STRONG, ANNA LOUISE. *China's Millions*. New York, 1928. London, 1936.

SUN YAT-SEN. *Memoirs of a Revolutionary*. London, 1918.
San Min Chu I. The Three Principles of the People. Translated by F. W. Price. Shanghai, 1927.

T'ANG LEANG-LI. *China in Revolt*. London, 1927.
The Inner History of the Chinese Revolution. London, 1930.
The New Social Order in China. Shanghai, 1936.

TAWNEY, R. H. *Land and Labour in China*. London, 1932.

TAYLER, J. B. *Farm and Factory in China*. London, 1928.

TAYLOR, DR., AND MRS. HOWARD. *Hudson Taylor and the China Inland Mission*. London, 1919.

TSENG YU-HAO. *Modern Chinese Legal and Political Philosophy*. Shanghai, 1926.

WILLIAMS, F. W. *The Life and Letters of Samuel Wells Williams, Missionary, Diplomat and Sinologue*. New York, 1889.

WILLOUGHBY, W. W. *Foreign Rights and Interests in China*. Revised Edition. 2 vols. Baltimore, 1927.

WOLFERSTAN, BERTRAND. *The Catholic Church in China, 1860–1907*. London, 1909.

VAN DORN, H. A. *Twenty Years of the Chinese Republic*. London, 1933.

Owing to the inconvenience of including Chinese characters in the main body of the book, works mentioned there are given here in their proper form. The list also includes works which have influenced the writer's views, but to which no reference has been made. Some are well-known, not to say standard, works, others are works which are off the beaten track but none the less significant for that. If a student wishes to go further, he will get all the help he needs from the *Quarterly Bulletin of Chinese Bibliography*, edited by the National Library of Peiping. The back numbers contain references, for example, to recent important works on the late Ming and the early Ch'ing Dynasties, to the rapidly increasing number of works on the Taiping Heavenly State, to compilations of foreign dispatches and other official records, and to the annual reports now issued by the different Ministries of State. The order adopted in this list is chronological, as far as is possible in respect to the period with which a work is most concerned.

明史佛耶機,呂棕,和蘭,意大利亞四傳註釋:張維華: Peiping, 1934 edition.

海國圖志:魏源: 1844: enlarged edition, 24 vols., 1852.

瀛環志略:徐繼畬: 1849: 1898, Shanghai edition.

太平天國之研究:楊逸棠: Shanghai, 1930.

太平天國文書:故宮博物院: Peiping, 1933.

太平天國雜記:簡又文: Shanghai, 1935.

曾國藩日記: Shanghai, 1909.

(The strict authenticity of this work has been questioned.)

郭侍使西紀程: first published about 1880: Chengtu edition, 1897.

中國近百年史資料:左舜生: Shanghai, 1926.

do.   ,續編:左舜生: Shanghai, 1933.

戊戌政變記:梁啓超: no date.

(Anonymous, but containing material mostly known to be by Liang Ch'i-ch'ao.)

仁學:譚嗣同: posthumous publication in or after 1898.

飲冰室文集類編:梁啓超: 1902.

南海康先生傳:張伯楨: Shanghai, 1927.

大同書:康有爲: Shanghai, 1936 edition.

翼教叢編: Hunan, 1898.

周禮政要:孫詒讓: Shanghai, 1904.

中華民國憲法史：潘樹藩： Shanghai, 1935.

清華大學報,非基督教專號： Peking, 1922.

梁任公近著：梁啓超： Shanghai, 1924.

中國歷史研究法：梁啓超： Shanghai, 1922: 6th ed., 1928.

中國哲學史大綱：胡適： Shanghai, 1919: 8th ed., 1922.

胡適文存：胡適： 1st series, 4 vols., Shanghai, 1921.

    do.   do.   2nd ,,   ,,   ,,   1924.

    do.   do.   3rd ,,   ,,   ,,   1930.

四十自述：胡適： Shanghai, 1933.

東西文化及其哲學：梁漱溟： Shanghai, 1922: 4th ed., 1923.
    (In 1927 the author withdrew the book as not agreeing with
    his later views.)

中國近七十年來教育記事：丁至聘： Shanghai, 1935.

近代中國留學史：舒新城： Shanghai, 1927.

近代中國教育思想史：舒新城： Shanghai, 1929.

中國現代教育史：周予同： Shanghai, 1934.

近五十年來中國文學史：陳炳堃： Shanghai.

中國新文學運動史：王哲甫： Shanghai, 1933.

中國新文學大係：ed. by 趙家璧： 10 vols., Shanghai, 1935.

中國新學史：戈公振： Shanghai, 1927: 4th ed., 1933.

中國文藝論戰：李何林： Shanghai, 1929.

科學與人生觀：張君勱等： Shanghai, 1923: 9th ed., 1936.

美的哲學：徐慶譽： Shanghai, 1929.

總理全集：胡漢民： Shanghai, 1930.

汪精衛集： Shanghai, 1930.

青年之路：戴季陶： Shanghai, 1928.

中國民族自救運動之最後覺悟：梁漱溟： Shanghai, 1933.

太虛法師文鈔： Shanghai, 1928.

INDEX

THE END